THE
BADGERS
OF
ASHCROFT
WOODS

Chris Ferris

Illustrated by David Astin

UNWIN

HYMAN

London   Sydney   Wellington

First published in Great Britain by the Trade Division
of Unwin Hyman Limited, 1990.

UNWIN HYMAN LIMITED
15–17 Broadwick Street
London W1V 1FP

Allen & Unwin Australia Pty Ltd
8 Napier Street, North Sydney, NSW 2060, Australia

Allen & Unwin New Zealand Pty Ltd with the Port Nicholson Press
Compusales Building, 75 Ghuznee Street, Wellington, New Zealand

British Library Cataloguing in Publication Data

Ferris, Chris
The badgers of Ashcroft Woods.
1. Great Britain. Badgers
I. Title
599.74'447
ISBN 0–04–440652–5

Typeset in 10½ on 13pt Times by Nene Phototypesetters Ltd
Printed in Great Britain by Hartnoll Ltd, Bodmin, Cornwall

Grateful acknowledgement is made to the following for permission to
reproduce material: 'Wendy my friend', *The Countryman*; 'Slugging!',
Dog & Country; and 'A Week in the Country', *Country Life*.

Contents

To Mícheál and Aodhán,
children of Ireland,
their country and its wildlife,
whose future we hold in trust.
May we not betray that trust,
nor that future.

🦡 BADGER FAMILY TREE 🦡

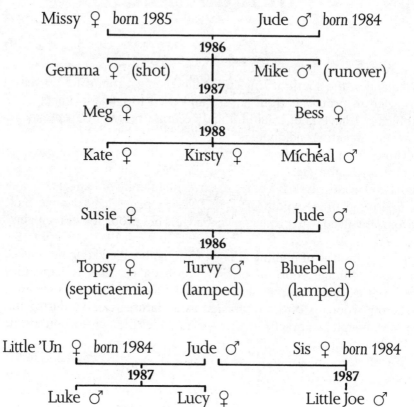

Missy ♀ born 1985   Jude ♂ born 1984

1986

Gemma ♀ (shot)   Mike ♂ (runover)

1987

Meg ♀   Bess ♀

1988

Kate ♀   Kirsty ♀   Mícheál ♂

Susie ♀   Jude ♂

1986

Topsy ♀   Turvy ♂   Bluebell ♀
(septicaemia)   (lamped)   (lamped)

Little 'Un ♀ born 1984   Jude ♂   Sis ♀ born 1984

1987   **1987**

Luke ♂   Lucy ♀   Little Joe ♂

Crisp ♀ born 1985

Introduction

Ashcroft Woods is the fictitious name of a very real and ancient woodland in the south of England. I have known it now for 30 years, struggled to protect it from misuse and tried to interest others in its problems. I have kept a faithful and accurate record of events there, now running into 22 fieldbooks.

Those from November 1980 to March 1985 were condensed and published as *The Darkness is Light Enough* – the first in the trilogy about the woods. In this book I discover the family of badgers, as well as foxes and other wildlife. By the closing pages local people have become involved with protecting its badgers but problems still remain.

Out of the Darkness – from March 1985 to April 1987 – describes the appalling upsurge of hunting at night with lights called lamping, as well as the traditional sport of digging for badgers. This is happening countrywide but I can only describe what I have seen in my own area. Ashcroft Woods is officially opened as a Nature Reserve during this period, though in a practical sense this provides little protection for the animals or the places.

The Badgers of Ashcroft Woods records the last two years during which time I moved to live in a nearby wood, and demonstrates how people's actions in real life can sometimes be stranger than fiction.

═══ 1 ═══

Canine Companion

Wendy was a Heinz of the beautiful variety. She had the head, eyes and soul of a black retriever and the body and tail of a pointer. The puppy was a gift to our children and became a wonderful family dog and companion. To me, who fed, walked and trained her, however, Wendy became something more – a devoted and faithful friend. At home busy working, I would look up to see her watching me and at my glance, her head would rise as her tail gently moved. Out of doors, she was a shadow rarely far from my side and always seemingly to know when I was unwell. A back injury allowed me little rest and when the pain was intense, I found that walking took my thoughts away from myself and actually eased it. Once the dog was old enough to be obedient, she began to accompany me on my walks both by day and night. It was to prove a friendship ending only with her death.

Very early on in my night walking, I had found the badgers, sometimes foraging in the fields or in nearby Ashcroft Woods. Some of my happiest early mornings were those spent concealed at their sett waiting for the sow and her three cubs to come home. At first, I was uneasy at having a young dog's company, but it was as if she knew she must never give us away or her night walks with me would be at an end. Looking back, Wendy's behaviour was like that of a guide dog; she was 'on duty' out with me at night, our daytime walking was quite different.

The Wheatfield badgers were the easiest to watch and gave us both the greatest pleasure. If they came along their trail through the standing crop, even I would hear them coming. There would be a rustle – pause – rustle and then in the distance, the corn would be waving as they passed through. They enjoyed eating the ripe grain and would rear up on hind legs to grasp the ears which they ran through their half-open jaws. This was usually done without removing the ear from the stalk, so the corn was left upright but grainless in the field. The cubs were not as accomplished at this as their parents, so they often ended up pulling the head from the stalk. The cubs would also play; one would find a pebble, toss it up and chase after it as a dog does a ball. Tag was a popular game and King-of-the-Castle another.

If the badgers returned along another trail, however, Wendy's whole attitude would let me know well in advance. Her sleek head lying on her front paws, would slowly rise as her ears pricked. Just occasionally, she would forget and allow her tail to wag, but my foot gently over it immediately curbed the involuntary and give-away action. These animals became special to both of us.

One early July morning I was walking with Wendy in Ashcroft Woods, when we startled a badger as it passed from the meadow on Colts Farm into the undergrowth on its way back to the sett. She was very excited and ran to me communicating her 'find'. Before I could stop her, she ran back to the badger, a big, handsome boar, who reared up on its hindlegs at her approach. In spite of the poor light under the trees, its striped mask, light-coloured, quivering snout and raised fore-paws with their long, curving claws, were clearly visible. In this attitude the badger greatly resembled a small bear and, in theory, the claws could have made formidable weapons. However, it is interesting that of all the badger to badger, badger to dog confrontations I've seen over the years, only twice were the claws used in self-defence. Wendy lay down when I called, her long tail still and her head flat between her paws. Still grumbling and growling to itself, but now on all fours, the boar turned and continued home.

A badger's usual reaction if it feels threatened with its escape cut off, is to tuck its head down between its front legs, so presenting heavy shoulders to the enemy. These shoulder muscles are strongly developed by digging and with its thick fur and rubbery skin, this part of the animal is less likely to suffer serious injury. Many an inexperienced terrier has gone for the shoulders, only to find the badger's head suddenly whip out sharply with a sideways, tearing swipe.

At home describing the night's events to my family, I needed only to mention the word 'badger' and Wendy's head would be raised my way, her tail wagging. Foxes, too, were watched together, but there canine enthusiasm was lacking, Wendy accepted that it was something I wanted to do, but rarely showed any great interest. In later years when she no longer shared my night walks I came to know a young vixen very well. On my return home the dog would display obvious jealousy at the fox smell all about me. The badgers that eventually musked me with their scent, she too would smell, but her attitude was never one of jealousy; only enthusiasm and a bright-eyed interest. Then, as I stroked her, I would feel a sadness that we could no longer watch them together.

Day walks with her were always a delight. She found so much that I would never have known was there, like the grass-snake in the act of swallowing a frog. She found it half-hidden by dead leaves and twigs and stood 'pointing' and whining softly to get my attention. Instinctively, she feared slow-worms and snakes, though she would find them for me to watch, only growing anxious if I picked one up to examine it. When I returned the snake to its hiding place, Wendy would jump up, tail wagging her relief at me.

One day she flushed a buzzard in the Old Orchard at Weldon. It rose up from the grass clearing and flew across my path, almost brushing my face. In the long grass were the remains of the meal from which it had been disturbed. The rat had flesh torn from its body exposing the ribcage. Its head was still intact, though the eyes were bloody. I called the dog and together we left the area so that the buzzard could return and finish its meal. A few evenings later whilst walking at dusk, Wendy flushed it again on the adjoining farmland. This time it flew up and perched in a tree on the edge of the disused chalk quarry. From then on, I began to watch it regularly, leaving the dog at home. I found that early mornings were ideal, before the sun rose too high in the sky and the day became hot. The buzzard favoured this particular tree overlooking the quarry and I would sit hidden, directly opposite it on the far side. The farmer used this place as a dump and besides the old cars, machinery and furniture that had been thrown down over the years, unsold lettuce, cabbage and other vegetables, were regularly deposited too. Shrubs, brambles, traveller's-joy and ferns grew from the chalky sides, covering most of the ugliness. The rotting produce attracted insects which in turn encouraged a great variety of birds as well as mice, voles, rats and foxes.

The tree this bird favoured had a dead limb which hung over the dump and from this it would drop onto some small creature scavenging below. This solitary buzzard, normally unknown in our part of England, had unlimited countryside in which to hunt, but the tree above the quarry was its roosting site and much profitable time was spent here for both the bird and myself. At first light it would sit preening and as the light increased to reveal colour, the rich browns of its upper plumage became visible, and its yellow talons and beak. Then it would rise with slow beats of its broad wings and sound its plaintive call. Dawn would find the bird quartering the orchard and fields in almost lazy flight, as it flew in effortless, wide circles, its sharp eyes intent on the ground below. Against the azure sky, the bird's wide, ragged-tipped wings gave an impression of great strength as it soared and hovered, then circled again. The hunter lived well; taking anything from rabbits, to worms and beetles. Once its pounce secured a slow-worm and on several occasions I saw it eating elderberries growing from the quarry walls. Somehow, the latter was unexpected, though whether this is unusual, I cannot say. The buzzard was seen by different observers some miles away over a period of several years. We all felt it was the same bird. It was most wide-ranging in the winter when food was scarce, though what had caused it to come here in the first place we had no way of telling.

Walking with Wendy one April morning she discovered a baby rabbit crouching terrified amongst the brambles. When they first venture above ground to feed, rabbit nestlings still retain this instinct to freeze. This one fitted easily into my cupped hands, its face babyishly rounded, the tiny ears laid back as the gentle thud, thud of its life pulsed against the palm of my hand. Of all those with myxomatosis here, I have never found very young rabbits affected. I put it carefully back into the undergrowth as we went on our way.

A few days later, the dog came towards me, head held low and tail moving gently from side to side. Putting out my hands, she carefully placed a tiny leveret into them and stood there bright-eyed and eager, regarding me. It was quite unharmed, though slightly damp from her soft mouth. My one worry was that I shouldn't find the form from which it had been taken, or the mother might not accept it when she next came to nurse. Wendy was content to lead me back and from the warmth of the slightly depressed grass, I felt I had returned it to the correct place. Recounting this later to my family, Karen, my daughter, reminded me of the dog with her guineapig. At certain times, the bitch would go broody and each time we would discover one particular guineapig had been taken from the wire run that it shared with the others, into Wendy's basket. Like the rabbit and leveret, it was never hurt, it even seemed to enjoy the change of scene. Eight-year-old Karen insisted that it was the other guineapigs who felt left out!

Wendy's knack of bringing me gifts held some surprises, as when she retrieved an injured woodcock left by an illegal shooter in Ashcroft Woods. The strangest, however, was the little squirming 'something' that jumped and twisted in the palm of my hand. It was the tail of a lizard. I have seen a lizard shed its tail when it was grasped by a gull. Perhaps a drop of fluid is emitted, but that is all and the tail comes away clean. A lizard chooses to break off its tail by a muscle contraction and though a fresh one will grow, the accident is noticeable from its stumpy appearance.

Like most dogs, mine loved ripe fruit and enjoyed coming with me to pick blackberries. Foxes and badgers carefully bite off each berry individually. Not so my greedy dog! She put her mouth squarely over a bunch and moved her jaws very gently. The ripe ones dropped into her mouth and she stood with eyes closed savouring the succulent berries as their juices ran down her chin. I once saw a family of badgers eat all the blackberries within their reach. Then, the adult animals climbed onto the bush and lay there eating the higher fruit as they straddled it, with their cubs scrambling around them taking their share. Wendy never

thought of that one, perhaps because she lacked the badgers' coarse protective fur and tough skin. Badgers, incidently, are amazingly noisy eaters and will slurp, smack their lips and burp – with gusto over something really juicy!

One night in the wood, we came upon the Old Cherry Sett badgers digging out fresh entrances and enlarging their home. Quite clear to us above came the sounds of digging with occasional pauses to listen (and, I imagine, to take a deep breath), then much snorting and grunting. As one backed out dragging the earth, there would be a rattle of small stones that a strong kick sent flying backwards. Over the years, these spoil heaps grow enormous as more and more earth is excavated. Badgers are capable of dragging out very heavy flints, as well as lumps of sandstone. Their claw marks show clear and deep on the latter. That night there were two animals digging out. Sometimes they would meet up below ground and then work would temporarily be halted and the sound, almost deafening in such a confined space, of prolonged purring could be heard. Sometimes, I could also hear roots being bitten through, or the familiar sucking sound of worms being eaten – the badgers' favourite food. There's nothing like finding the odd snack as you work!

One sunny morning, Wendy pounced fox-like in the tall grass and turned up the soft, chewed-grass nest of a long-tailed field mouse, complete with five grey, naked young. The mother leapt up and over the dog and so escaped. I called Wendy to heel and led her well away from the place. Then, telling her to stay, I went quietly back and stood nearby, careful to see my shadow didn't fall across the disturbed nest. The still-blind young wriggled haphazardly in the sun's warmth. Presently, the adult returned, first reconnoitring cautiously on hind legs; the prominent dark eyes and large oval ears straining for the slightest hint of danger, her whiskers all aquiver. Satisfied at last, the mouse carefully checked her offspring, then grasping one she disappeared through the long grass. A pause and she was back, taking the next away by a leg! And so on till the nest was empty. I then returned to the cause of the upheaval, now lying fast asleep and dreaming in the sunshine!

Wendy's fox-like high pounce had some amusing results like the day she upset a weasel. Immediately, there was a 'musk' smell and a very irate mustelid reared up on hind legs hissing and spitting at the startled dog. Together we stood and watched it sinuously disappear through the grass. Wendy had another weasel encounter when she chased one under a heap of dumped hardcore. Happily, she couldn't dig it out, but instead ran round the pile whining and crying her frustration. The weasel then darted out almost under her nose, reared up spitting and hissing, and leapt back to safety. The dog's ears shot upright, as tail between her legs, she slunk back to me. I told her weasels were wonderful! She did get her own back, however, a few minutes later, when I discovered a single fine specimen of the toadstool fly agaric growing under some birches nearby. Putting the close-up lens on the camera, I called her to come and sit as the sound of a motorbike drew nearer; then turned back to the fly agaric in time to see Wendy obediently sit fair and square on my specimen!

Later Wendy became ill and though she recovered from the resultant operation, she lost her stamina and thereafter could never be walked too far. One Sunday evening the late sunshine streaming through our windows was irresistible, and leaving the freshly baked bread to cool, I took her for a stroll round the nearby fields. We reached the farmhouse and, not wishing to return home awhile, crossed up to the Yew Tree Sett nearby. Together we climbed the steep bank to the fence and passing along it, reached the corner-post directly above the entrances to the sett. A 'nik-nik-niking' came to our ears in the dusk and peering round the corner, we saw the badger playing with a ball-like object which later turned out to be a little green cooking apple from the overgrown garden. The sow played with the apple as they do with a pebble, tossing it up in her mouth and scampering after it, completely absorbed, till finally it rolled down a sett entrance. As the badger disappeared after it, I gently edged backwards, with Wendy stealing after. Kneeling by her in the bracken, I was undecided whether to scramble back down the bank and so doing, perhaps frighten the young badger, or wait till it left to forage for food. Then there was a rustle along the wire fencing and the sow herself appeared in the meadow, at first keeping to the fence and then crossing into the open to dig under a cowpat – a favoured site of the cockchafer grub. Wendy looked at me, her ears raised and alert, her eyes shining, but so quiet and still. The old dog's face might be liberally flecked with grey now, but how she remembered our night watches together of her prime! With the badger's back to us and a distance away, we crept unseen down the bank and so home; the sky covered in black clouds, except for a streak of brilliant orange from the dying sun on the horizon and the daylight almost gone.

I have never owned another dog, but continue to go out almost nightly to the badgers and foxes that have come to 'accept' me in the area that I study. They have led a chequered existence of recent years

7

and their numbers have dwindled, mainly through hunting. We have probably more urban foxes than those living in the open countryside, since the latter can be easily dugout or shot.

By May 1987, however, the 800 acres of Ashcroft Woods and surrounding farmland contained 11 badgers, of which six were adult animals and five were cubs. More cubs had been born, but their mortality is naturally high with many dying in the first weeks of life, even before their eyes open at five or six weeks. So the one or two of a litter that venture above ground for the first time at eight or nine weeks of age, may well be the remainder of five or six cubs born to the sow. It is fashionable to be labelled anthropomorphic if one gives wild animals names, but names, rather than numbers, identify more easily in the human mind, so I named mine. The badger sows were Missy, Little'un, Sis, Susie and Crisp with Jude the only adult boar. Missy now had two cubs, Meg and Bess, Little'un had two also, Lucy and Luke, whilst Sis had Little Joe. Not all adult sows bear cubs yearly by any means; many miss some years and others remain barren. Crisp born in 1985, I had seen mate on several occasions, but hadn't produced cubs.

That May was memorable. At first light one morning, I found at the wood edge an unattended woodcock's nest containing four pale eggs laid amongst dead leaves. A few nights earlier, Little'un and her two cubs had startled a woodcock feeding on the irrigated field of young lettuce plants outside the wood. It had risen up with that curious jinking flight and I noted where it came down. Keeping the irrigation trolley between it and myself and gradually moving closer, I watched it for nearly an hour taking worms from the wet earth. Normally they probe deep with that long bill, but this was not necessary here as the wet earth had encouraged the worms to rise above ground to feed. Later, the bird returned to the wood and I had tried unsuccessfully, to judge where its nest was. Woodcock tend to fly high over the trees, only to drop down suddenly into a gap. They may scuttle some way along the ground before settling, especially if incubating eggs.

Waiting at the nest that morning, sure enough the 'cock appeared creeping through the bluebells. Once seated on the nest, however, it would have gone undetected amongst the dead leaves. Was ever a bird more perfectly blended? except for, perhaps, its eyes. So dark, large and prominent are they, set up high in the head for all-round vision, that it is normally easier to find the eyes first, then gradually note the outline of their owner!

At 5 a.m. there was a red-streaked dawn sky. All the Old Cherry Sett badgers (except one of Missy's cubs who kept popping her sleek little head out of an entance) were well below ground and, yes, there was the male woodcock roding his slow territorial flight. I went into the Chantry, the highest part of Ashcroft Woods, and collected tawny owl pellets for two young friends to dissect and discover what the birds had been eating. The Chantry was at its loveliest in May. Young beech leaves have a soft green peculiarly their own, whilst the less shaded places were carpeted with bluebells, wood anemones and large swathes of yellow archangel. With the morning well advanced, tiny fluffs of racing cloud dotted the blue sky and from Great Chantry Field outside the skylarks sang.

The previous October, these woods had been granted comprehensive by-laws as befitted their designation as a Special Site of Scientific Interest (SSSI) and a Nature Reserve. By-laws are valueless without someone to see they are complied with so, until the District Council could affort to pay for a warden, I had offered, with some misgivings, to voluntarily do so for at least part of each and every day. To some degree the misgivings were justified for as a small, middle-aged woman, I didn't impress anyone, least of all myself! But, as always, it was only a minority of visitors who insisted on disregarding the rules. I found many friends and allies amongst the local people who had a pride and affection for 'their' woods and were pleased that at last some attempt was being made to care for them. Each day I picked up the litter as I walked round and soon discovered that others were doing the same. There was a pleasure in answering queries on flora and fauna and, where possible, the history of this ancient woodland; older people recalled the place in their youth and so added to my knowledge. Finding lost possessions, children and dogs and returning them to their owners, forged an unexpected bond. Of those who persisted in riding their motorbikes, poaching, or digging-up saplings or wild flowers for their gardens, the police had agreed to interview if a vehicle number could be obtained. Gradually Ashcroft Woods was coming into its own.

Only the problem of the shooting remained a major headache that was largely unresolved. Although the 1968 Firearms Act made it illegal and indeed, a criminal offence, to shoot in a public place, because there was no one till now to stop them, owners of rifles and most particularly shotguns, came from a considerable distance to 'rough shoot' in these woods. Clothed in the popular camouflage gear such people are hard to detect. If dropped at the wood-edge by an obliging wife or friend to be collected at a pre-arranged time and place, there is also no vehicle left parked that might incriminate them. Too many shooters had for too

long looked upon it as a right to use Ashcroft Woods, so the shooting
continued.

It was perhaps as well that I no longer had a dog, or the vixen I
named Watcher would never have sought me out as she did. If by night
the badgers were with me, she would keep well away and only if I was
solitary, would I suddenly be aware of her. I might look round and she
would be at my side as if there had been no absence, or I might see her
emerge from the tree cover ahead. Then I would squat down for her to
come and touch noses with me in greeting. I knew she had cubs that
were kennelling at the Felled Logs Sett, long since disused by any
badger. Quietly wardening one afternoon, I came upon all six of them
playing together in the sunshine. At five weeks old, their boisterous
mock fights and chases were punctuated with gruff little barks and
occasional sharp yelps as some playmate was nipped too hard and
submitted puppy-like on its back with belly exposed. Then the victor

would run to the next cub and with bottom skyward and tongue lolling invite it to play.

The cubs were losing their chocolate-coloured fur and husky-puppy appearance; their faces were sharper and more fox-like. Watcher was beginning to wean them with food brought back to the den by herself and her mate. A rabbit bone was good to gnaw, play or quarrel over. Stick-chewing is popular with adult foxes in a playful mood as well as cubs. Stones, empty drink cans or other discarded rubbish might be brought back for her young to play with. This was another good reason for a daily rubbish collection on my part for I have known both fox and badgercubs come to grief playing with human rejects – glass, sharp metal and plastic bags can be dangerous play material.

I was careful never to have Watcher with me when her cubs were above ground, for I didn't want them becoming used to me or even to know I was there. So if I heard them playing, I kept well away and only ventured near when it was quiet to check everything was well with the den. The new by-laws protected all the animals of Ashcroft Woods and inwardly I prayed that neither mother nor cubs would be dugout or shot. Watcher, the beautiful vixen, had come to mean a great deal to me. Her family's play-area with the bluebells flattened at the Felled Logs was very obvious, as was that of the badgercubs. They too, enjoyed playing round their sett and at 13 weeks old were growing fast.

In May this place is carpeted with wildflowers blooming before the tree foilage should grow too dense and shut out the life-giving light they need to flower. There are red and white campions, bugle, speedwell, deadnettles, violets and magnificant spikes of yellow archangel. A few wild arum poke out of their pale green sheaves with charlock, herb robert, the stitchworts, dainty beadgrasses, and, of course, the chervils and cow parsley. The latter blow gently on the Briarmead borders amongst the flowering comfrey and may blossom. It is a lovely month.

Hares aren't plentiful in this area, but there are always some. The farmer and I take a pride in them, for they seem part of a way of life that is disappearing fast. Both of us have discovered very young leverets, but that May I was to see a doe actually giving birth. It was a mild, damp night on Sand Pit Field above the Old Cherry Sett and the time was just after 3 a.m. The hare bore four leverets, cleaned them and ate the afterbirths, then went a little way off into the wood edge to wash herself. Unknown to me, Missy had been foraging farther over and homed in on the newborn leverets; possibly the smell of fresh blood still lingered. She began to eat one, turning the skin inside out as she did so. The hare leapt out of the cover in two great bounds and kicked the sow violently on the side of her head. Missy cried out, but refused to budge from her meal and gave a sideways swing at the hare as she came in again. In desperation, the doe rushed in at an angle, grasped a leveret and leapt away with it, leaving Missy to eat the remainder.

First light was in the sky when I was met by Watcher. In a quiet way we were very good friends though she was never as demonstrative as her first mate Josh had been towards me. He would jump up at me in greeting or boisterous play and sometimes knocked me over. I followed after her as she walked across Long Field and turning, saw we had left a bruise trail where our passing had shaken the moisture from the growing stalks of barley, leaving it darker than the rest. At the bottom of the bank, the vixen pawed the wet earth – not digging, merely patting it and turning round as she did so to look back at the ground. She had discovered what birds and I myself have found; if you tap damp earth, the worms below rise to the surface. I have been told that they mistake it for heavy rain, but for whatever reason, it certainly brings them up. Three worms the vixen ate in quick succession before they could withdraw into their burrows, not pulling them out but rather holding them still before drawing them smoothly out unbroken. Then she trotted purposefully towards the winding Chantry path. High above us from an ivy-covered ash tree, a tawny hen cloaking her chicks, began kewiking to her mate nearby. He then called his low melodious, quavering answer, and seeing Watcher searching the ground below the ash, silently glided off his perch and over the foraging fox. Owlets are messy feeders and though their mother pulls pieces from the prey with which to feed her young, much goes overboard to end up far beneath for foxes to investigate. I looked on uneasily, wondering if he would attack *Vulpes vulpes*. I think he might have done, had the searcher shown any interest in the tree itself. But after finding a few morsels, the vixen continued on up the hill to the Chantry, I following closely behind.

I stood looking over Great Chantry Field at the rim of Old Joe's last home, the dark clouds of the morning sky run through with red and gold. Each tree was softly touched with green, yet each of a different shade, so even at a distance one could tell what kind it was though its shape might not be clearly visible. There was a noise close by my feet at the field edge; rustle, grunt, grunt and a hedgehog within the furrow was searching the wet crumbles of dark earth for a meal. How dewy wet its snout and how acute that urchin's hearing, but someone else with sense of smell and hearing quite as good was by me now and watching too! I felt her tense and gather, then a lightning dab of a quick paw and

the spiny prey was on its back. The vixen grasped her meal by its soft belly, biting deep. With one paw holding it down, she ate the hedgehog from its prickly case.

Looking at it again before I left for home that morning, the remains seemed at a glance like a small curled hedgehog, but on examination there was just nothing inside; no blood, no flesh, no vestige of anything at all. The spiny skin, but nothing more.

It was one Sunday evening in the same month of May that I watched a pair of nightjars. I was first aware of them when walking along the field edge above the Old Cherry Sett just after 9 p.m.; a churring mechanical sound, rising and falling, rising and falling for minutes on end. I stood quite still in the twilight, not daring to move for fear of disturbing them, but wondering just where exactly they were. The sound was coming from the bracken-covered birch stand, but I could see nothing till, suddenly, a long shape with buoyant flight passed in front of me, the white spots of wings and tail denoting it was a male. Then in level flight, perhaps two metres above the ground, it brought its raised wings down with a crack not unlike the woodpigeon's clapping when they leave their roosts. This was a single sound however, later to be repeated. I first heard a nightjar's whip cracking when badger watching at the Crater Sett many years ago. Then, I couldn't credit such soft owl-like wings made such a sharp noise. Last century, this field was a plum orchard and three ancient trees still remain at the wood edge in mute testimony to this. Just now they even bore a little blossom. From such a tree the hen nightjar was softly calling. Once more the male repeated the wing clap, then flying to her branch they copulated.

Much later, I watched them hunting over the barley and along the Briarmead verge. There were many airborne insects this warm night, especially those attracted by the plum and cherry blossom at the wood edge and also the damson blossom bordering the lane. The nightjars flew swiftly, beak agape to catch an insect (surely by sight only?) and sometimes swooped almost to ground level to scoop one up. I have rarely enjoyed a nightwatch more.

First light was now 3.45 a.m. An hour later, I watched two adult hares browsing on the barley field above the Old Cherry Sett. They seemed very brown against the growing green. Bluebells scented the air. At 5.15 a.m. an orange sun was losing its struggle with the black clouded morning. A strange, wine-coloured light seeped through the tree shapes, touching their trunks with shreds of purple and turning the ground cover of old, discoloured leaves to things of beauty. Now a wind was rising and that quality of light was gone. The birds were hushed... and, suddenly, the rain was here.

Wardening one morning I found a foxcub shot; from a distance I think, as the charge had splayed out. It seemed such a waste lying there amongst the bluebells. Some evenings later, another little dogfox was also shot, the 'tagless' one I had seen with no white tip to its tail that had so reminded me of my first Tagless whom I found shot and dying in the summer of 1984. Then during the Spring Bank Holiday, another was killed by a visitor's terrier and soon after, Watcher chose to lead her surviving offspring (two dogfoxes and a vixen), to safety well away from the woods. Four decaying straw bales had served as a hide in the winter months from which to shoot the pigeon that feasted on the growing oilseed rape. For the remaining months of that summer, whilst the crop steadily ripened, the family lived amongst these bales and hunted for itself hidden away from human eyes except mine and the farmer's. The young foxes grew more independent as each week went by. Only mice, voles, rats and rabbits shared their accommodation within the field and the nearest footpaths were a good distance off.

All the badgers regularly foraged at night for worms in the wet earth under the sprays of Colts Farm. This irrigation has the effect of heavy rain as far as the worms are concerned and foxes, as well as badgers, take advantage of this. In fact, starvation through drought is a common cause of badgercub death in many parts of the country. Worms are a badger's staple diet and though a lactating sow may continue to suckle long after the norm when worms aren't available for her offspring, her own milk may dry up if the drought is severe. Fortunately, there is usually no such problem in this area, since market gardening must have constant irrigation to support it. I enjoy watching worms come above ground when it's damp. They anchor their tail ends into their burrows and feed on any decaying vegetable matter in the surrounding area. Never really thought about it till I came to watch them at night like this, but to be able to expand or contract your body length as they do, is rather remarkable. The badgers like looking for worms too, though they were not so interested as I in their finer points!

The five badgercubs were now 15 weeks old and sturdy, playful young animals. The cubless adult sows, Susie and Crisp, often played with them too. Such 'aunties' may take over a young cub's upbringing if an accident befalls its natural mother. All badgers, including the boars, are playful and it was comic to see big, lumbering Jude good-naturedly take a battering in their rough-and-tumble. Crisp, as always, rather over-reached herself by first head-butting Jude's massive body, then my trousered legs! I left them to it.

June was interspersed with storms of thunder, lightning and torrential rain. The month continued cold and the amounts of sun were poor. In spite of this, the countryside had never looked more lovely. The wildroses, both pink and white, were all in bloom and the quail called lingeringly from its nest in the depths of the barley.

I decided to forsake my area for several mornings to do a concentrated search of the railway banks for possible badger setts. Summer is not the best time for this with its concealing vegetation, but the muddy paths had made Ashcroft Woods temporarily unpopular with visitors, so I felt I could be spared. The Permanent Way Supervisor at Oakley had given me permission *and* an orange jacket to wear, so starting from the railway station, I slowly worked my way along the side of the track. Some of the steep chalk escarpments were a nightmare to scramble over with their thick bramble covering hiding any possible holes. All had to be carefully checked, however, for I was determined not to miss one and badger setts vary greatly in size.

Normally, each clan or family group of badgers has only one main sett. This will be the largest and many contain a great number of entrances with at least some part of it in occupation. It is the main breeding sett. Annexe setts, as the term implies, are close to the main one and will also have several entrances. In contrast, subsidiary setts may be a good distance from the main sett with several entrances too. There may be several outlying setts with only one or two entrances; these mustn't be confused with rabbit burrows or fox earths. Not all badger clans will have all these sett types within their territory and, in common with other animals, badgers do not choose to fall in with man-made generalizations. However, the above is a useful guide in determining the number of badger families within a given area as usually there will be only one main sett per family.

In the first stretch of railway banks from Oakley to the next station, I only found one sett and that was a subsidiary. It was also badger-occupied and I was determined to return before light the next morning to see what it contained, then at dawn, I could continue checking the banks until well into the day. What I would have missed had I done this in the winter, was the profusion of birds, animals and flowers. There were butterflies and orchids in the railway cuttings that flourished nowhere else in the surrounding countryside. More important perhaps was that they were safe here from collectors on the dangerously sheer sides with busy trains passing below. It was easy to forget the danger myself in the fascination of these banks where each few metres seemed to yield some fresh marvel; the butterflies prompted me to buy a new book for their identification. Recent rains had made the chalk very slippery and had also caused abundant plant growth.

One morning I started embankment-checking so early that I startled a sow and her three cubs returning home about 4.15 a.m. The mother gave a great snort at scenting me and rushed up the bank with one of her youngsters in a clatter of broken flints; one cub ran downwards a way, whilst the other stayed all fluffed-up. I stayed too, quite still. The adult came down the bank to have a good look and decided I was probably harmless. This gave confidence to the one that had stayed. It came to within a metre of me squatted there and with snout raised tried, apparently unsuccessfully, to get my scent on the still air. Then, carefully, the sow skirted me and the family went on its way home with the cubs turning round now and then for a last look. I have noticed before that for apparently ungainly animals, badgers are very sure-footed on hillsides and rock faces. That same morning I saw a high-speed train hit three foxcubs playing on the track. There was something odd about one and, when I went over to inspect the bodies, I found it to be an albino.

Since their successful prosecution of two men for attempting to dig for badgers, the police had asked landowners in the area to notify them of any setts they might think their land contained. These contacts with the police and landowners were proving helpful. I would be asked to check if it was indeed a sett and whether occupied or not. If the owner had a problem with his badgers, this could be discussed on site and often resolved with mutual cooperation. To know *why* these animals are doing something, is half-way to solving it. The police needed to know exactly where an occupied sett might be and also the easiest vehicle access – important if a patrol was to get quickly to the scene of a suspected badger-dig. Our police were also keeping me informed of any badger road casualties which together we had started recording for the National Survey. We agreed to continue to do this indefinitely, however, as we were learning so much from it.

June ended with sunshine that continued well into July. Now the foxgloves and mulleins bloomed in the coppiced areas of Ashcroft Woods and the scent of honeysuckle lingered sweetly at night. One afternoon I came upon four youths riding their motorbikes on the steep slope of the Old Cherry Sett. They had been using it as a scramble track and, from the broken flowers and churned up earth, had been doing so for some time. They merely roared off at my approach though I knew they would be back, but with no registration numbers to their bikes, there was little we could do to trace them. Moreover, the damage had been done. Unnerved by the noise and trampling on the entrances of her part of the sett, Little'un moved her cubs Luke and Lucy to the more isolated one in the Chantry. This outlying sett will for me always have the association of the great boar Old Joe, father of Leslie and grandfather to Little'un, though she never knew him. In spite of leaves and debris the crowning-down hole, by which he was dugout and taken, still shows clear. Crisp, living further along the Old Cherry Sett, also moved away, which left just Jude still denning at the sheltered end where the trees grew too close for biking.

The hot, sunny weather continued. Soon the woodland paths were pale dust contrasting strongly with the luxuriant greens of the foliage and the many wild flowers. Once again, the great hanging curtain of honeysuckle was attracting many moths and insects to feed on the nectar lying deep within its flower tubes. This huge woodbine grows at the entrance of the Seam Path that connects the Chantry with the rest of Ashcroft Woods. The nightjars hunted the insects here for themselves and their two chicks that had now left the nest (a mere scrape amongst the dead leaves), but were concealed nearby in the bracken. Walking through this place at night, the heady, cloying scent seemed to be everywhere above my head, with figwort and enchanterers' nightshade below with me in the depths. Those other insect-hunters, the pipistrelles, hawked up and down Briarmead and over the barley where their prey was most numerous before dawn. These bats have well-defined feeding areas where they methodically fly in search of food. If another bat invades this territory, the owner will chase it off, before resuming its quest for airborne insects. They roost in the old, gnarled bark of the damson trees on the bank and that of the geans or wild cherry trees growing along the Wildflower Path. I liked to sit on the six-bar gate at the lane edge watching the pipistrelles catch insects all around me. I noticed they ate small moths and the like on the wing, but with larger prey, this bat takes it to a favoured perch to eat. The old dogwood tree by the gate has always been used for this, but only through bat watching did I find the answer to the moth wings and tough cases lying around its bole. The discarded remains of dor beetles I have commonly seen here, which is a large prey for such a tiny bat.

Coming across Colts Farm to warden one afternoon, I stood and watched birds by the irrigation sprays. They are usually attracted by the insects that breed and feed in the near vicinity, but that day they were acting strangely. The birds were flying upwards along the length of the waterjets and at first I thought this was a variant of their bathing, though less effort would have been used by standing under the jets with wings outstretched as they usually do. Then I noticed that only one jet was being used for this and the other birds were waiting to take their turn. Mystified, I viewed the jet from every angle and coming closer found that from where they were the sunshine through the water was rainbow-hued, the colours shimmering and translucent the higher into the air the water gushed. The birds continuously flew upwards along the waterjets, till the sprinkler head turned and the sun no longer reflected through the water. Patiently, the little birds waited as the minutes passed and the jets moved full circle. Once more the water became a rainbow and one by one, each bird flew up its length, out again and back to earth to take its place in the queue for another turn!

One night I found myself shadowed by Luke and Lucy and I wondered where their mother was. At five-and-a-half months they were sturdy young animals fast becoming independent, but still needing the reassurance of the adult's company and, normally, not straying far from her. Anxious that they should go to earth after daybreak before any dog walkers came to the woods, I led them back to their sett in the Chantry. There in the clearing under a great beech, lay their mother's body, her face all blasted away. A direct hit at very close range; the shooter must have known it was a badger. Man is so wasteful of life. The cubs smelt her body for a moment and then came whimpering to my feet. There was still some shooting here we knew, often with silenced shotguns which made locating them especially difficult. Probably she had been killed on emerging the previous evening.

I sat on the trunk of a fallen tree with Luke on my lap and his sister huddled against my legs. A moist snout snuffled beneath my chin as I stroked the rough fur and tried to adjust to this unexpected blow. How *could* we stop the shooting? I knew individual constables walked here off duty whenever they could and several shotgun enthusiasts had been caught, but 168 acres of woodland is a large area and the police had many more matters to attend to. If only the County Trust who managed these woods would hurry up with the notice-boards displaying the by-laws that they had promised to erect and also the 'no shooting' signs the police had suggested. A fence was needed as well to stop vehicles and 'bikes entering along the Wildflower Path. All these projects were visible signs of ownership and concern. But most important of all, was the Council's promise to employ a proper warden. At least the police tried to help in a practical way, but everyone else seemed bogged down with talk and red-tape. Now Little'un was dead and her cubs whimpered at my feet. I had to admit that much of my bitterness stemmed from my own sense of inadequacy. I was useless as a warden and I knew it.

= 2 =
The Orphans

By mid-July the blue skies had turned to black and it rained continuously for three days and nights. At first, after their mother's death, I had run away when I saw Luke and Lucy coming, hoping the cubless sows would take them over or, at least, show some maternal interest. They never did, however, probably because the cubs were already weaned and partly independent. Running away achieved nothing either. True, I could out-distance them, but loneliness didn't send them back to the company of their own kind. Instead, it gave them a dogged determination; snouts to ground, they picked up my scent trail and followed me night after night. My two snuffling, whickering shadows never gave up and reluctantly I came to accept that at least till the autumn, Little'un's offspring would regard me as a mother-substitute.

Some badger behaviour is instinctive like the practice of carrying bedding, shuffling quickly backwards to the sett. The foreshadowing of this inherent trait can be seen in cubs of a few weeks old, who pick up a leaf and carry it backwards a few steps before dropping it again. It is by observation, however, that cubs learn many of a badger's foraging techniques and though I know how these animals tackle different foods, I couldn't teach by example! Each time they found me, I would go look-about for the sows to encourage the cubs to forage near them. If I wandered away, however, I would soon hear their plaintive calling and a few minutes later they would be at my feet. Lucy was small, neat and very alert – the 'prettiest' badger I have ever seen. Luke was the male counterpart and heavier. Neither resembled their mother one jot, but both had Leslie's (their grandmother) ways and somehow reminded me of her enormously. Against my will and almost without realizing it, these two cubs had crept into my affection; I who wasn't going to be emotionally involved with badgers anymore! They loved the fallen birch at the Six Wents part of Ashcroft Woods and would bounce up and down, in and out its still-living foliage, only stopping when some delicacy was discovered, though they didn't always eat it. This was where their lack of a mother was most noticeable. One morning, Lucy pawed a large slug over and over, but finally left it uneaten. Never mind, perhaps it would eventually come.

A few days later at first light, I heard shooting coming from the Chantry and kept the badgers well away until the rain turned to a downpour. The shooting ceased at 6 a.m. and together we went 'home' and I watched them enter Old Joe's Sett. Not being a badger myself, I had no way of going to earth with them and had to sound angry before they would finally go below and stay there. Later that morning, I stood at the edge of the Chantry and Great Chantry Field for a while watching the rain. Continuing towards the Felled Logs, I passed what had been the body of Little'un – decomposition is quick in hot and wet weather. The foul smell had gone and there remained just a heap of shrunken-down grey. Checking the other setts as I walked home through the woods, I met Crisp still rooting about below the Scots Pines Sett and I stroked her as she stood on hind legs against me. How vivid this place was in rain – every shade of green, clearcut and clean. Bracken, bramble, grass, lichened trunks, leaves, all living and growing.

Another night, Lucy and Luke found me in Watcher's company and the vixen stole silently away. Although the little sow now ate small slugs, she was sniffing at a large one viewing it as possible food. Badgers, however, don't care for the excess mucus from the larger varieties, so they knead them first with their front paws, or rub them against something, before chewing them up. The cubs I felt, would never learn how to treat these gastropeds if someone didn't show them. So hiding my revulsion, I took it from her and rubbed it back and forth against the bracken. Then with what I thought was a crafty sleight-of-hand, I appeared to put the slug into my mouth and chewed hard and long whilst Lucy gazed intently into my face. A swallow on my part...

and still Lucy looked. Then, suddenly, she snuffled my hand, picked up her slug and padded along the fallen birch. She hadn't been fooled! A quick twist and the slug was thrown to land somewhere amongst the bracken and foliage below. I didn't think my potential as a badger mum was very great! Although the excess mucus made by larger slugs appears distasteful, I suspect the badgers' dislike is because of its stickiness to the fur of paws or around the mouth. In Victorian times, some dairies employed people to collect grey slugs by the bucketful which were then crushed up and put in cows' milk to give it a more creamy appearance. Even to keep strongly flavoured or smelling things near milk can taint it, so obviously the flavour of the slugs and their mucus couldn't have impaired the taste. However, I shall leave proving this to someone else!

By the end of July, the fields of rape with their ripened pods, had been harvested. The recent heavy rains had badly beaten down the barley and much of it was spoilt. The damp earth had encouraged the badgers to digout their homes afresh and Jude's digging at the Old Cherry Sett seemed almost the work of a small JCB! I missed Watcher's company for my two little shadows enjoyed chasing her off if I took any notice of her. Watcher, as she had no liking for badgers anyway, would merely slip away. I encouraged the cubs to catch the moths as they blundered about our heads and to find the insects living beneath the bark of dead trees, especially the Scots pines, by tearing the rotting 'plates' away. One cub would have been slower to learn, but the competition between brother and sister speeded up the process. We vied with one another for the tiny ripe cherries that fell from the geans onto the Wildflower Path and they gleaned the grain that had dropped from the spoilt barley. The year's first blackberries had ripened and I picked and gave them some, then refused to feed them further, merely picking for myself. Quickly they learned which were ripe and which were sour, possibly from a berry's softness, but more likely from its smell.

One night I discovered a fresh crowning-down hole had been dug into the tunnelling in Jude's part of the Old Cherry Sett sometime during the previous day. Two entrances had been stopped, that is the tops broken down with a shovel and the loose earth trodden in hard. Jude's other well-used entrances had peg holes round them; most likely 'fox' nets had been staked across each. Dogs' pawprints were every-where. The work had the appearance of haste, however. Had the terriermen been disturbed by people walking on the path below? The great boar was unhurt, but was now digging-out an entrance much further up the slope. Once more the fresh spoil heap he was creating showed clear amongst the greenery, advertising his move.

That day I phoned the village constable and found that this work by terriermen coincided with a suspect van seen by the police a few miles away. The van's owner and his friend had parked by a well-known badger sett, but had hastily driven off when the police approached. They had also been lamping and had been stopped with lurchers and terriers one night. I was asked if my area had any lampers now, but no, we hadn't. The police had caught some last winter and word had quickly got about amongst the others. We also discussed the shooting of Little'un. The constable promised to check for suspect vehicles and look round Ashcroft Woods as much as he could. He would let the rest of the Rural Office know and added, 'Now your diggers have been unsuccessful though they can see badgers are there, perhaps they'll try lamping for them again, especially with so many of the fields clear of crops.' It was a thought. We would all have to be on our guard.

The 10th August was the night of the full moon, everywhere was very lovely. I sat high up on the Old Cherry slope with a sleepy lapful of cubs and listened to the tawny owlets' hunger calls to their parents who were hunting for them over the barley stubble of Long Field. Lapwings and three of the adult badgers had been gleaning the grain there too, as well as Lucy and Luke. Now replete and their bellies tight as drums, the youngsters had scrambled onto my lap. Somewhere below us Jude was laboriously clearing and enlarging the inner tunnelling of his new home, though he seemed content with his single entrance in the stool of an old once-coppiced chestnut tree, long left to grow unchecked. Five great trunks grew around the edges of the stool and the sett entrance was in the very middle. From a distance would come the sounds of his digging, then a prolonged bumping with occasional stops to rest. He was dragging earth and debris beneath his body, holding it in place with both front paws and shuffling backwards on his 'elbows'; much the same action as for their bedding collecting. Backing out of the entrance, a few strong kicks of his hindlegs sent it flying onto an enormous spoil heap that was spilling through the chestnut trunks, across the stool-edge and way down the slope. His instinct to dig had made the three-year-old boar immensely powerful, the massive slope of his shoulders, conflicting with the small, short-sighted eyes and benign expression. Jude was in fact what he looked – a gentle giant, only using his strength to defend his territory, his clan or himself. That early morning, his spoil heap yielded something unexpected – the small skull and bones of a young badger. The bony ridge or sagittal crest of the

23

skull was still in the process of being formed which indicated the cub's age at death as about seven months.

As August progressed, the warmth and dampness encouraged the growth of many fungi with stinkhorns, parasol toadstools and the little branching *Clavaria cristata* sprouting from the woodland paths. Part of Newby Farm whose fields bordered Briarmead, was up for sale and I met the farmer one morning in the lane. Many farms were on the market and we wondered who, if anyone, would buy the land. He had noticed the shooting and bike-riding in Ashcroft Woods and asked about the badgers. I mentioned I would soon be away for three days and nights and had already let the police know. He promised to keep an eye on the setts and vehicles parked in odd places. That night there was a storm with the most beautiful lightning I have ever seen, often without thunder or rain. There were three groups of flashes branching and interlocking in the western sky, making a brilliant panorama above the land and lighting up the darkest places within the woods.

I need not have feared for the badgers' safety, for on my return Sis and her cub found me first and approached purring. The sow squatted onto my boots and musked me, sniffed her musking and tried again. This was repeated several times before she was satisfied with her work. Meanwhile, Little Joe decided my jersey had badger-potential and was tugging a sleeve. As I was struggling to regain ownership of my clothing, Meg and Bess appeared and Little Joe was stampeded in the rush to reach me. The jersey was saved with one sleeve half as long again as the other! The two little sows purred and whickered, Meg climbing into my lap to groom my hair. Later, I was musked by Missy, their mother, and Susie. The adults had been gleaning barley together. All the badgers here systematically quartered the harvested fields. Their latrine-pits filled with the husk-studded dung, had been dug under the Poplar Row and the Briarmead hedge. Crisp, Lucy and Luke made their pleasure felt by flattening me... well, at least it showed I had been missed! Jude's reaction was quite different. He foraged closeby till all the fuss died down and everyone had gone on their way. Then, he quietly approached me sitting on the great Cherry's trunk, and clambered up to my level and laid his chin on my knee. If he lived to a good age, Jude would be far more massive than Old Joe ever was, yet what a placid creature he was.

That night too, I had a barking contest with Watcher's three offspring over the width of Long Field. I was walking slowly along the top of the Bank Sett which is parallel with the Wildflower Path, when one young dogfox saw the movement and barked. I answered, forgetting that this is the one place in all my area that creates an echo. My bark from the bank top 'bounced' off the trees and resounded around. Now all three youngsters were barking as well as I; a pack of foxes were sounding. Just then Watcher herself appeared in the field below me and leapt up the bank, whining her pleasure.

My few nights' absence seemed to have had an odd effect on Jude. From now on, for some part of each night, he kept me company. Luke and Lucy were growing more independent and no longer shadowed me continuously. If Crisp or any of the cubs were with me and wanting to play, Jude allowed himself to be drawn into their games; he always had been a softie with the cubs. More often though, he would appear when I was on my own. One night he approached me purring, not the friendly purr, but his deep, sexual, throaty one, and walked round me stiff-legged. I spoke and stroked his head, but still he continued, I standing rather uneasily, wondering what was going to happen next. I soon found out when he tried to mount my leg and I got out of the way rather quickly. He persisted, however, and the only way out of the situation seemed for me to run off, dodging back and forth through the trees to escape him!

This incident reinforced my belief that badgers, in common with other animals, are well aware of human sex. I am also certain, that had I been a man I would have been less acceptable to this badger family and would never have had the success with them that I am privileged to enjoy today. Odour for the badger, plays an important role in this; also the woman's approach to an animal. *The Soul of the Wolf* by M. W. Fox (1980) explains the different reactions of a wolf towards men and women far more eloquently than I can. 'Squatting, remaining quiet, not staring directly and expressing with one's body language and whole presence – Come to me and let us be friends – usually break the initial fear/flight reaction and friendly contact is established.' This was with a wolf brought up in the author's household and walked in the local park. This passive, submissive approach of a woman can of course, be emulated by a man. The problem of odour would be more difficult.

A husband and wife took on the responsibility for two very young badgercubs, orphaned by diggers. They were determined to limit human contact to themselves and then make it as little as possible as they wished the badgers to be reintroduced back to their original home. For part of every night they drove their van to the area where they lived and gave the cubs the freedom of running about, before returning home. Eventually, the whole affair became so time consuming that a male friend helped them. As the cubs grew, their independence became such that they remained free for a considerable period each night and eventually reverted to a free-living state. The couple and their friend still took it in turns to drive up and walk about at night to check the badgers. One night, first the boar and then the sow yearling, were aggressive towards the friend and from then on would have nothing to do with him. Later, the same thing happened with the husband, *but* not with the wife. She continued to go out occasionally and both badgers still came up to her. None of this, of course, necessarily proves my point, but I find it very interesting.

By the 28th August, all the harvest had been gathered in with most of the Newby fields ploughed. Badgers, foxes, lapwings and seagulls were busy each night on the upturned earth. Recalling the village constable's warning, I was coming to the area by 9 p.m. half-expecting to see lampers' lights shining out, but happily all was peaceful. That night I did my usual badger headcount – Crisp, Lucy and Luke (horrors first!), Missy, Susie, Sis and Little Joe, then Meg and Bess playing together inside the woods. But where was Jude? Every night now he found me. I wondered if lampers had been here before me, but if so, it would scarcely have been dark.

I checked the roads and lanes for traffic casualties, but there were none. With Little'un's shooting in mind, I combed his favourite foraging places, still hoping his lumbering figure would appear. Ashcroft Woods seemed alive with young birds calling. The dark hours were scarcely long enough for the nightjar and tawny adults hunting food, to satisfy the ever-increasing demands of their growing fledglings. The young nightjars could fly, but catching insects on the wing is a specialized art. The largest owlet could also fly quite well, but the other two spent much of their time on the home branch, wing-flapping to strengthen their muscles. After such a session, one would lean forward, then jump. Once airborne, flying was least of their problems. Avoiding trees, crash-landing and taking off from the ground required skill and judgement. Normally I stayed to watch their progress, but the missing badger dominated my thoughts that night.

It was at his sett that I found Jude. He lay on the earth, tongue protruding between open jaws, his chest, front legs and lips covered in froth, the snare round his neck, biting deep into the flesh. His single entrance in the chestnut stool had been clawed bare of earth where he had twisted and turned in his futile efforts to dislodge his torment. A lesser boar, or one of the sows would have given up exhausted after a while, but Jude had grown enormous with a strength akin to Old Joe's. The snare that gouged deeply into his throat had been placed over the entrance, the end clipped round a thick stake driven into the ground closeby. The snare was soon unclipped, but the noose did not release its hold for it was buried deep into the boar's neck. It was a slow job to open and as the tension eased, glistening drops of blood appeared from the wound. Then gently lifting his head, I slipped the noose clear, laying his head back on the bloodsoaked ground. A long time passed before the sound of his breathing became easier. Only his eyes and occasionally his lips moved. It was still dark under the trees, but a lighter darkness was showing through the foliage far down the slope over Long Field. It was 5 a.m. as I sat with Jude's head in my lap and the male tawny flew on silent wings to his calling station nearby. A low, quavering hoot and a sharp kewiking as the hen answered from my left.

Should I go to get help? The nearest house was a distance away and the owner of the snare might easily return before I did. If a vet or the RSPCA came out, I would need to meet their van to direct them into the woods. And what could they do? To take him from his environment would be possibly the final shock to an already deeply shocked animal. Jude grunted with a sharp intake of breath and was still, but my hand felt the warmth of his tongue and his dark eyes knew mine. Dawn came as the sun rose high, sending deep shafts of flame to colour the trunks nearby. He grunted again and quivering, raised his head from my numbed leg in an attempt to gather himself for the final effort. Slowly, very slowly, he tried to stand, I keeping a hand on each side of his body, fearing he would drop back again and perhaps fall down the slope. At last he stood head lowered; then crouching, disappeared into the darkness of the sett. It was 8 a.m; no one had returned for their snare and its contents, or had they unknown to me? It was possible for the foliage was thick all around. I waited till well into the morning of that August Bank Holiday Saturday, but heard and saw no one there, nor on the way home.

I never saw Jude again and for the remainder of the Bank Holiday and early September, flies buzzed in and out his entrance. Lucy and Luke his offspring, returned to the Old Cherry slope, though at a distance away and very near the great tree itself. They were digging out and re-opening long disused entrances with the sandy spoil heaps bright on the lush, green grass. One day, before I left for home, I checked the sett once more, but all was peaceful. Light was stealing through the mist and touching the dew-laden spider webs on bramble and bush. Kneeling at Jude's entrance high up on the slope, I caught the sickly smell of decay. Poor Jude. One day another badger would digout here and *his* skull would lie on the soft earth. The snarer's stake had been well driven into the ground and pull as I might, I hadn't the strength to dislodge it. Somehow it seemed an invitation for others to do likewise at the cubs' entrances below me. Never mind. I had discussed the problems here with the head of Oakley police station and the Inspector had asked that I take him on site to see what could be done. Perhaps he could remove the stake.

Now that the badgercubs were independent, Watcher often accompanied me at night and I was enjoying her company again. She also joined me sometimes when I wardened these woods by day if it was quiet. I was unsure how to deal with this. The nights were a time of high winds and mountainous clouds, swift-moving to reveal a crescent moon and glinting stars. By autumn, all badgers are obsessed with eating to put on a thick layer of fat for the lean months ahead and mine were no exceptions! There were plenty of damsons dropping from the hedgerow trees and the acorns were big and plump, but this season's chestnuts were poor. I noticed that Crisp was standing on her hindlegs in the pear orchard, snout raised skywards. Badgers don't miss much where their stomachs are concerned! What Crisp did, Luke and Lucy were guaranteed to copy. The adult sow's habit of pushing her snout down the tops of my boots with her mouth full, became a favourite of theirs also, and I often returned home with wet and messy wellingtons.

The young tawny owls were independent now and soon would be leaving their parents' territory in search of their own. I had known the adults over a long period and, by imitating their calls, could often attract them to me. During the breeding season, however, I was hesitant to do so and particularly this summer when, invariably, the badgercubs were with me. Lucy and Luke were no respecters of birds, and tawnies with owlets to protect can attack without warning. One warm night, the mature tawny male flew round me calling as I stood on the Wildflower Path. His mate answered and they both flew round. I slowly raised my hand and gave the contact call. He went to alight, but swerved away as she perched instead. Only room for one owl on my hand and the lady was the boss! He was now in the ash tree just above us. He called and she answered into my face. How I wished I had my mini tape-recorder. Sometimes I record their calls and play the recording back to them. I have had the male perch on the recorder, all the while listening intently to the play-back!

Now they called and answered one another, she from my hand and he from above. Call, answer, call, answer, then he inverted his cry and she changed her reply. What do the slight variations mean to these birds? It would make a very interesting subject to study and perhaps it would be possible to fill the gaps in our knowledge of this species.

The afternoon of the on-site meeting with the Inspector was hot and sunny after the previous day's rain. I had drawn a rough map of Ashcroft Woods and arrowed in where we would be walking. Some time since the rain, trial bikes had been on many of the woodland paths. These the Inspector duly noted on the map, together with the routes taken into the woods. We were hoping for padlocked gates at three points and I particularly wanted a fence erected by the laneside bordering Long Field. A gate there would prevent lorries being driven in to fly-tip, or stolen cars to be stripped and set alight, but only a fence would stop motorbikes roaring up over the Briarmead bank and along the Wildflower Path. Once there, the favoured 'trials' course was the steep slope of the Old Cherry Sett. Neither the Council, who would need to find the money, nor the County Trust, who managed Ashcroft Woods, seemed to understand the need for this fence. However, the Inspector certainly did.

It was the first time he had seen the badgers' main breeding sett with its many curious entrances. The chestnut bough was only one of several dug into the bole of a tree. There was the disused nursery entrance, scene of Crisp, Sis and Little'un's birth, that led into the terriermen's old crowning-down hole. I showed him where Jude had been snared and he easily pulled the stake out for me, before we walked on to view the worst shooting areas and popular camping places. We picked up two bright shotgun cases on one of the paths, probably discharged that morning and agreed that policing such a large area of woods was well-nigh impossible. Having said that, however, the Inspector said the police would do whatever they could to help and I would continue to send them the monthly report of incidents here. Walking out at the top of Briarmead, the Inspector exclaimed, 'Just look at that view' and we stood looking over the farmland, the distant hillside and the gleam of river and lakes in the valley below.

I stood at first light the following morning, looking out over the valley and thinking of the history of the place. The wind blew through the meadow by the Old Barn ruins across the way, making the grass race, twisting and turning as it went. From a distance it was a strange sight, especially where the wind passed over the hill. One wave would catch up with another; one would turn my way, whilst yet another weaved in and out. Wind amongst grass or corn is a wonderful sight.

Originally, there were two cottages and their garden on the left-hand side of Briarmead Lane as it enters the woods, and a large barn to the right. The barn was by far the oldest structure in the area and was built on three sides of a square, the two 'arms' open-fronted to house wagons and carts and the middle side completely enclosed to take the farm oxen. In 1962 this building was still roofed and in use, a door in the adjoining wall of each open-sided portion leading to the main body of the Old Barn. Ten years later and before the tiles had fallen, I found appropriately perhaps, barn owl pellets piled together on debris in a dark corner. This led me to spend many happy night hours observing a pair of these ghostly birds, hunting over the top fields.

The next three years saw rapid deterioration of the Old Barn, one arm collapsing entirely, with nettles and rank weeds pushing up through the floor and partially destroying the runnel that ran the length of the main structure. Like many bygone buildings of an age when labour was cheap, it was well and sturdily made, with thick interlocking overhead beams, back windows looking out onto the woods in the main part and doors that, even in my time, closed perfectly. The Old Barn is shown on a 1769 map, but the cottages opposite were added later for the stockmen and their families to live nearby and so care more easily for the animals and carts. We tend to forget that oxen were the main beasts of burden for more than nine centuries and that their long reign was superseded by the horse for a comparatively short period. Then came the traction engine, briefly, which was in turn outdated by the tractor.

Oxen were used to plough in the south-east well into the 1920s, particularly in Sussex. There was much to recommend them, for they were fed on straw rather than hay, they were hardier, stoically reliable and, unlike the horse, required little attention after a hard day's work. Although undersized compared with modern cattle, they were nevertheless considered fit for meat when dead, whereas the horse was only carrion. In addition, the oxens' simple oak or hornbeam yokes and ash bows were easily made and mended on the farm and their shoes were often farm-made too. The variety of shoe design is enormous, and I still sometimes pick them up off the freshly ploughed fields. Oxen were generally shod on the front hooves only and the 'kews' as they were called, were separate half-moon shaped plates, nailed much as horse shoes. One kew went on each half of the cloven hoof. If a continuous shoe had been used so the hoof was locked and the two halves could not spread, then the animal would have been lamed.

But now, the cottages, too, have gone. That morning I stood in their overgrown garden with the sighing wind for company. It parted the long grass and in it I seemed to hear children's voices. Ninety years ago, little Elsie Lovell would walk through these woods on the old drover's track and so to the cottages, to stay and play with her big brother's daughters. Elsie was the youngest and only girl of a family of ten, so at six years old she was already an aunt several times over. Two of her brothers were ploughmen and lived far away, but her beloved Tom was head stockman here and his children, her playmates. It seems a sad reflection on our times that the child could walk safely unaccompanied the two miles of lane and isolated woodland, carrying a small bundle of presents for her kin and being neither at risk nor frightened. Instead, she loved the walk, her feeling of independence and the search for a 'few pretty flowers along the way' to give to her big brother's wife.

The children sometimes played in the woods behind the cottages, but these were keepered, so much of their time was spent in the old garden, even then a source of pleasure to the little girl who found its meandering paths and profusion of colour such a contrast to her garden at home, where only practical vegetables were grown. She could stand completely hidden behind the wisteria that sprawled over the wall and tried several times, unsuccessfully, to keep the Virginia creeper's brilliant autumn leaves forever in her drawer, only to find them later withered and faded. The downy-leaved spikes of great mullein or Aaron's rod and the slighter, white mullein she remembered well, and the pink-flowered bistort too, for the Easter-ledge puddings that were made from its leaves. But it was the musk roses, their colour and scent and the delicate fritillaries' chequered bells springing up from the grass, that at the end of her long life, she recalled so vividly.

It was the job of Tom, the head stockman, and his neighbour to feed and harness the horses ready for the day's work and although the Old Barn was out of bounds to the children, they were sometimes allowed to stand and watch. To the sound of jingling harness, the older man told them of himself at their age watching the oxen being yoked by his father. These were the small but sturdy red Sussex and he remembered them well. He gave each girl a crescent-shaped kew that had once fitted on the oxen span he recalled. At home, Elsie's father had polished hers till it shone and threaded it through by the nail holes to hang on her wall, for he too had memories of the slow and placid beasts. The Old Barn, like the garden, was a fascinating place for hide-and-seek. One day, Tom found the children playing there and gave them the job of cleaning all the horse brasses as a punishment!

Life wasn't all play for labourers' children though and generally at 11 years old, they left school to earn a few pennies bird-scaring or, that hated, back-breaking job of picking stones and flints from the fields. Elsie was one of the fortunate ones and escaped this to go into service. Whenever she could in adult life, she returned with her husband to the cottages and their garden.

But times change; families move on and buildings fall into decay. Why are forgotten gardens so evocative? This one had a feeling of timelessness, of beauty planned, perfected, enjoyed, then left to its natural devices. One can be alone, but never lonely in such a place. I only knew Elsie in her old age and quite by chance, found that she had played in the same garden I had discovered. Better still, she knew so much of its history. Talking, it seemed to us that a love of flowers had threaded our lives and bound them together.

Old Elsie, like the cottages and barn, has gone now and the woods, of course, are a Nature Reserve. And her garden? That was soon to be covered in asphalt and surrounded by rustic log fencing, for a car-park was needed for the visitors who drive up the lane to the woods.

Ashcroft Woods is used to visitors, though in the past, they haven't always been so welcome. Briarmead was not only a drovers' route, but a smugglers' too. A light at night from a high place was used as a signal for the smugglers and the position of a light, seen through foliage, was difficult to pinpoint accurately if customs men were about. The building in the Chantry had such a reputation, overlooking as it does, the winding lane and sloping countryside. Most local people, rich and poor, were involved in some way with the smugglers and many of the small farmers would never have survived on their poor farms without trading in some way. An old charcoal burner who worked the woods at Rendcombe, died very rich through assisting the smugglers on their route through the parish. In contrast, one informer was found 'roughly used' and another murdered in the woods around Oakley. The Court Rolls of the local Manor contained an interesting item in the late 1700s when the jurors requested 'that a pair of Stocks for the Detention and punishment of Offenders against the Laws, are necessary and wanted in the parish and that the same ought to be put up at the charge and expense of the inhabitants of the said parish.' The actual offence is not mentioned, but smuggling was rife at the time and a worsening problem. The recommendation for stocks was disregarded, not surprisingly, since most of the parish was involved. Who wants to provide their own punishment?

Briarmead through the woods is a beautiful route and one part of it is a sunken drove road bordered by pollarded beeches, all twisted and gnarled. Walking home along it, I've often mused on the exact location of 'the great Hanging gate in the Hollow way' and why there was one. This had gone by the 1700s and only the old documents remain to record its existence.

Ashcroft Woods have been 'managed' from medieval times at least, but possibly much earlier, when sweet chestnut and hazel were planted and coppiced. Beech, hornbeam and oak were left to attain their full growth amongst the coppicing and these are called 'standards'. These species, amongst the other trees, grew tall in their search for light. We were traditionally a sea-faring nation and long oak planks were needed for shipbuilding. Before these mature trees were felled, young oaks had

already been planted to replace them. Sadly, few oaks are planted today.

Rining was a crop, harvested in the spring, that was used for tanning. For this process, a special tool was needed to strip off the bark, usually in early May when the sap was rising. Oaks were particularly favoured for this treatment.

I suspect that most of the alder in the woods was deliberately planted, for alder is very tolerant of cutting and was once widely grown as a coppice tree. Not only is the wood easily turned for a range of articles from barrels to broomheads, but the poles obtained from coppicing were used for charcoal for the manufacture of gunpowder. Other trees were also coppiced for charcoal as it had many uses – for fuel, in the smelting of metal ores, as an absorbent, and, of course, for drawing. Charcoal burning was a craft traditionally handed down from father to son. Every forest and wood had its burners and the same kiln sites were used repeatedly as the earth below them became conditioned. Unlike other workmen in the woods, burners couldn't go home at night for the circular hearths had to be carefully tended to prevent them from bursting into flames. Some burners were nomadic and had their families living with them in rough huts, or more recently, in caravans. The man who last plied this trade in Ashcroft Woods was more fortunate and, until 1890, rented a small, timber built cottage on the edge of Great Chantry Field where it borders Briarmead Lane. It is probable his father and grandfather lived there before him and, like most early cottages, it had only an earth floor without foundations. By the 1920s, this dwelling was dilapidated and damp and inhabited by a man who paid no rent. When he died, it was pulled down and the small area on which it stood, reverted back to the plough.

These woods were worked for gravel and sand. The deep hollow inside them bordering Sand Pit Field, still yields pure sand each time a fox or rabbit digs out in the warren there. The gravel pits were later partly infilled and 'puddled' to create flight ponds. Main Pond was the largest of these. Ironically, this was probably the heyday of Ashcroft Woods for the wealthy owner was conscious of its value and had a love of trees, seeing them not only as an inheritance for his family, but living things of beauty also. The place was well managed and 'keepered with goose and duck on the flight ponds and pheasant, quail, partridge and woodcock aplenty. It is difficult to visualize this now with the ponds so rank and dirty; for the last 50 years they have been a favourite dumping ground for rubbish especially from campers.

There are the remains of two deneholes inside the woods and two on Colts Farm outside. Deneholes countrywide have been dug for different reasons and some are very old. These local ones, however, were dug to extract chalk for marling the surrounding fields and are of no great antiquity. The pick marks on the walls were made by square-headed picks and are no earlier than the eighteenth century. These 'chalk holes' were made in the form of a deep well with a pulley and bucket at the top to draw up the excavated chalk. In Ashcroft Woods, when a shaft had been sunk into the chalk it led to a single chamber, whereas those outside in the fields, have several chambers spreading away horizontally in different directions. Whole families were engaged in this dangerous work, particularly children, who were very nimble, though accidents were commonplace. These families travelled the countryside, hiring themselves out to local farmers. Prices would be haggled and disagreements were not unknown. In one incident, here, the diggers downed tools and left a shaft of less than four metres to puzzle successive generations as to its purpose! Long before fertilisers were used, acidic soils were neutralized by the process of marling which involved spreading alkaline chalk on the fields. The result was described as 'cowspit' and looked like earth mingled with lime, leaving many small white specks on it. Farmers also sometimes used the chalk for road-making, first leaving it to dry out in the farmyard.

The history of man in the woods goes back beyond recorded time. Early settlers had a hill or lookout post before the Romans made one at its highest point, the Chantry, overlooking the valley. Flints and a beautifully worked Palaeolithic handaxe have been discovered by modern man, whilst Romano-British tiles, shards and oyster shells, have been dugout by modern badger! My great boar badger Old Joe, returned to the Felled Logs Sett one night and had a massive digout. When he had gone to earth there and the rising sun filtered through the trees, I noticed it glinted and reflected on many, tiny, glazed fragments of decorated tile amongst the old bedding and fresh earth of his spoil heap. Most of these were crumbling and all quickly lost their bright colour once exposed to the light and air. Three pieces only I successfully retrieved and these were pronounced Romano-British by a curator of the local museum. The other setts have yielded, amongst all the broken pieces, a tiny, perfect Victorian vase, a glazed pot of the same period, a smoothly-baked clay marble and, most recently, a small inlaid wooden box, brass-sided and intricately made. Cubs, both badger and fox are very playful and will carry off small objects to the den or sett. These may be played with for a while and then abandoned, or more likely taken to earth. The vase was dugout by a badger living in the Chantry and the charcoal burner's house was at the far edge of Great Chantry Field. Could it have come from here and if so, who brought it? A child looking for flowers... or a cub looking for a game?

= 3 =

The Great Storm

October started mild and wet with the badgers worming on the freshly ploughed fields. With food so abundant and easily obtained at this time of year, there was plenty of opportunity to return to the sett half-way through the night and sleep off a heavy meal, or to digout old entrances and extend the tunnelling. Their instinct to eat and so lay down fat for the winter ahead is as strong as that of digging. Not only will the area's main breeding sett be re-dug and cleared for winter use, but, most if not all, of the outlying setts too. If a badger is disturbed at its chosen winter home, the resulting stress may cause it to move to another within the territory, so this autumn digging makes strong sense. One can be forgiven, however, for believing an area is full of badgers, or indeed, that all such setts are badger-occupied. Two badgers here were responsible for re-opening as many as 16 entrances in a couple of nights and not sleeping in any of them!

The rain continued as the month progressed. Friday and Saturday, the 9th and 10th October were very heavy, cold and with gale force winds, so that by Sunday morning, 12 cms had fallen and the River Bourne rose steadily. Only the badgers loved it and they foraged deep in the wood, protected from the wind. The paths became streams that converged into the lane. Briarmead was a torrent of water that gushed off the fields and through the banks of the winding lane sending earth, flints and leaves down to the main road.

With brief sunny periods between, the heavy rain continued till the night of Wednesday 14th when it ceased about 3 a.m. The incessant wet had finally stopped the badgers' digging some nights earlier when the earth became mud. Missy, with Meg and Bess, were well settled at Colts Farm in the sett there. Missy was a lovely, gentle creature and I fervently hoped that nothing bad would befall her. Crisp, Lucy, Luke, Sis and Little Joe were spread out at the Old Cherry Sett which left just Susie on Cliffords Bank. I suspected Susie found the three tearaways, Crisp, Lucy and Luke, rather wearing and preferred a loner's existence to a noisy one and I sympathized! The badgers generally met up at some point during the night in any case, though I was never quite sure if it was because I was about, or whether they would have done so without me. I watched them take worms, grubs, berries, chestnuts, acorns, windfall pears and damsons that night and marvelled at their capacity for eating!

The next day was bright and gusty, the glint of water all around and a busyness of birds. They seemed to be making the most of the first rain-free day, their flitting shapes and continual calls held an urgency. That evening there were many birds in the sky, the dying sun accentuating their vast numbers. I stood a long while watching them, noting with unease that they were all flying northwards. (I didn't connect this until much later with the atmospheric pressure preceding the storm that probably warned them of impending danger.)

Soon after dark that night I walked the land, enjoying its fresh scents and not heeding the fine rain as Thursday passed into Friday. By 2 a.m., however, I sought the shelter of the woods from the heightening wind that seemed intent on blowing me off my feet. An owl called through the tumult; the trees bent and rasped together as his quavering cry sounded from above. I answered him standing below and held out my hand. His wings rose as he dropped. At least I was a more steady perch than a swaying tree! The rain had ceased with a weak crescent moon struggling through tattered clouds. The tawny yawned gape wide, leaned forward and grasping the material of my anorak with his curved beak, climbed onto my shoulder, so relieving my hand of his not inconsiderable weight. There he sat preening and I walked on carefully, knowing from experience that he would stay quite happily till I reached the boundary of his territory. Then he would become uneasy, swivelling his head this way and that, raising his broad-padded feet and placing them down again like a shuffling human. Next there would be a sudden

lift off as he flew back on silent wings, only calling when he reached his own piece of woodland again. This night was the exception, for he chose to stay with me as I passed through his territory into his neighbour's and so through the length and breadth of Ashcroft Woods, till together we returned full circle.

By 3.15 a.m. the gale was fearful, like none other that I had ever known. The badgers were underground as the wind screamed through the trees, twisting and bending them with frightful strength. I didn't want to leave; I belonged to this place, so went to shelter against the Old Cherry's massive bulk, curling up small. The sheer volume of noise was deafening, and then with horrid fascination I saw the ground above me heave and crack open. The split ran like water down the slope, widening as it neared; something beneath me heaved and shuddered

... and the split disappeared again in a rush of earth and twiggy debris. The wind howling over the Cherry Sett slope from the open fields above was lifting the trees momentarily from the sodden ground as it went. Once passed, their great weight settled back once more, but not often in exactly the same spot. The forced-up roots tore the ground that closed again as the trees eased back. I wasn't afraid, indeed I had been out and enjoyed too many gales to fear them and knew from experience that it could be far more dangerous to try returning home across the open farmland. Yet something beyond myself was urging me away.

The journey home *was* frightening, as twice I was plucked up and thrown down again. My once familiar landscape had gone. A giant's hand had snapped in half each tree of the Poplar Row, with some uprooted and stretching far across the fields. Obstacles impeded my progress and branches torn off trees and blown into others, hung precariously suspended.

Navigating Ingrim's Fields, I met a curious object; a shed roof neat and unbroken on the footpath. So buffeted but unhurt, I reached home and going round to the back door by which I always enter, found the two mature trees in our garden had been blown down. Still, there was no rain, but the wind forever worsening was of a terrible ferocity; surely more a hurricane than a gale. But we were the fortunate ones and only sustained broken guttering and tiles to our roof, whereas others lost their homes.

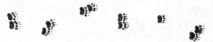

All was quiet in the mellow sunshine when I returned that afternoon to Ashcroft Woods. How can I describe the immensity of the damage? Like bodies on a battlefield, the trees lay strewn about; some flat, some at crazy angles, some uprooted with platforms of earth held in their roots, some snapped off. A desolation of trees. A catalyst, not a hurricane, had screamed through these woods. The destruction had been at its greatest for the earth was already sodden before the winds came. Great, sturdy monarchs with many years ahead of them had been wrenched up by their roots leaving gaping craters. This was probably our greatest loss. The overgrown coppicing had been pushed over in places, but not in the way one would have expected. In the main, it had been felled by great trees falling and only the dying and rotten coppicing had suffered. That which was vigorous had merely swayed back and forth, springy and pliant.

The Old Cherry Sett seemed to have disappeared under a rain of trees, earth and foliage. This is an eastern facing slope, that looks down through its green living cover to Long Field below. Trees had been ripped out of the wet earth undermined, from the tunnelling only a metre below. They had either crashed criss-cross over one another or, causing certain death to any badger below, had dropped back crushing chambers of the ancient sett. Two animals were missing from here that had gone underground before I left at 3.40 a.m.; the male cub Little Joe and his mother Sis (Lesley's daughter). I never saw them again. Parts of the slope had subsided or collapsed, elsewhere there had been a great earth slip. Clambering about searching, there was not only a danger of trunks moving as I struggled up, over, round or under, but an even greater danger of disappearing into the soft earth riddled with cracks. I took photos knowing they would never be a faithful record of the impact of carnage the hurricane had wrought on the woods that were my life, but I had to have some record, however inadequate.

When I first witnessed the desolation, my heart rebelled and I felt betrayed. For 27 years I had loved and tried to protect this wood, only to have an 'act of God' destroy great tracts of it in a few hours. The trees of Ashcroft Woods will never be restored in my lifetime, nor in my children's. Now I was picking up the pieces, though the sense of betrayal remained.

The next day I met a friend and together with her indomitable old dog, we scrambled up, under and round our woods for the paths had disappeared completely. We couldn't call it going for a walk. Margaret was upset at the destruction, but in her practical Scottish fashion said, 'We should be thinking about the trees to be planted and what kind.' My heart warmed to her – and to the little dog with his short legs that was bravely jumping over the felled trees. He wasn't going to be beaten either! The weather that had been a mixture of sunshine and showers, suddenly poured ... and shone. A radiant colour crept through the still-standing trunks as a beautiful rainbow appeared in the near-black sky. Its light reflected in the droplets still falling from the leaves above, sparkling and multi-coloured and with Margaret's words still echoing in my mind, I remembered God's promise to Noah.

> I do set my bow in the cloud, and it shall be a token of a covenant between me and the earth. And it shall come to pass, when I bring a cloud over the earth, that the bow shall be seen in the cloud: And I will remember my covenant.

It is a strange fact that I know such a God does not exist, yet just as I believe in a natural order of things, so I believe in this covenant and was comforted.

Two days later, I spoke to the man clearing the old cottage site for the new car-park. It was his lunch-break and we met as we both collected – he picking up chestnuts and myself, the inevitable rubbish. People were coming from far and near to view the damage to the woods and though the blocked paths made it impossible to walk very far, the fallen trees made ideal seats and the fine weather encouraged picnics. The man told me he had seen two terriermen the previous afternoon who had stopped their van near his car and walked into the woods, 'I don't trust that sort myself,' he said.

Shooting seemed to have increased after the storm and with all the fallen trees and the paths gone it was virtually impossible to locate anybody provided they stayed still. However, even if they did move and therefore become visible, the tangle of branches, roots and under-growth made following them difficult. Since the fateful 16th, the remaining Cherry Sett badgers were denning under the mass of felled trees and had been seen at unaccustomed times during daylight. This proved disastrous for the young badger Luke whom I found shot three times through the head. He appeared to have been using a fallen tree as a bridge on the slope and must have made a clear target against the light. I recalled his mother Little'un, shot last July and feared for Lucy, his sister. Luke's death left just six badgers in my entire area; Crisp and Lucy still at the Old Cherry Sett, Missy, Meg and Bess on Colts Farm and Susie on Cliffords Bank.

The 22nd, nearly a week after the Great Storm, as by now it was known, my young friend Stephen came for a walk with me in Ashcroft Woods. He, like so many local children, was home from school as their buildings still had no electricity. We took something to eat and a can of drink and I saw he was now as tall as me as we strode along. At 11 years, he was a good companion. Steve borrowed my instant Canon camera, I having the Olympus; he had his binoculars and I, the monocular. White clouds scudded by in a vivid blue sky as we gazed at the damage all along our route. Many trees were gone forever; we would not see their like again. Trees planted in the 1700s and mature fine giants of last week were the worst hit and, in falling, had done great damage to other trees and property.

It has been suggested that a species of honey fungus, *Armillaria mellea*, increased the scale of wind damage as it causes a fungal infection of a tree's roots which weakens them. This could also explain the patchiness of the damage where several trees, or an isolated one, were left standing and the rest blown down. However, other factors could account for this and it is not easy to answer at present. Fungal infections can also cause premature yellowing of foliage, but so can aerial pollution and a lot more research would have to be done to substantiate this suggestion about fungus. Of one thing I am certain: trees with well foliaged crowns were made top-heavy by the added weight of their wet autumn leaves.

Standing with Steve that day, my heart ached for our woods. I was to see many children, not only this one, who grieved for the trees. We have an altered landscape on a far greater scale than the Dutch Elm disease and this was so sudden. Never mind, when eventually (and it will be many months, even years) the wood is carted away, we must plant, not for our children, or our grandchildren, but for future generations. *We* must be the landscape architects of the future. Where there is room and light, there will be natural regeneration and some trees will be good to leave and rot, but where acres of trees lie criss-cross over one another denying light and space, only the invasive bramble will creep across. Steve took photos and I took Steve taking photos.

We found sections of some of the paths in Ashcroft Woods un-affected by fallen trees and when, after scrambling through branches we came to such a stretch, we had a sense of shock to realize it had all been like this barely a week earlier. Returning home we looked through the local paper and the photos of the hurricane damage, mentally counting our blessings. It *was* amazing that more lives were not lost. If it had occurred during the day, the human casualties might have been as great as the trees. As it was, cars were blown against buildings and other cars. A local driver barely escaped with his life when a tree fell in front of his car, then one behind. He got out and ran for it, as a third fell across the vehicle. There were many such accounts and near tragedies with buildings and power cables. We were all very lucky.

Through my interest in local history, I remembered the recording of the gale and destruction of 1703, though this was a storm with lightning and thunder. The recorder was an architect who never published the 'memorandum' of his village, merely leaving it as a document for posterity. He wrote,

The remarkable storm rose about 10 o'clock at night on the 26th November 1703 and continued to rage with extraordinary violence till 7 o'clock the next morning. The devastation extended through-

43

out the whole Kingdom. The damage done to London was estimated at 2 millions sterling. Two thousand stacks of chimneys were blown down, steeples toppled to the ground, the leads on the churches and public buildings were rolled up like skins of parchment. The roofs were in many instances carried entirely off the buildings. Twelve men-of-war with 1,800 men perished on the sea coast. All the boats and vessels were sunk or destroyed.

He doesn't mention the trees, but with such horrendous loss of life, he probably didn't think to. Or were the trees less damaged? Others, too, recorded the storm of 1703, but nowhere did I find a mention of trees.

Towards the end of the month, Crisp and Lucy began digging out two entrances and the inner tunnelling in the remains of their home and thankfully, were denning below ground once more. I spoke to a couple of farmers, one of whom had had a large modern barn and the other who had a listed seventeenth-century barn on his land. The latter, in Newby's farmyard, had stayed intact throughout the hurricane, apart from two tiles being blown off, whereas the modern one in Colts farmyard was completely demolished, the walls falling in and the roof sitting on top like a neatly folded cardboard box. Perhaps not so strange, for the great chestnut beams (not oak as is often supposed) and carefully pegged tiles were built to last. Modern buildings are relatively flimsy affairs.

On that last October afternoon, the sun came out and showed the woods in their autumn colours. There was no one walking as I cleared rubbish, though I was soundly scolded by a grey squirrel with much foot-stamping, churring and tail-waving. The ponds were overflowing and I stood for a time in the sunshine looking up at the ivy-clad oak nearby where the male tawny roosted. Wardening the woods that year, I had found he often called about midday if the weather was dull, though he didn't fly far. Today's sunshine was too bright for his liking, however, and he slept on in its welcoming warmth.

One mild, damp November night with the moon nearing the full, I went into the Chantry and climbed round, under and through the great fallen beeches in an effort to penetrate the centre. Their girth was so great that often I had difficulty pulling myself up and over them. Like stricken giants they lay, the white lunar light softly touching their smooth, grey trunks. Beech roots grow deep into the earth. Young beech are helped by the shelter of other species, but once, well grown, become wind-firm and sturdy trees. Their wind-pollinated flowers open in May after the leaves, but are borne only at two or three yearly intervals and with good crops of seed or 'mast' occurring perhaps once in four or five years. The base of large beech such as these becomes buttressed as time passes, though the bark remains grey and smooth through to old age. This buttressing combined with the roots that begin above ground before descending deep into the earth, encourages rainwater to collect from which birds and mammals will regularly drink. The badgers here use these drinking pools and, when those on the ground become dry, will climb some distance up the gnarled buttressing to seek out fresh ones. The bark of some trees bear numerous scratch marks from their long claws.

These stately beeches that had been planted 200 years ago had taken the full force of the winds sweeping across the open farmland. With the ground so saturated and the Chantry so high and exposed, the trees had come up roots and all with many tonnes of earth adhering to them. Up to four-metre craters had been left and immense 'walls' of bright earth,

like the side of a house, stood upright to face me as I carefully skirted these deep pits. Standing sorrowing with my hand and cheek on one smooth, horizontal trunk, something moved in the now open centre of the Chantry and there were Missy and Meg regarding me quietly. This was the first time since that fateful Friday more than two weeks' earlier that I had seen any badgers here. Together the three of us went carefully outwards to Little Chantry Field and the Warby side.

A mild night with a fresh breeze and the clouds sometimes hiding, sometimes revealing, the full moon; a beautiful skyscape with soft sounds everywhere. All the badgers were on the move, not truly settled at any place. Partly the time of year, but not altogether. The hurricane had left them disquieted and uneasy. Fallen trees were still settling and up to a year later the slightest wind would send an apparently sound one hurtling earthwards. Digging out fresh entrances could be hazardous or, at least, have startling results. A perilously poised oak under which Susie was working one night, suddenly chose to rise, taking badger and all in its branches and a very frightened animal found herself several metres off the ground!

I was with Susie, Crisp and Lucy at the margin of our woods, when suddenly I saw a man in the meadow and realized he was shooting. I took the badgers into the trees and watched them disappear through the undergrowth. Beyond my line of vision someone else was luring foxes, giving the rabbit squeal over and over again, so there were two men. These poachers were not interested in the rabbits all about, or the odd hare. One had shot a pheasant clearly visible against the skyline in the moonlight, but the foxes were wily and though around, kept well out of sight. These men were not lampers; their guns were equipped with night-sights and silencers. I had never seen them before and as they didn't seem to know their way about very well, I felt they came from a distance and, therefore, would have a vehicle parked somewhere. One finally shot a young dogfox and with that and the pheasant, they began to move and talk quietly. Certain they were going, I raced down to the farmyard nearly a mile away. The phone was dead, probably it had been so since the storm. I came back to the area only to find the nightshooters gone. In desperation, I ran all round to each possible parking place, but there was nothing parked. By now it was 5.30 a.m. and, of course, they would have been long gone. There was nothing for it but to see the badgers safely below ground and return home. I think the poachers were after fox pelts, though a badger might have been acceptable if it had been in their sights, and the pheasant was a good bonus. In the Spring of 1986, I had been given the use of two-way radio, but things had been quiet for so long that we had ceased to use it. Perhaps it would be wise to let my contact know of the night's events and bring my set out with me again.

This was a prelude to a period of illegal shooting with night-sights around Oakley and the neighbouring villages, though the guns were not always equipped with silencers.

It was about this time, too, that I was shown pictures of two dead sow badgers photographed in the back of a landrover. They had been snared and the snares were still clearly visible round their necks, though the cause of death was 'the insertion of a sharp instrument into the abdomen'. The vehicle's owner professed to finding the badgers already dead outside their sett; he had merely picked them up, he said, on finding them.

I was particularly interested in this case and not just because Jude had been snared. We were going through a spate of snaring in our own police area which, besides Oakley, includes 13 villages. Anything and everything seemed to be falling victim, from cats and dogs to livestock and wild animals. The Rural Office were doing their best to combat the problem, but even local teenagers were making free-running snares from wire obtained from hardware or DIY shops, and snaring isn't illegal.

I was still continuing with my sett mapping for our police and local RSPCA Inspector and a careful search of hedgerows and banks was turning up horrendous evidence of rotting bodies trapped in snares. The law requires that snares be checked at least once every 24 hours to prevent unnecessary suffering. The obvious drawback to this, of course, is the impossibility of enforcing such a requirement. Self-locking snares are illegal; these are ones which lock as they tighten. In theory, free-running snares are less cruel; when the victim ceases to struggle, the tension on the wire eases. However, this rarely happens.

The cheapest snares, home-made from fine wire, cut through flesh as cheese-wire does cheese. The stronger snares, bought from fieldsports shops and catalogues and made from several strands of wire twisted together, soon rub fur and skin off the frenzied animal and, once buried in its flesh, the agony is the same. No, there is one great difference. The victims caught in these professional snares will take days rather than hours to die. Myself, I hate snaring; it is cruel beyond belief.

My experience of snaring led to me being invited to write an article on the subject for *BBC Wildlife Magazine*. The RSPCA headquarters provided statistics and wrote a countrywide analysis for the article. Apart from the deliberate and illegal snaring of badgers on their known runs or trails and at sett entrances, many badgers are accidentally snared every year. Snares, after all, cannot differentiate between species. Even the Nature Conservancy Council have expressed concern at the 'significant number of protected wild animals injured and killed in snares'.

It was particularly disappointing that the County Trusts were so uncaring on the subject. The Royal Society for Nature Conservation (RSNC), with its 48 Trusts, forms the largest voluntary organization concerned with wildlife conservation in the UK. Many of its trusts have their own Badger Groups and the symbol of most of them, as well as that of the RSNC itself, is the badger. At the request of the National Federation of Badger Groups, the RSNC carried out a survey of all its trusts about snaring. Sixteen months after the Federation's initial request only four had bothered to reply. Of these four, three supported a total ban on snares and one, while recognizing the danger to badgers, felt them a better option than an increase in the use of illegal poisons. Due to this lack of interest, the RSNC felt that they had no mandate to support a ban. This disinclination to even bother to reply to the head of its own organization was surely apathy at its worst. I wondered if members of the public who belonged to trust badger groups were aware of this.

For every genuine pest controller, gamekeeper or farmer with a vermin problem, there are many, many poachers who set snares in parks, playing fields, railway embankments and on farmland. If the *possession* of snares was made illegal, as well as their setting, it would make the enforcement of such a ban more practical. Cage traps and multi-purpose traps have now been tested and approved by the Ministry of Agriculture, Farming and Fisheries as an effective and humane alternative to snares.

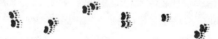

A typical November day – no sun, no moon, no clouds, just gloom. Wardening in the afternoon I spoke to two coppicers trying to get warm round their fire. All right for me walking round, but cold sitting in the machine collecting logs. They asked about the badgers and foxes.

A week later we had fine, steady rain for 12 hours and how my badgers loved the wet! Not so the coppicers, however, who had to pack up and leave as I arrived to warden at noon. Everywhere was so muddy that they could no longer extract the wood felled before the hurricane. Indeed, the paths were so bad that I had the place all to myself and walked round in the grey, murky conditions very happily. The wet bracken was a fiery glow and the late flowering herb robert made cheerful splashes of pink in the undergrowth. A wren chink, chinking and the twittering titmice busy searching for food were the only sights and sounds.

I collected Scots pine cones to take home and grow new trees from seed. Although there was talk of providing fresh trees for Ashcroft Woods, I was particularly concerned for this species. Our woods are unique insomuch as we have Scots pine 'standards' and, though native trees, they do not germinate easily so far south. From fossil remains we know they once grew here after the glaciers retreated, but as the climate became warmer, so they germinated less readily in the south. Past owners here have planted them for the love of trees and their beauty, enjoying the sight of their 'plate' bark, tall towering trunks and scented smell. I believed, too, when it came to it, there would just not be enough young oaks, beech, hornbeam and so on to go round. Ornamentals and quick-growing species yes, but not these. After all, nurserymen were not expecting the hurricane and trees are grown according to demand. I have spent many years collecting seed and returning it here as young saplings, which I then watered regularly in dry weather until they were mature enough to survive on their own.

I stood later in the fading light, watching and calling the tawnies. They hadn't been affected by the loss of our big trees as there were still a good many standing. Collecting the pine seeds reminded me to take home the two small plastic pails I had hidden to water the saplings here from the pond during the summer. The little trees, though leafless of course, had healthy buds at their twig-ends and were straight and sturdy. No one yet had vandalized them; long might they grow unnoticed. The first pail was hidden safely at ground level behind a contorted stump. The other, and smaller of the two, was still wedged at shoulder level in a hazel bush. But whereas in the summer months it had remained quite hidden by growing leaves, now it showed most conspicuously. I took it down and glancing in saw fine pieces of bracken inside 15 cms deep, almost concealing the plastic scoop at the bottom. I picked the scoop up and there were two of the most perfect yellow-necked mice I have ever seen inside it; one on all fours staring upwards, the other on hind legs, one front paw raised and whiskers all aquiver! Very gently and carefully I re-covered the mice and wedged their home back in the hazel, then covered it with dead bracken. I would leave *that* pail all winter. Good to feel man sometimes has his uses!

The wood was a strangely muted place, shrouded in grey mist. Muted, too, was the distant hum of motorway traffic. A bird twittered almost nervously at its own voice and was silent. Nothing stirred. This was one of those moments I hold most dear, when the wood and I are one and there is nothing else. Walking through the trees, the smell of damp, freshly-sawn trunks hung cloying on the moisture-laden air. Woods are wonderful places.

One frosty night, my breath was vaporizing and making my face ache as it cooled, so I went up into the Chantry to Old Joe's sett and stood under the remaining beeches there where it was warmer, looking out over the valley and the twinkling village lights below. The branches above my head still had a few leaves clinging and old mast etched against a lighter sky. It was very peaceful with no animals or humans about. Just a gentle wind passing through the great trees and the tawnies distantly calling from the Briarmead edge. So much had happened in the years since old Joe was taken from here. Deep in my thoughts, I was gradually aware of a gentle eruption near my left boot. A molehill was about to be created! I stood hardly daring to breathe whilst the dirt continued its upward surge and, little by little, a mound was constructed to match the others round about; the master builder completing the job, thereby entirely obscuring my boot.

Earlier that week, the vixen, Watcher, killed and left a mole which I picked up to look at closely. For their size, moles are surprisingly bulky, substantial creatures, the males averaging 14 cms in length and the females slightly shorter. The forelimbs are large, broad and open (the paws can't be completely closed) and are set at a palm-outwards angle. To me that night, there was something pathetically human about the dead mole's 'hands' with their broad palms and five digits and the long claws like uncut nails. The velvety coat is legendary and rightly so for it is difficult to imagine anything more soft or luxurious. I could stroke it in any direction and the nap still stayed the same. A mole's fur is always quite free of dirt and grime which, for a creature that spends so much time digging, is rather remarkable. Not for the mole is the badger's obsession with grooming! Though their eyes are tiny and eyesight very poor, they can detect movement and degrees of light and dark above ground.

Still and warm in my hand, that night's mole seemed helpless and vulnerable. Yet they are marvellous digging machines, earthmovers, can give a strong bite and move, if necessary, in surprising bursts of speed above ground with propulsion from the more finely made hind limbs. A mole digs at a depth no greater than a metre and often far less; from the deepest tunnelling comes its main source of food. Just as mammals above ground patrol their territories in search of prey items, so the mole down below patrols its labyrinth for the worms and insect larvae that burrowing in the earth, pierce and drop into the tunnelling.

The small, hairy tail of the mole is a sense organ and is always carried vertically to touch the roof of the tunnelling. On the open spaces at the foot of High Ridge in late February, I have seen the runs, or tracks of earth, they make above ground leading from a molehill which tear up the turf. These are caused by the males in search of receptive females with which to mate. Apart from this brief period, moles are solitaries each living out its life in its own underground system.

The small moles I occasionally see here in July and August moving above ground are almost certainly youngsters who have left their mother's territory to seek one of their own. At this time the owls and foxes supplement their diets with the prey, though the latter seem to prefer carrying them back for their cubs, rather than eating the moles themselves.

After a heavy fall of snow, I have watched, fascinated, as fresh, dark earth appears, pushing chunks of snow away. Deep snow acts as an insulating blanket so that the earth beneath remains soft. A thin layer of snow may trap the sun's infra-red rays which will also keep the ground below it warm. Moles will sometimes store live worms by first paralysing them with a bite to the neck and leaving them *en masse* in caches. This may particularly occur in winter as a precaution against deep frost when food is hard to obtain. I have watched more than one badger find and eat not only the mole's 'larder' of worms, but its owner too!

The last weeks of the year continued mild with the badgers above ground each night. All six animals were very playful and I noticed that Lucy's company seemed to have made the nervous Crisp more stable and confident. I was sure that young Lucy admired her big friend and after a game of 'Let's both hang onto Chris' anorak' one night, I decided that Crisp was not really a good influence! I regularly stayed over from the hours of darkness to warden Ashcroft Woods during the day and found that Watcher often waited for me in the Briarmead hedge nearest the Sand Pit at noon. I might urge her away, only to find her quietly at my side shortly after. She was a wonderful vixen and a beautiful sight in her winter coat. I prayed she wouldn't get shot. One dull, grey, mild morning we stood by the lane with a kestrel hovering

above us in the nearby field and no one else about. We three had the world to ourselves. Another morning, at first light I came across one perfect primrose in bloom; the pale, pure colour seemed to glow from the undergrowth around. The two tawnies appeared and chose to fly a few paces ahead of me to the Crater Sett where they perched waiting on the canopy of last year's dead black bryony leaves that overhang the hollow. As I approached, the two birds sat side by side at my face level, regarding me solemnly. My joy in this woodland is made of such small moments.

The hurricane seemed to have encouraged a period of timber stealing and both the coppicers and myself would come across groups of men complete with chainsaws and, where possible, lorries or vans which they had driven right in amongst the trees. By now we had gates at two of the main access routes, but no padlocks and chains! It was fortunate that I knew the coppicers well, as all these folks insisted they were contracted by the owners. Noting vehicle numbers and promising to pass them on to Oakley police, however, worked wonders! The split trunks known as 'rails' had been taken down near to the lower car-park to be collected at a convenient time by the contractor and driven away on great trailers.

Evenings come early in December and often people would drive in to walk their dogs at dusk and leave when it was almost dark. One local builder drove in sometimes to walk his dog before driving out again. It was a while before I connected a gradually reducing pile of rails with his visits. The lorry came in with a tarpaulin lying loosely in the back, only to leave shortly after with the tarpaulin stretched over a load. It is one thing to suspect someone of stealing and quite another to catch them in the act. I could only warn the contractor who tried to move his timber as quickly as he could. In the meantime the local man became even more greedy (did he have a good outlet for his loads?) and confirmation, vehicle number and description, ended the source of his revenue.

Perhaps the saddest thing for me was the insistence of people cutting holly by the sackful to decorate their houses. This, and the cutting or digging-up of young yews as Christmas trees, I still find difficult to understand; that year particularly, when we had lost so much to the hurricane. Visitors were self-righteous in their claims that they had always come each year for their holly, that they loved the woods and their little bit wouldn't make any difference. Their yew tree didn't hurt, they had always taken the small ones at this season and there were still some left! None of these people was poor, if their smart clothes and smarter cars were an indication. Somehow, I find it easier to understand what motivates badger-diggers, shooters and snarers than I do these people justifying their greed. Their abuse, too, was quite as colourful as any I had heard. Notices displaying by-laws forbidding what they were doing only made them more determined. The two weekends leading up to Christmas were a nightmare from dawn to dusk. When the holly trees' lower branches were devoid of berries, fathers climbed onto higher ones and sawed them off. It was easier for the wife and children to pick sprigs from these.

With car-parks at opposite sides of Ashcroft Woods, as well as other parking places, and only myself to warden, the whole affair was hopeless and the police could scarcely be expected to patrol the nature reserve too. In desperation I notified both councils, parish and town, as owners of these woods, who phoned the County Trust – the managers. But, of course, everyone was too busy at these weekends leading up to Christmas, they had families and presents to buy and, presumably, their own houses to decorate also. The police drove up into the car-parks to help as much as they could, but the Christmas period with shoplifting and extra traffic is their busy time too. How I longed for The Day to be with us and all this to end.

The 18th December was a lovely, damp night with gentle rain. The badgers were very weighty, even dainty Lucy wasn't quite so dainty with her winter accumulation of fat! They didn't really need to forage for long, but there's nothing quite like a mild, damp night to set them all worming. The foxes, too, would hunt at night (or dusk and dawn) when it was mild, but if the winter weather should become bitter, they changed to the day. Only I am the foolish one that still comes out whatever the weather, even if only for a few hours. However, I miss not coming and I miss the night; my daytime wardening can never make up for the tranquility of the dark. Often there were insects in flight. Even in winter when it turns mild, they seem to be everywhere, especially at dusk and first light. I followed the track leading down to Glebe farmyard and stood on the rise of land as a stoat below me slipped along the rows of autumn-sown barley that had grown quite high. Reaching the first fence post, it disappeared into the weedy verge close by. I followed the paddock edge that leads onto Briarmead and sat on the six-bar gate till first light. Two pipistrelles, tempted by the mild air and its insects, hawked above me in the quiet of the lane.

One weekday I met two local men, Frank and Dick, long since retired, who often walked the area together and kept an eye on the badgers locally. We talked first of the hurricane and then of the woods years ago. In their childhood, they would wait till Mr Hills, the gamekeeper, had gone by, then go for a swim in one of the ponds which in those days were all of three metres deep. The 'keeper lived in a cottage at the bottom of the hill and the boys would stretch a length of black cotton across the path the evening before, to see if it was broken when they came in the morning to play. Once Mr Hills had safely gone by, then off *they* would go! Dick had explored the dene holes and said that the vertical shafts had niches dug into their walls, though whether for lights, or resting-places, he was unsure.

Christmas was a beautiful day with sunshine slanting through the trees and the birdsong tumultuous. There was just one car belonging to a man from the city who drove by every day to his work and had always meant to stop and explore the woods. He queried which paths were free of fallen trees and I showed him the best routes, then left him to explore for himself. His pleasure was my pleasure also and in spite of all the damage, both hurricane and human, I saw the woods through his eyes and knew them to be still lovely and a joy to behold. Walking home deep in thought that day along the winding lane, I was hailed by two red-masked figures, complete with red and white robes and hoods, in a van. Father Christmas – and Mother Christmas too – had been delivering presents to a local children's home and offered me a lift back into town. I enquired where Rudolph and the others were and was told they had all gone lame. That's what comes of asking silly questions!

4

Problems with Poachers

The mild, damp weather continued well into 1988. I hoped that Missy would have cubs this year, the result of her mating with the now dead Jude. I had seen Crisp, too, mate with him for a long time last year, but doubted whether she or any of the other sows were in cub. The badgers 'pottered' and wormed a little in the dampness, then played and went to earth. Missy was very careful with herself as she scrambled into my lap. I put my arms round her gently and felt her stomach, sure she had cubs tucked away in there. Her snout pushed softly against my face; gentle Missy, so much depends on you.

One bright, very gusty day with showers and few people about, I cleared branches blown down by the high winds across the car-parks; last October's hurricane had undermined the trees so much. Then I took some of the larger rubbish from the sett on Colts Farm and deposited it in dusty-bin at the yard. The hurricane had hurled motorway litter straight across the field which had become wedged in the trees round the sett as well as the edges of Ashcroft Woods itself. I decided that sometime I must have a grand clean-up, but some of the articles were big and heavy and I am small and light!

Besides the animals of my own area, I try to keep a check on other vulnerable badger clans. One outside the village of Weldon particularly concerned me. Their main breeding sett had been the scene of the county's first badger-digging case co-ordinated by Oakley police. The sow and cubs there had survived that ordeal 16 months earlier and now I hoped the mother would cub again.

Ideally, one maps all the setts whether occupied or not in the area of a clan and does a regular check at each. Badgers are most territorial in the first five months of the year as this is both the season of birth and of mating. The dominant boar will actively defend his territory if necessary, though more often his scent-markers round the perimeter of the area will be sufficient to warn trespassers off. The scent-markers take the form of dung pits and the anointing of objects – tussocks, trees or posts – with drops of musk from the sub-caudal gland beneath his tail. It is common at this time of year, too, for these scent signals to be 30 or 40 cms up a tree where the boar has rubbed this gland by backing up and doing a neat 'handstand'! To human observers, the dungpits are the clearest sign of the limits of a particular family of badgers, though a good 'nose' will confirm the visual evidence. It is far more satisfactory when watching to know their range and number of homes, than merely to observe the occupants of one sett. Then, if a badger disappears, you will probably find it at another sett within the territory, unless it has come to a violent end.

Walking the setts at Weldon had been a sobering experience. At some time every one had been dug for badgers and some outlying setts had been completely destroyed by the crowning-down holes, which although infilled by the hunters, now showed clear where the earth had settled leaving the disturbed ground several centimetres lower. Some had been dug before the event of locaters that are now fixed to the terrier's collar. These emit a bleep and tell those waiting above ground exactly where to dig. The crowning-down holes of those earlier days are often gaping pits or long trenches covering a wide area. Using the modern locator, only a neat hole scarcely more than a metre square need be dug. From the few badgers now living here and the many ruined setts, it was clear that for years this little family had suffered a long and steady level of persecution. Terriermen will have a wide knowledge of many areas and may travel long distances. A district will be worked and then left for two or three years, or sometimes longer, for the animals to breed again. After all, if a patch is too overworked, hunters and dogs would be out of business.

I had no wish for the Weldon badgers to become used to my presence, but I was determined to keep a regular fieldbook of their numbers and movements against the time when they would surely be hunted again. Their setts were partly in private woodland and partly on open farmland. Permission had been obtained for me to check the whole area which I often did by day. I was also discovering afresh the challenge of watching strange badgers unaware of my presence and, whenever time allowed from my own area, I would go out at night to watch these too.

Wardening for part of every day I had come to know the coppicers well. They were cutting down some of the overgrown chestnut that through years of neglect had become the height of normal trees. They were concerned that nothing was being done about the hurricane-toppled mature trees. If these were left too long with roots exposed to frost, they would merely become so much timber. If cut some metres up from their boles, however, and so relieved of their top heavy weight, many would drop back into their craters roots and all (or could be sling-pulled back as in other woods) and the earth trodden firmly around them. These would, in effect, become pollards which would have a very long lifespan. Many pollarded trees live for hundreds of years. The woodmen felt this was far more urgent than the coppicing plan drawn up before the hurricane, which could safely be left for a season. Their boss had discussed this with the managers of Ashcroft Woods, but to no avail. Sadly, these trees are now all dead.

Two of the coppicers were brothers in their mid-twenties who worked together deep in the woods. The other was an older man working not far from the Old Cherry Sett, who sometimes brought his young son to help him on Saturdays or in the Christmas holidays. They were friendly and hard-working; it was good to have them here. They would arrive every morning at 7.30 a.m. except Sundays, and as their car headlights appeared over the hump of the winding lane, Watcher my shadow would slip away beneath the trees.

Wild arum shoots, primrose and bluebell greenery were well advanced in the mildness with hazel catkins lighting up the bare trees. Many very young rabbits and squirrels were venturing into the mysterious world beyond the fastness of their nurseries. They tend to 'freeze' when so young, rather than run for cover. Once over their initial fear, however, curiosity takes hold and I spent long periods very happily, slowly walking as a young squirrel tried to keep up with me along the way. His claws were still very short and his judgement of distance poor. He would jump to the nearest low branch and cling desperately, getting back his breath and probably his self-confidence. Finally, I would take pity on him and just stand under his tree. Still holding on with one tiny paw, he would lean forward gazing into my face as I 'clicked' gently, tongue against the roof of my mouth. Head inclined, he tried clicking back, till a dog barked in the distance and I hastily walked on.

Now came a time of deep, penetrating frosts, near silent dawns and, by day, a reluctant sun vainly struggling to pierce a misty sky. The badgers stayed below ground apart from brief emergences to potter in the vicinity of their homes. At such times, they ate and defecated rarely. With no fresh dung in their pits and no signs of digging-out, one might be forgiven for believing their setts were empty. Badgers do not hibernate, merely become sluggish, and with a layer of fat to sustain them, have little need for food.

The night of 16th January, I saw Watcher running with a 'dusky' dogfox on Glebe farmland. Now was the time of the rut and this male (whose near-black markings, instead of the usual white, made him so conspicuous), had obsessively followed the vixen for several nights. Only for a brief 72 hours of her three-week oestrus would she be fertile, but that night they mated. It was very frosty with a light wind and only Lucy above ground to say 'hello'. I wandered through the whispering woods with the young badger scampering after me. Sometimes attacking my boots or nose-diving a wind-blown pile of old leaves, my progress with Lucy was far from quiet. I sat on a fallen tree and next moment the youngster was beside me growling and worrying my sleeve, mischief in her every movement. Wickedly, I tipped her off the trunk to land at my feet with a look of surprise and I couldn't help laughing. She glanced up startled and realized I had been the cause of her downfall! Next moment a chunky little badger came bounding up again, leaving frost-white pawprints all over my anorak. Then forsaking me, she padded along the tree, barking and snuffling, nearly lost her balance and came galloping back. I sat there a long time that night with a sleepy badger warming my lap and the tawnies distantly calling. Life had been good for Lucy; she of all her family had survived.

January continued mild and wet with occasional frosts at night. The grey partridge coveys had already broken up and paired which was early for the time of year, but undoubtedly due to the very mild weather. At first light, I watched a pair on Colts farmland and once their feeding ground had been discovered, it was relatively easy to observe them in the early morning and late evening, their main foraging periods. Insects, when available, form a large part of their diet, together with small slugs, snails, seeds, grain, buds and greenery. Once paired and a territory established, the cock bird will defend this, if necessary, from other cocks, with considerable aggression. Looking at a grey partridge cock in close-up, it is a boldly marked bird with those barred sides and orange-brown face, that blends into the farmland wonderfully.

Favourite nest sites here are the edges of Ashcroft Woods at ground level, where the long grass and vegetation conceals. Once her clutch is laid, the hen alone incubates and neither summer storms nor approaching humans will cause her to desert. She will merely flatten and stay put, her duller plumage rendering her nearly invisible on the nest. She covers her eggs with dried grass and leaves before going to feed, neatly pulling these over with her beak. The male escorts her to their feeding ground. I have never seen him on the nest, though he is a good father and, together with the hen, will protect the young chicks stoutly from predators or feign a broken wing to lure away the danger. Later in the year, I have discovered their lying-up places away from the heat of the day and their shallow scoops in the dirt of the farm tracks, for like the pheasant and their cousin the red-legged partridge, these birds enjoy a good dust-bath.

By day the sun shone briefly, lighting the hazel's pollen-laden catkins. The catkins on the alders, in the woods' wet places, grow higher than the hazel and unless the birds are busy at them, might not be so readily noticed till they fall. The alder is a pretty sight with the old year's spent cones still hanging amongst its tasselled catkins, especially on a dull day. The spurge laurel (*Daphne laureola*) had bumblebees busy on its yellow-green flowers and a mallard was already nest-building near the pond.

I was anxious to continue with the sett mapping and one Sunday decided to divide my time between wardening the woods and checking a 90-acre area of private wood and pastureland by the river if I could obtain permission. These are the grounds of Cleates, a Grade One listed Tudor hall, now restored and converted into offices by the new owner. Years ago, I had known of a badger sett there.

I walked down Briarmead in radiant sunshine as two car owners called out 'hello' and a man from one of the bungalows near the lane's end stopped to speak. Walking his spaniel the previous evening, he had been concerned by the occupants of a van who, with their terriers, appeared to be waiting for him to leave. He had hesitated to telephone Oakley police, but had done so. Later, his call was returned. The van owner and his companion were well known and the appearance of a patrol car had speeded their departure. I was getting to know people as never before and it was paying off, not just for Ashcroft Woods, but for the badgers too.

I spoke to the head gardener at Cleates who showed me the badger sett, not occupied now he thought, and told me of two incidents there in the past. In one, a terrierman had threatened to kill his dog when he approached them and he had not realized till then, that most of these people carried knives.

We agreed I should come and go that day between periods of wardening, but was also welcome at any other time.

Back in Ashcroft Woods, I found three youngsters riding trials bikes up and down the part of the Old Cherry Sett slope that was unaffected by fallen trees. We still hadn't the fence and gate I had asked for and it was a temptation for local lads to ride straight up the lane, along the Wildflower Path and so onto the sett slope. We all ended up sitting on the old tree itself, discussing the finer points of the badgers beneath us. They knew it was a badger sett, but had felt that provided they avoided the entrances and didn't break them down, they were doing no harm. Granted, not all youngsters are as willing to talk as this and, for some, only police intervention has stopped the problem. However, I have never seen these lads riding here since, though I have met them several times walking.

That afternoon I returned to Cleates and had a glorious time exploring its grounds. Trees, shrubs, ferns had been planted here which were a great novelty to me, used as I am to the flora of my county. The harts-tongue ferns growing from crumbling walls centuries old, the exotics that have survived the demise of the great greenhouses, the statues, rose-garden, lime avenue and so much more. Though much of the grounds were semi-wild now by Victorian standards, they are a naturalized wildlife habitat by today's. Everywhere were wonders; an ornamental coping topping an ancient vari-bricked well – how old was that?; mistletoe growing from apple trees; great fallen limes slain by the October hurricane; and the little river, for once, a wide stretch of rushing water in full spate. The river probably more how the Elizabethans would have known it for, after all, Elizabeth I came here to stay and she came by barge! A ruined picture gallery remained on its bank, old lichened steps leading to a gazebo now hidden amongst trees; the secret garden behind Tudor brick walls. All seemed to slumber, forgotten in the sunshine. Tiny clouds chased one another in a vivid blue sky to be reflected in the diamond-leaded windows of the stately old hall. Snowdrops showed their white heads amongst the grass. A beautiful place fashioned by man and mellowed by time.

I found a line of dungpits beneath some fallen trees running parallel with the river, as well as single pits dotted about. The badger sett was occupied, but at the far side now, with fresh entrances dugout under a fallen Lawson cypress; what beautiful trees these are. I could have spent days rather than two short hours here, so many foreign trees and plants all unknown to me. Examining some fungi, I chanced to look up ... straight into the face of a vixen! With a feeling of guilt this reminded me that I hadn't seen Watcher for several days and nights. I returned to thank the head gardener and exchange telephone numbers. I asked if the fallen cypress could be left. The tree meant the badgers had a stable roof to their newly-dug entrances that wouldn't subside in the wet. Also the entrances would prove impossible to get to by terriermen, so they couldn't be stopped-up. He was more than pleased to agree to that, then asked me if I didn't get despondent over the badger abuse I see. I could honestly say that I had no right to be, when I met help and interest like his.

Walking through the woods to warden briefly before returning home, the sun by now was gone and the air chill. All was quiet but for a bewildered dog that came up to greet me and was obviously lost. It was anxious to keep me company, so together we walked down to the farther car-park and waited by a solitary vehicle still parked there in the dusk. Time passed as stars pricked in a velvet sky. How strange to have the company of a dog again. It whined softly and pushed its muzzle into my hand. Then a sad little family came trudging along the track that leads from the farm. They had asked everywhere for their missing dog. An ecstatic canine was united with its owners, that somehow seemed a fitting end to a very full day.

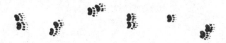

Watcher and her mate were keeping close together; whenever she came up to greet me Dusky would be nearby. She had chosen the old den in the Sand Pit and both took turns to dig it out, one resting whilst the other worked. Sand is easily dug, but as anyone playing on a sandy beach will know, the grains find their way into some surprising places! After a digging session, Watcher would stand with four feet firmly planted and give herself a sustained shake. Sand had worked through the long guard hairs and short under-felting of her thick winter coat and weren't easily dislodged. A prolonged rolling session followed, as she squirmed and rubbed her shoulders against the rough ground and arched her back as she wriggled. Normally, both foxes would be denning below ground now till the birth of the cubs, when the dog would be banished. The unusually mild weather made this unnecessary and, instead, they curled up together amongst the bracken above the Sand Pit.

Missy seemed obsessed with an urge to bring in bedding, mostly soft grass bitten off at ground level from the meadow with some bluebell greenery that had already grown tall in the mildness. I knew she was soon to cub. One night I left the badgers, to walk over the fields very quietly and softly to see what else was around. I can get so close to lapwings feeding at night, yet cannot by day. Just above the farmyard, I came upon some Canada geese grazing on the autumn-sown barley; 11 beautiful birds all told. I could hear little owls crying on the still air and distantly, from the woods, came the tremulous call of a tawny.

Now a wind was rising and it began to rain as I made my way back to the shelter of the trees. The trunks of the chestnut coppice bowed down their long slender heads as the wind passed through. From the slope behind me came a loud rushing sound as a wall of rain came over the ridge top. The tawny couple who till now had been dueting quite

unbothered by the weather, were silenced and flew deeper in amongst the trees. A few minutes after, the rain had passed as quickly as it came and once more the owls were calling. By now it was first light and the badgers gone to earth. The rain had made everywhere fresh and glowing, accentuating the vivid colours of the living green and last autumn's dead leaves. The tawny male was circling me, so I raised my hand and called. For a few brief moments he perched. I felt his soft, wet feathers against my cheek as he lifted a wing, inspected beneath and preened a flight feather. Off he glided to finish the serious business of 'calling his bounds'. Then home to roost.

Walking home myself, I heard a steady croak-croaking from the willow edged soakaway in Holmoak Lane; the male frogs were already waiting for the females to arrive. The mild weather was confusing everyone, birds were nest-building and the daffodils were in flower.

Two nights later, Missy came up to me purring. She was lactating, the strong smell of milk, heavy on the night air. I stroked the long, black fur on her chest and could *feel* the sound vibrating there. Purring is a bad description for the whinniny-purr is not really cat-like, but unique to badgers.

This was surely the loveliest of seasons with its promise of the year to come. Each morning I noted the progress of a pair of long-tailed tits nest-building in one of the damson trees that line Briarmead Lane. They both shared in the work. They were attractive, tiny birds with that astonishing length of tail. Their eyes were almost jewel-like, the reddish coloured rims giving them a bright, pert look. Watching the pair brought to mind the May morning when I came upon one of their nests, blown out of a tree. Normally, it is an oval-shaped nest hanging from a branch, but as time goes by, the eggs hatch and the young develop and so it stretches longer and longer with their growth and movement. What I picked up was an intricate piece of 'material' about 15 by 20 cms. One side was lined with many tiny feathers, soft and downy. On turning it over, I saw it was interwoven with strands of moss, hairs, feathers and, yes, even cobwebs! A fairy-fine texture, yet springy and strong. I would imagine the fledglings had left their nest by then for there were young long-tailed tits about that May looking strangely stunted with their still short tails. When the female is incubating the eggs, her long tail is either raised up to fit the nest, or can sometimes be seen protruding out of the entrance hole. Indeed, seeing one of these birds with a kinked tail is a sure sign that the hen bird has been incubating!

One winter I found, tucked away in a jumble of dead branches near the Old Cherry Sett, a huddle of these tits roosting. Such tiny birds must have a constant struggle against the cold. Even feeding they tend to concentrate in groups and are constantly calling to one another. Obviously, there is safety in numbers and many pairs of eyes are better than one. They have no song as such even in the spring. Theirs is a spluttering call and a thin, high 'si-si-si'. A wood in winter is always several degrees warmer than the land outside (just as it will be shady and cooler in summer). All the animals and small birds that are so vulnerable in the cold know this well. That winter morning's long-tailed tits stayed huddled together till the rising sun touched the far horizon sending long fingers of flame to warm their branch. Then first one 'titmouse', then another, fluffed its feathers, moved slightly away from the group and preened. Soon the whole roost was feeding on the remains of the spindle trees' berries at the wood edge.

One warm, gusty night I was greeted by Missy. I had only seen her briefly since she cubbed, so we made a great fuss of one another. I left her to choose the way and she meandered, foraging as she went, whilst I followed. Everywhere was wet and the grassy places spongy, so there was no shortage of food. It was as we rounded the wood-edge just before midnight that we came face to face with two men and their lurchers. Their beam was off, so I imagine they had been lamping the meadow above Cliffords Bank. One man I recognized; I had seen him walking his dog here sometimes in the day, but the other and his dogs were quite unknown to me.

In a moment there was uproar as the lurchers went for Missy and I turned away as a lamper tried to dazzle me with his light. My gentle badger, now so aggressive, was fighting for her life, but was no match for the great, towering, nimble dogs and their owners urging Fleet, Jacko and Tiger to 'carve it up'. In vain I shouted above the uproar for them to call the dogs off, but it was hopeless. After all, this was great sport and a bonus to their poaching. Had I interfered, I would have been bitten by badger and dogs alike, so drawing the radio a little up from my anorak, I tried to make contact with the villager who held the other.

The moment they saw I had a radio, the whole situation changed as they both tried to take it. Not for nothing was the strap across my shoulder, under jersey and anorak and no way was the webbing likely to break. Instead, I was dragged across the ground, through dogs and badger which broke up; the dogs moving off and a bewildered sow trying to stop my progress. I think it was the poacher's lamp that hit my radio with a great thud and the answering voice was lost abruptly. Missy jumped growlingly at the man holding the strap and with a yelp he let go and both men and dogs ran into the wood. Still lying on the ground with a confused Missy snuffling me, I tried to make radio contact, but was far too near the wood itself. Going nearer Cliffords Bank, I made contact and asked if a patrol might check Maddon Lane for a vehicle. The little sow was by my side and seemed covered in blood. Confirmation came that the police had been phoned and a patrol was going to the destination. It was suggested I go round to meet them. Easier said than done for by now I felt exhausted, but, leaving Missy to wash herself, I made my way back across High Ridge and reached Maddon Lane in time to see the patrol car leave! I walked slowly up and down for half an hour in case they should return and might expect me to be waiting. This had happened before and it must be very irritating for officers busy with other calls. There were no further developments, however, so by now tired beyond belief, I returned to find a very sorry-for-herself little sow with a long strip of fur, skin and flesh hanging from her side and deep bites on flanks and neck. The strip would need to be gently cut off lest it catch on brambles and the wounds needed hydrogen peroxide in case they festered.

It was a long journey home to find my son on his way to look for me. My worried radio contact had feared I wouldn't make it, but all was well. By now it was 2.30 a.m. and I phoned the police station thanking them for their help, but, no, a vehicle hadn't been seen. Then a slow, slow return to tend my badger at the Old Cherry Sett suckling her young ones, now barely two weeks old. I called her up, gently cut off the hanging strip from the flinching sow and bathed her weeping wounds; she licking the scratches from the brambles on my face and hands.

Later that morning a constable came asking for details and, subsequently, the sergeant phoned too. I explained that the next day I was due to go into hospital and, being unwell, had been slow to get about. The sergeant was fine though, said he hoped all would go satisfactorily and to let him know when I came home. That day alternated between black skies, heavy showers and high winds, then blue skies with sunshine, but no way could I warden or go across to my area. Hopefully, Missy would keep herself clean and now the poachers knew I had a radio, they would most likely keep away. I suspected, too, that Oakley station would keep an eye open for trouble and the sight of a uniform was a better deterrent than anything I could do. We shall see.

On my return I found a van had been driven into Ashcroft Woods and set alight, together with a young oak and cherry tree nearby. It could have been far worse, but for the wet weather soaking the undergrowth. A short way off grew a stand of great holly trees with their thick, waxy leaves. Fire consumes hollies in a matter of moments, the flames shooting high into the air. If the fire had spread to these, acres of trees could have burnt. All but one of the by-law notices had been torn down and a fortnight's accumulation of rubbish awaited me. All the badgers and Watcher were fine, however, and that was a great relief.

Missy's wounds were drying well with most of the bites nearly healed. She washed herself leaning backwards on my lap as I sat on the chestnut bough above the nursery entrance. Grooming over, she turned her head to listen, nibbled briefly at the hand lying on my knee and jumping down, disappeared into the shadowy hole. Immediately came the cubs' fretful trilling at their mother's welcome appearance and moments later, the sounds of suckling. Then a prolonged whimper, renewed suckling and the sow's purring murmur; reassurance to her young or the contentment of a nursing mother? It was good to be back. I had missed the night world with a deep sense of loss that had become an acute ache. I had missed the pleasure in small things; a lone leaf spiralling earthwards, cloudy skies in dappled water; and the solitude and peace of this woodland after dark.

Watcher was soon to cub; her narrow hips and normally slender belly were tight with her unborn. She kept close to the Sand Pit now. Since their mating, Dusky and she had hunted together, often sharing their kills. Now he continued to hunt, but took the food back for her – groundnesting birds, wood pigeon feeding on the oilseed rape, part of a rabbit – whatever he might catch. I knew from watching other fox families that he would continue to do this once their family was born. As they were weaned, both parents would hunt separately for themselves and the cubs; she in the vicinity of the den, whilst he would range farther afield to the limits of his territory, if food was scarce.

Wardening one evening, I discovered two youths from the village who had sent their terriers into the badger-occupied entrances of the Old Cherry Sett. They said they were only after rabbits and, indeed, I'm sure they were, but it certainly wasn't a rabbit that one dog was baying at below. Then the barking turned to a bomping as if something was being dragged along and a 'yip-yip-yipping' as the terrier backed out, its nose and the right side of its head was covered in blood and its right ear appeared to be missing. The lads grabbed up their dogs and made off looking frightened; their ignorance had cost the dog dear. Something similar had happened here before with a terrier and its

66

owners ferreting. Then the sow had vacated the sett and I wondered if this would happen again.

That night I came upon Missy in the process of moving her cubs one by one to Colts Farm where her yearling daughters Meg and Bess were already denning. Fortunately, it was still mild and her three offspring, at five-and-a-half weeks, were covered in fine fur, or the outcome might have been tragic. Younger naked cubs or a bitter frosty night could have meant death on a long journey from sett to sett. It had taken her an hour to carry the first carefully through the woods, avoiding thickets and brambles, holding it with her head unusually high, then across the open farmland, with pauses to set down and rest. The cub had its eyes open and, though bedraggled by the time it reached its new home, seemed alert enough. At this age it was heavy and Missy was well tired on her return to the Old Cherry.

She brought the second cub above ground and put it down as a third appeared, whimpering anxiously, in the entrance she had just left. Badger cubs are not usually above ground so young, though at this age they can sometimes be heard exploring the tunnelling of their home. The mother growled her disapproval as she tried to nose it back, then growled louder as it still persisted. This time it retreated hastily. Missy took up its sibling in her mouth and padded along the trail leading horizontally across the sett slope. As she did so, a dark little shadow re-appeared at the nursery entrance, the white face with its two black stripes showing clear. I called softly to Missy who stopped short and looked back, another tiny striped face hanging below her large one. Then, I did something that I would never normally dream of doing – knelt down and carefully picking up the crying cub, put it down the front of my anorak. Much as Missy trusted me, how would she react to this? But I need not have worried. Except for occasional checks when she rested, the sow seemed content that her problem was solved. Each time she put her cub down, she would snuffle into the top of my anorak and give the youngster in there a quick wash. Walking along, I had carefully put my hands under its body to protect it from the inevitable jogging as we moved. Once motionless, however, it took to exploring the confines of its new 'home' and I was snuffled and nibbled in some uncomfortable places. I can confirm that at five-and-a-half weeks, badgercubs have teeth and sufficient jaw muscles to make them felt! Their claws, too, especially the front ones, are already long for their owner's size. This cub, even now, was showing signs of its future ability to dig. Best of all, I noticed, before I returned it to its mother, that this little chap was a male!

At the Colts Farm sett, I sat on the ground whilst Missy went below with her burden. Time passed. There was movement inside my anorak and snuffling. I felt something warm – and wet! – against my body, then all was still. Missy returned and I gently undid the zip. The cub was curled round, fast asleep. He strongly objected to being picked up by his mother and the sounds of his discontentment could be heard all the way into the sett!

It was well into March and Missy seemed settled and contented on Colts Farm with Meg and Bess. There was plenty of room at this sett and I had to admit things had turned out for the best. They were all so much safer here under the watchful eye of the farm-manager and his men, most of whom lived nearby. I often found Susie from Cliffords Bank in the company of Missy and her daughters, but it was Lucy and Crisp who gave me the greatest pleasure. Like a stressed child that in adulthood finds it hard to form stable relationships, so Crisp's early life with the troubles here had cost her the companionship of the other badgers. It was a vicious circle. Her odd, irrational behaviour at the enforced isolation had grown more marked, till last autumn and her friendship with the orphaned sow. Dainty little Lucy, still a mere yearling, was now the inseparable companion of big, bumbling Crisp who at three years old, seemed at last to have matured and lost her nervousness. This, in turn, made her more acceptable to the rest of the badger clan.

By now Watcher, too, had her family safely housed in the Sand Pit den. For the first two weeks of their life she remained with the cubs, keeping them warm with her own body. Unlike those of Missy, her cubs were born with coats of short, dark fur, but unlike the badger sow, vixens give birth on the earth floor of the den and don't provide the thick, insulating bedding that keeps young badgers warm. I didn't see Watcher at all during this period though doubtless she came above ground briefly to urinate and defecate. I did see Dusky bringing back food for her several times and Watcher's daughter also. This vixen and one dog were all that had survived of last year's litter of six. The daughter had produced no cubs herself, though physically capable of doing so. This isn't unusual as the presence of a dominant vixen may inhibit reproduction in subdominant vixens; possibly nature's way of limited numbers? In Watcher's case this proved fortunate for one Friday evening, the dogfox ceased to appear. The young vixen responded to the situation by redoubling her efforts that weekend and even imitated Dusky's habit of entering the den a few paces, before dropping the catch and backing out. Only injury or death would have caused Dusky's disappearance. I wondered if he had been shot and taken for his pelt.

Between wardening I searched the woods and surrounding farmland. The chances of finding his body or, indeed, any signs of his disappearance, seemed remote. By 3 p.m. Sunday, it began to rain and gradually people were leaving the woods. An hour later it was raining heavily and I was about to leave for home myself, when a colourful movement caught my eye in the undergrowth and there was the missing dogfox, snared by his right hindleg. The wire was deeply imbedded in the bone and the victim had begun to gnaw in desperation at his own leg; sure signs it had been caught more than 24 hours ago. The snare had probably been set on Friday afternoon or evening. I had the greatest difficulty getting the wire out of the bone though the fox offered little resistance, exhausted as he was. At first his lips had curled back from the teeth, but once I spoke and knelt down by him, Dusky merely regarded me steadily. It was one I know and I suspected the blood supply was cut off in any case, hence the gnawing at the limb. For a long while he sat licking the injury as I hunted round for more snares and found them. One contained a dead rabbit that the fox readily accepted. There had been 12 snares set altogether, five the hand-made, single-strand wire ones and seven the brass-woven type. I pulled them up together with their pegs to hand in to the police, noting as I did so that the hurricane-blocked path, gradually being cleared by the two young coppicers, was not far away. They were interested in Ashcroft Woods and its wildlife and had commented on the poaching here and the spent shotgun cases they were finding as they worked. I would tell them what had happened.

A man in one of the villages found two of his chickens dead and believed that the badgers in a nearby sett had killed them. When the RSPCA Inspector went to investigate, however, he was told that the owners had meanwhile found their neighbour's dogs to be responsible. The Inspector asked to view the badger's sett in scrubland on the hillside a short distance from the garden and together we went to map it. At one time, this had been a large and active main sett. Now there was possibly a solitary badger in a very small portion of it. All the entrances bar two had long since been disused, the vegetation grown up hiding them and their spoil heaps. We found a few smooth-sided snuffle holes, badger hairs and grass balls of bedding discarded along a distinct trail. We could find no dungpits, though the sett area contained dense blackthorn and hawthorn scrub which made checking it difficult.

We spoke to a man living on the lower road and found his comments interesting. 'You won't find any badgers about here now, only perhaps the odd one, though I doubt that. I used to see them around here regularly, but not any more. Up to a few years ago, we had lampers up there on the hillside and they took everything – fox *and* badger. I shoot on the beam myself for rabbit, so often saw them. Can't understand the mentality that puts his dogs to badger. Badgers aren't nice, gentle, furry things and, when they get going, they're savage. They'll tear a dog right up. I keep Staffs myself, but I'd never let them get near a badger. I can't see the point in hunting badgers. They don't do any harm and they're dying out anyway.' He added, 'There's a great big sett off Church Lane. You follow the lane into the Forestry Commission wood, then go through the fence and its under the big trees. It used to be full of badgers; that's mainly where they came from, but it's empty now. They took them on the beam as they came out to feed in the meadow. You'll be lucky to see a badger in these parts now.'

Whilst we had been searching the sett on the hillside earlier, people had called to us from a garden on the lower road, so we drove along to explain why we had been there. They said that strangers had gained access from the track at the side of the road and recently there had been a spate of break-ins. It was difficult for the police to catch anybody owing to the open pasture and scrubland behind. The same, of course, would have applied to the lampers a few years ago if anyone had thought to contact the police. I still had this village area to map for setts. It would be interesting to find which were empty.

I was spending much of the night on Colts Farm watching Missy with her three cubs. At first, they were merely soft shadows appearing at the nursery entrance when their mother came and went. If she stood close to them they wobbled out and under her, peering this way and that. She would glance down, decide one needed a wash and, loudly protesting, it would wobble back in! They were almost eight weeks old.

I had a grandstand view of the sett and the field below as I sat high up on the slope. The nights were mild, there seemed to be hardly any motorway noise and the moon was becoming a fine crescent of silver as it waned. Many rabbits fed below the sett bank and the large stretch of water that collected in the dip there served birds, badgers, foxes and rabbits as a drinking place.

Two tiny leverets had their forms in the bracken where the sett joined the meadow and their mother came at dawn, dusk and occasionally during the dark hours, to nurse them. Hares are not territorial, though a doe coming into oestrus will be guarded by the dominant male against the attentions of lesser-ranking bucks. He will sometimes chase off other males from his favourite feeding ground, but otherwise hares seem content to feed at a short distance from one another. Several pairs of ears and eyes on the lookout for danger are better than one. Their mating involves little courtship and often the doe will get angry at the buck's attentions and turn to 'box' him. This boxing doesn't seem to involve male with male for *their* disagreements start with a chase and end when the victor bites the vanquished hard on his rump. Boxing on hindlegs is the prerogative of the incensed female, warding off the unwanted attentions of an impatient Jack. In spite of the doe's ability to bear three litters a year, hares are not as plentiful as they once were. The leverets are born fully furred and with eyes open and can fend for themselves at a month old.

It is easy to overlook grazing hares at dawn and dusk, owing to their method of feeding. With flattened ears, they crouch low and motionless, eating only the vegetation within reach, before taking a step forward and grazing there.

Missy's cubs had no inkling of my presence high up on the sett slope, but their mother knew I was there. Sometimes she came onto my lap to groom, leaning back on me whilst she licked and pawed through the hair on her chest and belly, then nibbled at her legs. She had long, black fur on her neck and upper legs. I have noticed this with some badgers, yet others may be very short of fur in these places. One night, Missy went down to the field pool to drink and whilst doing so, her cubs came out onto the spoil heap of their entrance. One whimpered for her mother, but doubtless couldn't see her for they are still very myopic at this age. She took a few steps more and fell down the slope; not a very bad fall, but frightening for such a wee creature. At its cries, Missy rushed back, licked it all over in a worried sort of way and taking it by its bottom! carried it back into the sett. Its brother and sister had disappeared below at its first cries.

Susie came back to live at the Old Cherry Sett with Lucy and Crisp and dug herself three entrances. Lesley, the mother of Crisp, had used one of these as a nursery 'play-pen' for her cubs – how many years ago? Originally, it had been a crowning-down hole made when *her* mother was taken from here. It was last closed by men on the Friday before August Bank Holiday in 1985. Somehow it seemed a good omen for the future of these badgers; the last stopped entrance being opened and used by them once more.

The wild cherries would soon be in bloom, frog spawn was in the ponds and the great toad migration at Holmoak Lane was well under way with the males' soft and quite melodious onking (not really

71

croaking like the frogs) a feature of my night walk over to these woods. Two mallard drakes were feeding on the ponds and their ducks were incubating their eggs now. I watched a slow-worm in the early morning sun, basking on the tarmac of Briarmead; not a very wise choice. I picked it up and returned it to the field edge before motorists came up the lane.

══ 5 ══

Dormice Days

Collecting rubbish from the Maddon Lane car-park one early morning, I spoke to a coppicer coming to work. I knew that he had been born in one of the villages and had often walked to High Ridge and Ashcroft Woods. We discussed the effects of the hurricane and he said that beech and ash will rot if left lying, but not oak. Oak can be left several years and though the bark and outer wood may deteriorate, the heartwood (the wood that is used), remains sound and will, in fact, season. He had spent eight years re-building a 24-metre long Danish trawler of oak in his spare time. As a lad, he had longed to build one from scratch completely of oak and used to walk about speculatively here! It was a double-edged sword; the love of seeing trees grow and the love of building in wood. But the hurricane had given him the opportunity to buy some of the felled oaks here from the owners. He had a friend who worked for an organization giving holidays to disabled and blind people. 'Holidays round our coast and abroad. It's a wonderful experience for the disabled and one they never forget, but for that I need a larger boat. The extra length will make room for hoists and pulleys to get the passengers up onto the deck. Eventually, I will sell the first boat to equip the second for that will cost a lot too.' I felt the great oaks lying here couldn't have a better destiny and he smiled, remarking that he had loved the place all his life and would call his boat *The Ashcroft*.

Earlier that morning, I had met Watcher taking back part of a rabbit and I went with her to the den in the Sand Pit. Her four cubs still had their dense, chocolate coats, but their faces were altering. I was sure their eyes could focus better; when very tiny, they have a weak, purblind look. Their mother watched them pulling at the rabbit. They growled and quarrelled amongst themselves and one, scrambling onto the carcase, threatened the others. None of them had the strength or co-ordination to follow up their threats, let alone cope with such a large prey unaided! Watcher pulled a piece off which one cub snatched and took a short distance away. There it chewed and sucked and licked, doubtless taking in some nourishment, before a tawny flew over with a sudden wavering hoot which sent the young foxes rushing underground. Their mother continued at the rabbit, turning it over as she tore pieces away and soon the cubs crept out again, reassured by her lack of concern. One carried his portion into the bluebells and another ran back into the den with his piece, to eat away from the others. The fourth cub fared the best. He licked and pulled at Watcher's mouth, standing on the dismembered carcase to do so. The vixen coughed twice and regurgitated partially digested rabbit that he ate standing by her.

Keeping in the shadows at the top of the sandpit, I could watch the family unseen. The den was dug in the wall of the pit, beneath a stunted beech growing near me and the family played in and out its vast root system. The sandy earth sloped away to the bluebells and yellow archangel growing at the bottom of the pit which, in turn, sloped gradually up and out again to the open field that bordered Briarmead Lane. Many trees had young leaves unfurling and soon the place would be screened from curious eyes. Watcher often met her daughter here. On hot days, both vixens would lie in the cool of the bluebell greenery, letting the cubs clamber over them. They would groom the cubs and one another, half hidden in a sea of blue and green. Dusky had lost his paw and part of his leg in the snare. It appeared to have withered from the point where the wire had been embedded. Whether it had rotted away or the fox had gnawed it off, there was no way of telling. The injury was only noticeable when he moved slowly; trotting or loping, it made no difference to his speed.

The sun was high in the sky when I met a man coming out of the woods along the Wildflower Path with his dog. He was rough-shaven and wore a dirty broad-brimmed hat. We knew one another well! That

74

morning he swore he hadn't snared here recently and seemed very agitated; sweat ran down his face as if he had been running. Seeing I had made no comment whatsoever when he first appeared, I wondered what might have happened! No, he continued, he only snared along the river; couldn't even do it round his garden now as he had caught his neighbour's cat. Why didn't folks leave him alone? Later, the coppicers clearing the upper path called to me and the mystery was explained. They had seen him acting suspiciously in the undergrowth and on asking him, had received a torrent of abuse. One retaliated by approaching the poacher waving his chain-saw, whereupon the man and his dog had disappeared at speed! To have met me as he came out of the woods, must have seemed the last straw and considering how often he had threatened me in the past, I found the chain-saw incident highly amusing. More to the point, I have never seen him here since.

Warwick Reynolds of the Surrey Badger Protection Society, had promised to erect reflector posts where badgers regularly crossed roads to get to their foraging grounds. Four badgers had already been killed that year by passing traffic on the main road between Oakley and Weldon; one in January and three within five days of one another in March. The only sad consolation was they were boars and not lactating sows with cubs left below ground to starve. Two had been mature animals and the others yearlings. Their main sett was in the bank of the road where it sloped into a neighbouring field. It had been there long before Oakley existed, when the road had only been a winding country lane. Then the town had mushroomed with a by-pass to take the traffic that threatened to choke it. Worst of all for the badgers, their leafy lane became a straight, wide road with a 40-mile speed limit, which at night was regularly exceeded.

The lady who owned the field and its bank, was concerned for her badgers who had suffered the depredations of badger-diggers several times. The little colony were just beginning to build up their numbers once more, only to fall prey to the traffic. Warwick, his friend, myself and a Highways Inspector, walked this stretch to decide where the reflectors fixed to black and white posts might be placed. They had to be lower to the ground than those used to deter deer, so they reflected the light of oncoming vehicles into the eyes of the badgers who would, hopefully, stayed dazzled for a few moments, till the traffic had passed. Badgers tend to turn and face any danger which is why so many road casualties suffer head injuries. There are obvious drawbacks to these reflectors and it is still difficult to equate how successful they are. However, if they only saved one badger, I felt they would prove their

worth. One must bear in mind too, that a fully grown badger can be a considerable danger to drivers travelling at speed.

Where the dead badgers had actually been picked up, didn't necessarily correspond with their trails which were clearly visible through the vegetation. It appeared that the animals came down to road level, then meandered some way along before crossing. For maximum effectiveness, the reflectors had to be exactly positioned, but we had to agree where the posts should be placed with the Highways Inspector who, understandably, wanted them well out of the way of pedestrians for safety. He was interested and helpful and a compromise was reached. On one side of the road, the positioning wasn't ideal, however, for the posts were really not close enough to the traffic. Warwick decided the Dutch models would be best here; reflecting light from the other side of the road. There would be room to cement these in.

We moved on to another problem area; this time, a quiet lane following the River Bourne and leading from one of the villages. Again, the main sett was in the bankside, but this time sloping steeply upwards to fields above. Earth from the spoil heaps sometimes dropped down onto the tarmac and the whole area was obviously badger occupied. In spite of its close proximity to the lane, however, a lady driving home one evening had stopped men digging into the sett; one terrier was already underground and two others were coupled to a tree. There had been several genuine badger road casualties but local people had also found badgers dumped with injuries not consistent with traffic. The whole area was a popular beauty spot with tourists yet it had its darker side too.

Warwick felt the Austrian type reflectors in conjunction with the Dutch would best serve the badgers of this lane. The Austrian are made of red glass prisms set in angled casing and they reflect light from the same side. Again, the positioning wasn't ideal nor was the location with its steep banks. The bank containing the sett sloped down to the lane, the bank on the other side dropped away to the meadow and river. The reflectors here couldn't be cemented in.

The Highways Inspector suggested that with vandalism a popular pastime in the locality, it would be best not to draw attention to what we hoped to do. Like most people involved in badger groups, Warwick had a job to go to and weekends, with more people about, would be unwise for the work. He had already spent his fortnight's holiday cleaning and cutting the vegetation back from six miles of reflectors he had installed the previous year in Wiltshire! My reflectors were on order and he said he would meanwhile paint the posts and as soon as they came in, and he had a free day, he would phone me.

Everywhere was becoming very dry. There had been no rain of any consequence for some time and the recent winds made it even drier. The young trees I planted two years ago needed watering twice a week. I took the water from the ponds, generally collecting it just before first light and had come to know one of the mallard pairs very well. The duck who had made her nest in an old, long-coppiced oak two metres up from the ground, would make soft noises at me, quite unlike her usual quacking, as I went by. Her drake took to the pond at first sight of me, but now he also was used to my presence, following behind when I left the pond to go with my water to the clearing. I never saw *him* incubating the eggs; with mallards this seems to be done solely by the duck. Watering the trees I would talk softly to him as he searched about in the dead bracken nearby. It must be very easy to tame mallards. One morning he choose to go ahead and beat me to the saplings. I was glad there was no one to see us for I felt silly carrying my plastic pail and walking behind his dumpy little body!

When the sun was well up, I photographed the foliage of the small-leaved limes and wild service. The beauty of leaves unfurling; oak and hornbeam are a deep red, sweet chestnut and beech, as they pull from their long, brown sheaths, are a vivid green. How many shades of green in a living wood? The variety seems endless. Many of the young oak leaves had been bitten off by the squirrels at dawn. They also eat some of the unripe catkins but squirrels are very destructive – the base of each and every oak was strewn with bunches of young leaves with many of the catkins untouched. I wondered if they did this for the sap, but sampling the twig-ends I discovered they had no sweet taste at all. A squirrel high above me was trying to raid a woodpigeon's nest in a Scots pine. The bird hissed and screeched at the marauder as she sat on her eggs, but the squirrel came back again and again, approaching from beneath the nest as well as from behind. Then another pigeon alighted next to the nest and the agile squirrel disappeared.

Walking home there was a cuckoo displaying and calling from a birch stump at the wood edge, his mate, nearby, was sounding her bubbling trill. On the footpath near Holmoak Lane, I nearly trod on a slow-worm basking in the morning sun. These legless lizards are very much a feature of this countryside and they feed on slugs, snails, worms, insects and their larvae as well as spiders. They are slow and deliberate in their actions as a rule, though if attacked will struggle violently and, like other lizards, have the ability to break off their tail if grasped by it; hence their Latin name of *Anguis fragilis*. Though they feed at night, they will bask in the sunshine just as other lizards and snakes like to do. Perhaps their favourite prey are slugs and these are first 'smelt' by the slow-worm's flicking tongue before the slug is grasped around the middle and chewed up. Smaller slugs are swallowed whole and their choice of food is governed by size because unlike the grass-snake, for instance, their jaws cannot dislocate to accommodate a large victim. They eat snails by gradually pulling them from their shells as they swallow. Like other lizards, slow-worms have eyelids so close their eyes when asleep. Once I was fortunate to see a female give birth to 13 young and still have the record I wrote at the time: August Bank Holiday Monday at midday. The slow-worm writhed convulsively till an opaque bubble appeared with a four cms long perfect slow-worm inside. This wriggled and thrashed about as the bubble collapsed and dried. When the newborn emerged it was a vivid golden colour with a dark line running along its back the entire length of the body. This birth was repeated till 12 more emerged, one by one, but the last made no movement inside its transparent membrane and never emerged. None of the young slow-worms appeared to remain with the mother, but instead moved away into the grass.

The following night was mild and starry with a clearcut visibility and I confirmed for the first time, beyond any doubt, that Ashcroft Woods *does* have dormice! They live so high up in the tree canopy and are so completely nocturnal, that I've never been sure. I have found hazel nuts with the kernels extracted that have looked the work of dormice; the gnawed holes are very regular with their edges almost completely smooth. I knew they weren't uncommon in the south, but I have never seen one before. These were delicate and tiny – much smaller than I had imagined. They had recently come out of hibernation so had lost their plump roundness. Dormice hibernate usually from October to

April though during that time they may briefly awake for a few days. In the summer they occupy nests low down in the shrub layer and can be encouraged to live in bird boxes. The proportion of dormice to any area is low, unlike other rodents.

Woodlands are fascinating. Woodmice and yellow-necked mice eat similar food, but survive without competition in the same area by living at different levels – woodmice on the ground and yellow-necks higher up. Squirrels and dormice live in the tree canopy, the dormouse never normally descending to the ground. Ashcroft Woods at one time had plenty of hazel and honeysuckle, the basic necessities of life for them. The shy little dormouse shreds honeysuckle bark to make its nest and eats the buds, leaves, flowers and fruit. Sitting amongst the flowers, its head becomes dusted with pollen which will later be transferred to other flowers. Besides honeysuckle flowers however, I was later to watch a dormouse eating hawthorn blossom and the haws too. I have not heard of this before, but feel they probably have a far more catholic diet than is generally supposed.

I decided to ask the County Trust, who managed these woods, for permission to erect tit-boxes in very secluded places where the public didn't roam. If the entrances were turned to face the tree's trunk leaving very little space, tits wouldn't have an opportunity to enter, but the dormice would. The removable lid type were ideal to check the occupants without disturbance in order to do a proper study of dormice numbers and behaviour. The coppicing was going ahead quickly with nearly a quarter of Ashcroft Woods already felled. This could spell death to the dormice who would lose their honeysuckle as well as the tall overgrown coppice poles which make such wonderful habitat for them. I had already asked if the coppicing could be slowed down as pollution and noise from the motorway was becoming worse. So far my request had gone unanswered, but perhaps a plea on behalf of the dormice would succeed where pollution had failed?

That night gave way to a beautifully sunny Sunday morning; the distance hazy and shimmering. Light touched the stitchwort's star-like flowers speckling the ground beneath the trees. It was a morning of vibrant birdsong and amongst all the others, sounded a chiffchaff, then a nuthatch with over all, the softly cooing turtle-dove. Yellow brimstones, small tortoise-shells and an orange-tip were busy in the sunshine. Soon there were people arriving and enjoying the woods. This was my favourite part of wardening – seeing families and couples walking and taking pleasure in the place.

A programme was being made for Central Television on badger-digging and baiting and I had agreed to talk about the lamping of badgers. I was also looking for somewhere else to live as our house was being sold; my son and daughter had already moved right away from Oakley and nearer to their jobs. Nowhere could I find rented accommodation within walking distance of Ashcroft Woods. For nearly 30 years I had known and loved this place and, my family apart, I held it most dear.

One night Missy's three cubs played round the nursery entrance as their mother collected fresh bluebell greenery for their bedding. At ten weeks old they were inquisitive and boisterous; one little sow copied her mother as she backed a short distance with her few pieces too. Missy had limitless patience with her offspring tumbling and jostling beside her. They had lost their fluffy appearance and were tiny miniatures of their parent. A crescent moon hung in the starry sky; from the wood edge, the nightingale was singing and the pervading sweetness of bluebells lingered on the night air. The scene before me held a special poignancy, bound by the knowledge of all I would lose should I be forced to move far away. My life was changing. What had the future in store?

It was the last Sunday in April with the evening sunshine casting long shadows. Lilac and the fragrant white flowers of the wayfaring trees were opening. The whitebeam is well-named; the undersides of its leaves such a silvery-white and so conspicuous as they softly unfurl. Crab apple buds are pink, though they open to white. The flowering fields of oilseed rape shone a vivid yellow on a patchwork of green. The orpine was growing tall on the Colts Farm side of Ashcroft Woods, surrounded by the stitchwort's tiny white stars. The goatsallow leaves showed pale and furry and the gorse was in vivid bloom at the wood edge. Watcher found me silently wardening and with no one about, decided to accompany me. She bit off and ate the choicest dandelion heads as we went and I recalled that the big dogfox Josh had liked these too.

Along the lower path, the hurricane-felled Scots pines had been sawn up to reopen the way; the fresh smell was wonderful, though their demise saddened me. Now the trees creaked and groaned in the rising wind as the sun dropped below the horizon and birds began searching for a roost. There was a family of very young rabbits living at the far end of the Colts Farm Sett and another one below the entrances of

Missy's family; not all this large sett was badger occupied by any means! The dungpits near the bottom of the slope were full to overflowing; about time the family dug some new ones, I told my fox. Watcher was taking an unhealthy interest (at least for the rabbits!) in the small lower holes and I called her away, walking towards Ashcroft Woods as I did so. At the Sand Pit den near Briarmead Lane, the young foxes greeted their mother and I continued on my way alone over the fields of Newby Farm. I knew this land had been sold, but even the farmer didn't know who now owned it; the agent had only said it was someone living abroad.

The daylight had quite gone with a slight rain falling and the distance hazy. The lights of a van that had been left in the car-park all evening, disappeared over the hump of the lane. Everywhere was very mild. There was a snuffling movement in the long grass; a striped head startling in its clarity, poked out of the nettles and Crisp was beside me. She was very nervous, chittering incessantly and I strove to calm her by kneeling and stroking the side of her face. Where was Lucy – the two were inseparable; where one sow was, the other was guaranteed to be. I returned back through the woods with Crisp close by my feet, almost tripping me in her anxiety not to leave my side. The radishes were being irrigated nightly on Colts Farm and the badgers usually followed the sprayers as they moved across field, taking the worms as they rose in the 'rain'. Sure enough, there they were, their bodies shiny and darker-looking with the wet; all that is, except Lucy. Crisp partly rose on her hindlegs scenting the air for several long minutes, almost as if checking carefully for her lost companion. Then, down on all fours again, she trotted purposefully off through the lower part of Ashcroft Woods with me following.

Badgers can move quickly on their trails through dense undergrowth and I would soon have lost her had I not realized she was heading for home at the Old Cherry Sett. Coming out at the top of the slope, I called nonetheless; so many trees, so many entrances. Two badgers answered from below and there was Crisp... with Lucy caught fast in a snare fixed over her entrance hole. Three other entrances also had these home-made snares, but, luckily, neither of the other sows denning here, Crisp and Susie, had been caught. Badgers emerging for the first time of an evening will often spend many minutes scenting the air and listening, half in, half out their homes. Once confident all is well, they may move quickly outside to use a dungpit or to groom before going off to forage. The wire had passed over her head and front legs till it came to her back ones and there it had tightened, cutting into her stomach.

Lucy was fortunate, not like poor Jude. Miraculously, she didn't appear to have struggled much. I had the most curious feeling she had waited for my coming (as Wendy did when snared in this same wood all those years ago) and yet . . . could a badger react like this? Jude was a great, strong, dominant boar and patriarch of all he surveyed. He had fought the snare in anger, frustration and then pain, but I doubt if he had at any time been afraid. Jude was a Samson going down still fighting and so he was strangled and eventually died of his injuries. Little Lucy's behaviour was something different, though unlike his, her snare was made of fine wire; Jude's had been a 'fox' holding snare.

I went home for the hydrogen peroxide and returned in good light at 4.45 a.m. to wash the cut clean. Crisp helped, her long tongue parting the belly fur with Lucy lying for ease on her side, then her back in the bluebells. It is possible that the snarer *did* come through the wood and saw us, for I was far more concerned for the victim and had forgotten anything else. At last, the sows went to earth with the birdsong tumultuous, stock-dove and woodpigeon, chaffinch, goldfinch, yellowhammer, chiffchaff, blackcap and the titmice all competing with the penetrating calls of the Old Cherry Sett wren; such a tiny bird for such a call. From the end of the Wildflower Path, the pheasant 'korr-koked' and a carrion crow flying over Long Field made his presence known too.

Walking home I remembered the van parked till dark. There was nothing to connect it with the snarer and people often walked their dogs very late. Force of habit had caused me to note the number; only time would tell if it appeared under suspicious circumstances again. Apart from entering what had occurred on the monthly report for the police and telling the farmers and one or two vehicle owners who helped me with Ashcroft Woods, there was little else I could do. I did contact the man who held the spare radio, however, and he promised to look round some evenings when he could. We also agreed to use the two-way radios again, at least till I moved.

This monthly report had proved informative. It is easy to forget the exact circumstances surrounding an occurrence. Writing it down whilst still fresh in the mind not only avoids exaggeration or distortion later, but may link it with another incident, perhaps months afterwards.

A week after Lucy was snared, she was still far from well and this, in spite of her being half-way through a course of antibiotics. Her 13 cms long wound that had begun as a hairline cut, was now 4 cms wide and badly infected. I cleaned it and she was very good at washing it herself, but being a low-slung animal given to foraging in wet earth, dirt inevitably penetrated and the skin died back. Probably for this reason, septicaemia through wounds or bites is often a cause of badger deaths. Finally, I used an antibiotic powder in a puffer canister which dried the injury well. One Saturday night, I had just persuaded Lucy to roll onto her back to 'have the treatment' when a thunderstorm sounded distantly. The radio slung over my shoulder under my anorak, kept bumping against her, so I took coat and radio and laid them next to us. Crisp often felt neglected when her companion was attended to and stole the limelight that night by going to earth with my radio at the next clap of thunder. As it happened the radio was on (we had some difficult youths camping in the woods) and for 24 hours my radio contact heard bleeps, odd bumps and sounds of heavy breathing gradually becoming fainter as the battery ran down!

Crossing High Ridge that morning, I saw a strange confrontation between a weasel and a green woodpecker. The woodpecker was aware for some while of danger, but since it was in a wide open space and the predator was at a distance, it wasn't inclined to move in a hurry. The weasel gradually crept closer and then from behind a tussock of grass, reared up to reconnoitre, its slender shape and neat white underparts showing clearly. Still the woodpecker remained, though very watchful. Suddenly the mustelid darted snake-like across the open space and, as if waiting for this signal, the bird rose upwards with a few strong wing beats, emitting his sharp alarm note and with bounding flight, disappeared over the birches.

Weasels are good swimmers, though they don't like to swim and won't go far. A young bird fell out of its nest overhanging the Main Pond one evening and a weasel repeatedly tried to reach it. After each attempt, it came ashore flattening its body against the ground to press the excess water out of its fur, then swam out again to the chick now in the middle of the pond and fluttering feebly. At the fourth attempt it reached the bird and swam on with it to the farther shore.

Going home that same day, I spied a kestrel preening on a post of the motorway fence. It ran its curved beak along each primary, carefully separating and cleaning as it went. Next, it turned its head one way to clean its back as far as it could reach, and then turned the other. Suddenly, its fierce, sharp eye caught sight of me standing silently on the path and it was very still. Then up, up, ever higher, it rose far above my head. For seconds it hovered as I gazed up, then gracefully soared away.

There was a great canopy of honeysuckle in bloom overhanging an old hazel tree well inside the woods. The ground slopes steeply from the hazel and on the rise, an oak fell during the hurricane. Its branches had disappeared into the higher reaches of the overhang and I liked to sit as far along the broadest of these as I safely could, almost five metres off the ground. Sitting here I looked over the cultivated fields with their nightly irrigation and foraging badgers and would find myself up amongst the bats at dusk and first-light. This tier upon tier of pale but clearly visible blossoms was nightly visited by moths and most special for me, the shy dormouse. There were few of them; I was never to see more than two at any one time. It is impossible to describe the pleasure derived from watching these tiny, plump creatures leaping with delicate agility from slender twig to even finer stem, or running dextrously up and down the old, overgrown coppicing beyond; this last so smoothly, that the minute figure appeared to flow. Thus I learned to distinguish at a distance their movements from those of squirrel or weasel. Their large tail was not used to grip, rather it aided their balance. I discovered the dormouse enjoys insects as well as oak catkins. Should the weather turn cold and damp, even in the height of summer, the dormice can no longer been seen feeding and I suspect they become torpid till warmer conditions prevail. All in all, they well deserve their country name of 'sleep mouse'. It must be very easy to destroy their habitat without even realizing they are present.

By May the swallows were back swooping to drink, bathe and catch insects over the Main Pond and the quail called hauntingly from the depths of the concealing corn. We were still in the period of hot weather with day temperatures in the mid-seventies and heavy dews at night. By midnight, mist would creep into the hollows and at the very bottom of High Ridge where it meets Maddon Lane; it always seems to accumulate just there. Thus the air was cooling, but a breeze blowing through the elmbrush of Cliffords Bank as I walked along the top path, sent warm air trapped from the day, onto my face! The long, meadow grass between the wood edge and the bank came above the top of my wellingtons, making my trouser legs wet with fallen dew; so was Watcher's fur. The fox was looking patchy in her moult and her cubs had kneaded away her belly fur. She would run her teeth through her thick coat, pulling and teasing as she did so; the old fur was intensely irritating in the heat. Wads were left behind from her grooming, the small holes visible where her teeth had combed. At 2.30 a.m. a cuckoo called repeatedly from the lane as the vixen pounced on a woodmouse in the grass. I watched her cubs playing with it; they had already had their fill that night. Later, their mother cached it, tupping earth lightly over with her nose.

Missy greeted me purring and, for the first time, her three cubs came up to me also. Nervously, their moist snouts lightly touched my boots, then backed away. The boots hadn't hurt or frightened them, so they were smelt again. I squatted down to purr back at their mother, resting a hand on the ground to steady myself. It is good practice to ignore the timid and I concentrated on Missy who by now was washing my hair. The hand was softly smelt, then the young boar, bolder than his sisters, inspected my trousers. These cubs I had named after children who write to me about *their* countryside and wildlife. There is Kate from Oxford and Kirsty in Wiltshire. A seven-year-old Irish boy sent a badger glove-puppet he made and the 'badger-file' he was writing for me to read. Would I name a cub after him and give his puppet to the chosen cub? Mícheál's enthusiasm involved his school and his mother, who started the local badger-group, the second of its kind in Ireland. She wrote, 'Perhaps their generation or their children's children will be less arrogant than ours and learn to share this earth with their fellow animals.' When I look at Mícheál, son of Missy today, I recall the Dublin lad who cemented my concern for the dreadful persecution of Irish badgers. Though small in years and stature, children can be great in compassion and love. It is their environment and future we hold in trust. Ours not to beguile them with platitudes, nor betray that trust and future with the Judas kiss.

At first light the cuckoo was still calling from Briarmead and I came upon Crisp and Lucy digging out their entrances at the Old Cherry Sett. Again my boots were smelt, this time with sandy snouts before their owners musked them, then back to the serious business of extending their home. Something caught my eye on Crisp's spoil heap; a bedraggled, dirty something, but my radio nonetheless! I scooped it up quickly before she turned to notice and walked back along the lane as the sun rose. There were dogroses, comfrey and the campions blooming on its banks which already had many bees in attendance. How tall and verdant everywhere was now! Cliffords Bank had become a living, green wilderness and beneath its sheltering foliage it was dark and cool in the heat of the day.

One mild night with low cloud hiding moon and stars, I stopped on my way to Ashcroft Woods to watch nine badgers, five of them cubs, foraging at the side of a field. I recorded them as the Embankment badgers with their main sett in the railway bank and the subsidiary sett in private grounds. Coming and going to my area, I often watched this little family, though with no desire to be accepted by them. Indeed, it was a challenge to see just how close I could get to observe without them being aware. At the corner of the field a dogfox appeared, a large rabbit dangling from his mouth. He also watched the badgers, adjusted

his burden and, by a circular route, stole silently on and under the railway chain-link.

My badgers too were foraging, except for Lucy and Crisp who, unusually for this time of year with no cubs present, were collecting soft, dry grass as bedding and backing down-slope to their sett. This reminded me of the sett I had mapped the previous day, dug under the piles of an old burnt-out house. Freshly dropped pieces of bedding lay in one entrance hole that proved on examination to be bitten off iris leaves from the overgrown garden. The nearest bedding to this is the finer bluebell greenery so beloved of badger mums for their offspring. However, they will make use of whatever is available. I have heard that badgers in the Bath area not only used rushes by a lake for this purpose, but also left the surplus in piles to dry for future use.

In Ashcroft Woods the previous day, the council's men had been busy erecting the permanent metal by-laws notices, and 'no shooting' ones, clearly displayed, each on a square metal post cemented into the ground. The bank between Briarmead and Long Field now had a strong fence and an even stouter barred gate and stile. No more motorbikes roaring in from this part of the lane to race over the Old Cherry Sett. At last we were getting somewhere!

The day's first sun over the sprayed fields of Colts Farm was bringing forth the insects. Swallows swooped and dived after them in their aerial quest for food. They skimmed and twisted across the track where a large puddle remained from the night. Sometimes they forsook insects momentarily to sweep down and sip water, then rise again. Their blue-black backs and russet throats were glorious in the rising sun. The highest standing barley was that of Long Field; its whiskered heads had a pinkish look as a breeze rippled through. Now every roadside bank was awash with nodding rough chervil and cow parsley whitely dappling the living grass – surely green is the colour of life?

Wardening later, I watched a sparrowhawk above the trees near the Chantry. It was circling high in search of something, then appeared to fly off and I lost sight of it. I walked slowly through the woods picking up litter, happy at being on my own in such a lovely place. There had been problem campers the previous week in a dug-out site who the police had moved on. I wanted to check that all the litter had been cleared, so I could carry any down to the bottom of Briarmead where a lady living there let me leave it with her rubbish awaiting collection. Moving silently along the path, I stopped to watch a chiffchaff just ahead, the sun shining on its plumage giving it a golden look. Something from above dashed along the ride – a flurry of feathers and a sparrowhawk was flying through the woods holding a glimpse of yellow, its short, rounded wings ideal for dodging and twisting amongst the trees. I took the little winding path to the recent camp site past the old beeches amongst the bracken and on to a birch stand, when nearly there I stopped. Something grey and fierce-eyed was there before me plucking feathers from its victim on a broken birch stump and occasionally looking round with yellow eyes alert, only to resume its occupation. How long and cruelly curved the steel talons were, set in yellow claws and the hooked beak. Suddenly it spied me and flew off with its prey to disappear amongst the trees. I stood some time at the plucking post, marvelling I hadn't guessed before that a bird (rather than a mammal) had been responsible for these feathers. Several times in the last few weeks I had seen fresh feathers lying about – jay, thrush, great tit and now the chiffchaff – so this was the culprit. Had it a mate incubating eggs somewhere in our woods?

Returning home that day along the Sleet House Path, I met the farmer who asked me how the Embankment badgers were. He had noted pawprints, some of them small, and hoped they had cubs. He had just come from the footpath at the side of the railway; if I hurried I'd see the foxcubs out in the sun on the farside bank. Sure enough, there they were, gekkering one to another in the dappled light beneath the trees. Two were quarrelling over the remains of the rabbit their father had left that night. The winner set to eating, tearing from the throat and chest, all the while looking up towards the den and his vanquished brother in case of trouble.

A while later I had a phone call from a Weldon friend to say that the two acres of land containing the main badger sett near them, had been cleared and bulldozed by the owner whilst they were on holiday. The occupied sett remained with a shelter-belt of trees around it for the landowner knew the badgers were there. That night I watched the little family. Just as the terriermen digging for badgers in this sett 20 months earlier had failed to make the dominant sow move, so had this clearing of the land around her home. Her young boar cub and a yearling sow were still safely living with her. This would probably have been a different story were it not the main sett. Subsidiary and outlying ones are not the centres of badger family life in quite the same way. Discussing it with the RSPCA Inspector, there seemed little one could do. The owner *had* left the sett undisturbed, she naturally knew of the badger-digging case centred on her land, she had even left the immediate shrubs and trees and the badgers still had many acres of wood, meadow and farmland on which to forage. I would continue to quietly watch the Weldon badgers at night whenever I could and check everything was well.

Central Television's Cook Report on badger abuse was televised on the last evening in May. Many people contributed with their knowledge of the cruelties inflicted on this protected species. More than any other programme or article, this brought home to the public that digging and baiting are alive and well; nor do they just occur in isolated country places. Incredibly, it also brought forth in the editorial of a terriermen's magazine complete agreement with the correspondent who desired 'the reinstatement of the badger as a legitimate quarry species, but with a close season during the breeding period, since no serious fieldsports- man wants to see any species under threat.' After all, you need badgers for the sport of badger-digging and terriers bred to work badgers, need badgers on which to work. The editor ended on a sorrowful note commenting, 'the Badger Act has only curtailed the sport of the genuine terrierman.'

$==$ 6 $==$

Warning and Revenge

June began unsettled with sharp showers and sunny periods and the
badgers were busy in the wetness. The hours of darkness are brief at
this time of year and badgers can be seen in good light.

One morning I walked up Briarmead with Watcher. The quail called
lingeringly over the fields and I thought how my whole life was to alter.
Soon my daytime wardening here would come to an end and my
rubbish collecting, as no way would I be able to do these things when I
moved so far away. I would come for a while at least several nights a
week, to see the animals and after that ... I knew not. The vixen
looked up at me standing daydreaming, saw me smile down at her and
giving a grunt, stood up on hindlegs with front paws at my waist. We
touched noses, I stroked her head and we continued on our way into
the dawning.

The following day we had thunderstorms and prolonged rain well
into the evening. Crossing Ingrim's fields about 1.30 a.m., the noise of
metal clanking upon metal sounded clearly for a few moments. Was
someone breaking into the horses' stable? I ran on to their field and
jumped over the fence. Clearly no one was there for the horses were
quite unbothered, though pleased to see me as they snuffled into my

89

pockets in search of their polo mints! Just as they gently pushed and breathed around me, a vehicle – heavier than a car – drove off towards Rendcombe village. It sounded at though it had been parked near the soakaway, but the high hedges and the horses themselves blocked my view. A driver sleeping for a couple of hours parked off Holmoak Lane? Not unusual, especially in the summer months. Walking on I checked the goats, but nanny and kid were grazing higher up their field so I continued to my own area.

There was mist again in the hollows and my breath as well as the badgers', vapourized before us. The paths seemed to have grown smaller as the growing burden of the verges sought to cover them. Their wetness soaked us. For me it was a lovely night nonetheless and watching the nightjars, I realized there were in fact, two pairs. I had rarely known this here before. In a scrape amongst the dead leaves and bracken above the Old Cherry Sett, were laid the usual couple of eggs. Now I must wait and see!

Walking homewards that morning, I found the answer to the mystery noise hours before. The heavy wooden gates onto the goats' field were gone; the chain that padlocked both together must have rattled as it was taken! Oakley police promised to let the owners know. Nanny and kid were grazing well away from the space now open to the lane, but unlike horses, they can be left several days without attention, so the missing gates could go unnoticed for some time. I was still concerned for the animals' safety though and later that morning returned to find a man erecting temporary fencing to seal the gap. He said the hinges had been capped to prevent the gates being lifted off, so instead, they were removed taking posts, cement and all! How I wished I had found the source of the noise in time.

The 7th was a lovely night with stars beginning to shine as the rising wind swept clear the sky above the tree-line. I had Lucy and Crisp for company and together we walked along what was left of the Poplar Row, the badgers snuffling beneath the broken trees as we went. At 3.15 a.m. a skylark called from its shelter within the wheat stalks; a rush of wings and another rose singing into the lightening sky. Lucy froze at its passing, snorted sharply in surprise, stood a few moments scenting the air, then trotted hastily after us.

Newby Farm had a forlorn, unkempt look in spite of its inturned weeds of last month. Wheat and barley should have been standing high in its fields; the protective haven of quail, pheasant, mouse and rabbit and the hunting ground of weasel, stoat and fox. Untenanted farmland is a sorry sight. Heavy dew had soaked the overgrown farm tracks, so badgers and I walked on the neglected field edge to save ourselves a wetting.

The Briarmead banks seemed bursting with wild flowers and an amazing variety of seeding grasses towered above our heads, for the lane curves deeply sunken through the countryside just here. A mist was creeping over the fields as the day began and cascades of song floated down to us from the skylarks somewhere high above in the grey. Crisp thrust her snout into the bank, then sneezed violently as the swaying plumes of cocksfoot released their thick russet pollen to dust her face. I chuckled at her discomforture. She seemed to stare a moment, then bounded up muddy and wet to stand on hindlegs against me and be stroked.

Homeward bound through the dull, misty morning, there were two mallard drakes on the Holmoak soakaway and a duck feeding nearby amongst the growing wheat. I gave the farmer's horses their polo mint each and spoke to the goat and her kid in the field opposite, just as the sun succeeded in piercing the greyness, sending shafts of light to bejewel the tall, wet grass.

Wet summer evenings are marvellous after dark when the rain keeps all other humans indoors! I met up with my badgers soon after nightfall and a funny thing happened. In spite of the heavy rain and wet foliage soaking me, I was very happy in their company and some music I had been playing much earlier that day, was running through my mind. Almost without knowing it, I burst out singing to myself. In full spate, I was aware of a frozen tableau of brockies each staring my way; in retrospect, I can sympathize. I stopped, spoke softly, then went on, curious to see their response. Crisp recovered first. She put her head down and charged meaning to butt my legs, but I jumped aside in time and she flattened Susie instead! I must admit to feeling guilty as the older sow snapped back and Crisp the Terrible was put firmly in her place.

By daylight it was still raining as I walked slowly along the path of the contorted oaks in Ashcroft Woods. A faint twittering of birds and a stoat bounded across my path. I watched it unseen as it ran through the bracken before disappearing into the deeper undergrowth. The rain pattered on the foliage above my head as Watcher's mate came into view, his leanness accentuated by his wet and moulting fur as he hunted at the Six Wents clearing. He was suddenly aware of my presence, turned to run back in the direction of Colts Farm, then cautiously retraced his steps, sniffing the air as he did so. No scent on the rain-laden morning, so he began to skirt round me. I made the soft

'mmmmmmmmmmm' and he slowly came up in recognition. I bent to touch noses, the vulpine greeting, and was accepted. Walking on my way, I turned to see him looking after me. Sanicle, the campions red, white and bladder, and the tall, towering foxgloves now graced the woodland rides, with figwort yet to flower.

Standing awhile enjoying the place, the fine rain on my face and hair, the vividly green, mossy boles of the old oaks themselves and the wet fragrance of a wood in June, I was conscious of a squeaking noise accompanied by a rustling. There was a silence for a few moments, then the noises again. They came from the smoothly rounded hole near the base of one oak, so I knelt down and looked in. The dead leaves and wisps of grass inside were quite dry for the overhang caused by the tree's odd growth, protected it snugly from the elements. The 'nest' inside heaved and convulsed as the squeaking broke out once more and gently I lifted a few pieces away. I didn't know what I expected to find, but there was a hedgehog writhing, twisting and turning as it lay on its back. Its hind legs were pressed hard against the inside of the tree so that stretched out like this, its head and shoulders were forced against the opposite side. A convulsing and ... there came the birth of its first young, enclosed in a membrane, the head pushing out first, the slightly curled newborn clearly visible through the placenta. The mother commenced licking her vulva, next the placenta, which under her urgent tongue soon sloughed off and was eaten. She washed the curiously bloated looking baby that was about 7 cms long. The tiny limbs, released from the confining membrane, stuck out stiffly and under the skin of its back and head were tiny white, flat spines. I would hazard a guess that the water beneath the skin is to protect the mother internally from the spines both in the womb and during the act of birth. The mother 'purred' (how many animals do this!) and holding her newborn in her mouth, put it in front of her. For a while she rested curled up slightly, then began to lick her vulva again and the whole process repeated itself. An hour later she had seven, two being breech births, the others frontal, with a few minutes between each one. By 5 a.m. I concluded she would have no more, as licking the last she placed it against her nipples. She did this to each in turn until all seven were suckling. I noticed she had five pairs of nipples. Then I silently moved on. At no time did she appear aware of me, although hedgehogs are rather oblivious of humans if we are careful.

Later, I told my neighbour of the hedgehog births. We often laugh together at the antics of our garden hedgehogs. He puts out milk near his backdoor step for a little black cat and one morning as I came home from Ashcroft Woods at 5 a.m. and walked round our sideway, the noise of tin striking cement was almost deafening in the quietness. A squeaking, grunting and there was an urchin with the tin in his jaws. He ran a few paces and threw it perhaps half-a-metre away, then trotted after and repeated the performance, occasionally stopping to sniff and lick inside it. The noise he made suggested a much larger animal (a fox turning out a dustbin springs to mind), but I've noticed this before with hedgehogs. Discussing this, we concluded that the hedgehog had come upon the container smelling of milk but empty and was venting his ill-feeling on the offending tin.

Our own hedgehog had been 'trotting about' (they raise the body well clear of the ground when they walk quickly) in bright sunshine a few weeks earlier. Ours was a lively, healthy and very heavy specimen, indicating that if he continued so, he would easily survive a winter hibernation. He was something of a character and I had rescued him from our terrapin's pond where he had gone a-slugging. Not that the hedgehog was in difficulties; they are good swimmers. But having had his fill of slugs, he had dared to sunbathe on the Spanish terrapin's rock, which upset the latter a great deal. The pond-owner hisses at birds that invade his 'island' and clambers out of the water to push them off, but this great creature with spines outstretched to allow the sun to dry him ... for once, an immovable object had met another immovable object; armour-plated reptile attempting to push off prickly-armoured insectivore. It was a case of stalemate and nobody was going to win.

Hedgehog behaviour is notoriously eccentric. There was an old overgrown orchard at Weldon which covered many acres and a very tiny portion was used by a local model aeroplane club. This was a well mown area 23 metres square with a mown path leading from a corner of it to the footpath a short distance away. Walking at dusk one August evening in 1980 I spied a movement in the square and, on investigating, found a hedgehog trotting round and round in an anti-clockwise circle. It continued for a long time, grunting occasionally and I tried to judge the size of its circle – about six metres across. By now it was almost dark, but it still continued. I wondered at the time whether it had been affected by the spraying of pesticides there, but this was in the midst of acres of neglected orchard that hadn't been tended for years. The matter of hedgehogs running in circles had been discussed, I found, in the 1960s and a short paper even appeared in the *Journal of Zoology*. Pesticides, illness and other causes were suggested. However, despite the interest and publicity this aroused, I don't think anyone was much the wiser.

It was an evening again, this time in May, when I was walking along the top of Cliffords Bank and came to a part of the meadow there that had been nibbled down by rabbits, giving it the appearance of a lawn. In front of me out of the concealing elmbush, a hedgehog ambled. On reaching the flat surface of turf, its speed accelerated and it shot across the open space, disappearing into the long grass. No sooner had it gone when another hedgehog and another appeared all from this stretch of hedge and all apparently with the same destination in mind, and rushed across in the same way. In all I counted 11! These were adults and I had no idea till then, how many of these creatures could be found in a given area of suitable habitat. It was for all the world as if children were having a race with clockwork toys.

I witnessed another rather eccentric example of hedgehog behaviour one December night when walking past the orchard by Sleet House, I saw a hedgehog eating one of the fallen apples there. After a time, he attempted to carry the fruit away in his mouth. Lifting his head as high as it would go and walking tall he tried to raise the apple above grass level as he passed through. This made his legs appear quite long and thin as, of course, he was raising his body too; looking very unlike a hedgehog in fact. Then he would rest, descending to his usual squat position and have another crunching session. I was surprised he had not hibernated, though the spell of mild weather we were having then might have had some bearing on that. I have since found that they do, in fact, wake and find food in mild spells, only to return to hibernation again, though there is a risk to this and death may result. I have never seen a hedgehog attempt to carry an apple on it spines as is frequently reported. Nor for that matter have I seen one self-anointing, that is applying saliva to its spines. Perhaps I will one day.

Many years ago, my neighbours and I were often woken during the summer at 2 or 3 a.m. by empty milk bottles rolling about. One night I quietly went downstairs on being woken and opened the front door. There, most unconcerned at my appearance was next door's half-grown cat and a hedgehog. The cat had knocked over our bottles and both animals were drinking the 'rings' of water on the cement that had formed by the warm air condensing on the cold glass and running down. When they had finished, the cat led the way along our path and on to next door where they repeated the performance. This is the only time I have witnessed mutual co-operation between a hedgehog and another animal. From my own experience I know fox and cat relationships are not unusual and have been told that cat and hedgehog associations are not unknown, but co-operation is something rather different. Not only can hedgehogs move very fast when they wish, they can also swim and climb well too. One of these animals even climbed into an upstairs bedroom via the ivy growing on the wall! I have never seen one climb down however. They merely drop, landing as a curled up ball (that often bounces) and cushioned by their spines.

A friend and his wife kept a hedgehog as a pet, giving it the free run of the garden as well as the ground floor of their cottage. They had discovered it apparently abandoned at two or three weeks old and it lived for some years with them. This hedgehog, however, seemed incapable of finding slugs, worms, and so on for itself (though would eat them when offered) and all its life had to be fed. Baby hedgehogs open their eyes at 14 days and start leaving the nest from about three weeks. They are weaned between four and six weeks. I have watched sow hedgehogs with several youngsters in tow, foraging amongst leaf litter in woods and beneath hedges, as well as looking for slugs on our lawn. This would indicate that they are taught to hunt by the mother and their vital time of learning by parental example is from six weeks onwards.

Early in June 1986 at 5.30 a.m. I watched something rather amusing. Walking from the Briarmead direction, along the winding trail of the Old Cherry Sett, I came across a hedgehog on the path with his back to me. A large, white pigeon's egg lay before him, the shell of which he appeared to be licking. Next to it lay the far smaller blue-green speckled egg of a song thrush. Even as I stood there, a squirrel with another thrush's egg in its mouth, came down a nearby tree and seeing the hedgehog busily engaged, put down its egg and scolded the urchin soundly! The egg-licker took no notice whatsoever, though the squirrel bounced up and down in its fury, tail waving and feet stamp, stamping. Then suddenly in the midst of all its anger, it saw me quietly standing there. Immediately, picking up the little egg it ran back up the tree. The hedgehog turned to see the cause of its alarm and hastily disappeared amongst the fading bluebells, leaving me in possession of the two eggs! In the middle of the large white one were two neat teeth marks that had pierced the egg and held it. The wrong shape for the hedgehog's, but right for rodent teeth. The small egg had scratch marks on each side where teeth had held it. True, hedgehogs are good climbers and love eggs, but in this case I think it safe to say that the squirrel had raided the nests, only to have its booty discovered and the hedgehog had been licking the white escaping from the bitten shell.

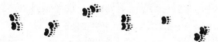

Our summer seemed to have left us with a succession of dreary, wet, cold days though the cuckoo still called and the geans' tiny cherries littered the Wildflower Path. Missy's three cubs were robust and adventurous. There had been no man-made problems in their young lives and they were emotionally well balanced. Perhaps a rather curious remark, but an important one. Most animals are liable to stress, though some individuals can cope better and some fare worse. Young stressed animals, and those with stressed parents, become nervous, tense and have difficulty forming normal relationships with others of their species. It is known that stress can inhibit reproduction; it can also leave the animal more liable to infection. Patterns of behaviour laid down in formative months may never be resolved in adulthood. This is particularly true of badgers.

Watcher's four cubs were a few days older than the badgers and by now were beautiful young animals. As usual at this time of year, they were more vivid in their colouring than the parents. The adults were well into their moult and appeared greyish, tatty and very thin by comparison. Foxes in their first year do not moult; the long guard hairs that give the animal its glorious colour, gradually grow through the early woolly felting.

I was deep in a part of Ashcroft Woods that was almost untouched by the hurricane. High above me a wind was blowing the tree-tops in a grey, dull dawning. On my lap Susie was grooming herself – and me – as we sat hidden in the undergrowth and listened to the whispering wood. A gap in the fringed foliage showed a lighter sky. Something flew in and dropped – the woodcock – but I couldn't mark the place without disturbing the busy badger on my lap. I leaned my back against a trunk as Susie's tongue worked its way over my face, my arms round her warm body and the feel of rough fur on my hands.

There had been no dew-laden grass these past nights, for it was neither hot by day, nor misty in the dark hours. By 10.30 a.m. the June sun shone warm for the first time that month with the wind surging through the barley far below me as I stood amongst the flowers brightly scattered in the Colts Farm meadow above Maddon Lane. The patches of scarlet pimpernel, cuckoo flower, ribbed melilot, herb robert, meadow cranesbill, green alkanet, vervain, large Venus' looking-glass and ox-eye daisies were wonderful as they peered in multi-coloured triumph above the swaying grass.

Distantly, I could see the silver sprays irrigating the far-off fields and, moving my head, catch the sun rainbowing them through. Behind me in Ashcroft Woods were foxgloves, tier upon tier of stately purple pink and sometimes white spires and the figwort, so beloved of wasps, was slowly coming into bloom. Walking home across the land, a tractor caught me up. The farm-manager and I talked badgers, foxcubs, a 'wild' ferret he had seen in the woodland bank, long-tailed tits, weasels, stoats and the sparrowhawk. Then off he drove to his dinner now 12.45 p.m. and I was homeward bound.

Crisp and Susie had been quarrelling one night. It all started over a very 'high' pigeon one found. Crisp ran off with the prize and later Susie was picking on her, the older sow really being the more dominant. At 3.50 a.m. they were bickering with more noise and 'threats' than physical contact. The querulous voices were sharp on the quiet air and suddenly they came to grips in the grassy space where once the Old Barn stood. Susie bit the other on the back just above her

tail; Crisp yowled and turning, swung her head to bite back as the other dodged clear. A whirling tangle of grey, a 'yakking' and snarling and one broke free and ran against my legs – Crisp trying to hide behind me. Susie went to run round and I jumped to one side shouting and clapping my hands. They both stopped and stared at me and, as if for the first time, I heard the birds in full song. Just as suddenly as it began, the fight ended, Susie swaying home through the wood and Crisp trotting off down the Briarmead Bank.

Another night I was with Missy and her family as they foraged by the motorway embankment. The cubs played amongst themselves until they saw their mother on my lap and *all* decided they wanted to climb aboard! As usual about 2.30 a.m., the badgers headed for home, Kirsty well ahead, Kate next with Mícheál pottering happily after his sisters. Already their individual characters were well marked with the young male having his mother's easy-going, quiet nature. Kirsty was the adventurous leader, whilst Kate loved a game and would have one at any price.

Together we crossed silent Maddon Lane and, in single file, passed along the hedge onto the farmland. Just ahead were the freshly drilled radishes and the irrigation pipes disconnected from the hydrant, but still joined together from the previous day. Kirsty gave a great snort of surprise at a tall figure ahead and one farther away tinkering with the pipe-couplings. 'Look it's a bloody badger,' exclaimed the first, doubtless seeing her black and white mask. She turned and rushed back into my legs as the man came towards her. 'Here, what do you think *you* are doing?' I involuntarily exclaimed and the nearest man swore and turning, rushed off with the first. There was a surging of fearful badgers round my feet and I tripped over one (I think it was Missy), as a vehicle parked on the farther field track was started up and bumped hurriedly off along the wood edge. The sound of metal rolling and banging came from the tipper part of the light lorry as it sped off towards the lane.

When the badgers and I had sorted ourselves out, I looked carefully at the pipes, but everything seemed still coupled up. The radio's range didn't extend this far and, in any case, I had no vehicle number. The time, 2.50 a.m., was too late to be starting a 'job' at night on the land for it would shortly begin to be light. Had they been checking out the outhouses and barns of Colts Farm first (recalling that the lorry *had* contained something) or had the two been on their way home from somewhere else and thought to drop in on this farm for a few 'optional extras'? We went on slowly to the sett in the meadow where I left the badgers grooming whilst I walked on through the wood.

Later that morning I spoke to the farm-manager and we discussed the recent spate of thefts from local farms. The owner of a vehicle seen in the vicinity of one such incident was a lamper and poacher. The summer months are out of season for these activities, but stealing equipment for resale is an evergreen occupation. I mentioned that police patrols at night were common for I had met several in the last fortnight. I also mentioned the gates taken from Holmoak Lane. The manager said that his gates off Maddon Lane had topped hinges, but thieves had unscrewed them recently and tried to lift off a gate without success. There must be a ready market for gates and farm equipment and the chance of anyone being caught in such isolated places at night was remote.

A quail had laid her eggs deep in a barley field off Briarmead Lane and each morning I would watch the pair through my monocular. I had found only one other solitary quail in the entire area. This timid little bird, not unlike a small partridge, has a mottled neck and a distinctively streaked pattern on throat, head and face. We had a succession of lovely mornings with the sun quite hot. Swallows skimmed over the whiskered barley in their airborne quest for insects. There were many bees and butterflies on the dogwood blossoms, woody nightshade and bladder campion of the Wildflower Path. The swallows' sickle shapes twisted and turned in the sunshine as a distant wind raced through the corn below. A crow cawed above the other birdsong and long fingers of shadow pointed across the field. Towering clouds formed, dissolved and reformed, as they hurried over the sky and the wetness from the dewy night evaporated quickly in the warmth.

Swallows had nested in the horse stables off Maddon Lane. It is always stated they nest in buildings, but what did they do before the event of man-made constructions? I wondered this, as some of these

99

birds seemed to disappear into Prossers Wood, the little wood by the railway. Might some of them nest in trees? There were sandmartins in the bank of the railway cutting where it runs into the wood and martins were nesting in the outbuildings of Glebe Farm; it would be interesting to find out more. Passing by the barley, I saw the wind was surging through it like sea swell. It is the most lovely grasses, especially at this stage in its growth before the ears begin to droop. It has a sheen like no other cereal that I know.

One morning on Briarmead, I discovered evidence that a badger had narrowly avoided being rundown there sometime during the night. A large ball made up of bitten-off blades of grass, lay neatly on the tarmac. On the field side of the lane, tyre marks and flattened vegetation were visible where a vehicle had swerved. A few paces along the other side of Briarmead was the animals' up-and-over path onto the bank. Who had been the bedding-collector? Had he or she been knocked? But thinking back, I had seen all the badgers that night and none appeared injured. Examining the ball, most of the blades of grass were of the same length, that is around 15 to 17 cms, and were probably taken from near ground level. Grass like this makes a compact bundle to comfortably carry, unlike leaves which tend to leave a trail. Someone had a lucky escape! It seemed an odd sight there in the lane with the dawn light touching it.

Many fungi appeared with all the dampness of these June nights. Field mushrooms, shaggy parasols, *Boletus impolitus*, magnificent specimens of *Ganorderma applanatum* on one of the Chantry beeches, and many more. As I walked slowly through this wood in Watcher's company, gnats and insects danced in the early morning sunbeams that were stealing into its deepest shadows. The fragrance of honeysuckle hung on the air. All was a deep, deep green enhanced by the greyness. Looking out over Warby from the entrance to Little Chantry Field, three pipistrelle bats flew almost over my head, with one flying in front of my face. They were fascinating and I saw one rest a moment as it ate a large insect.

There were only a few great crested newts now in the Main Pond; so many people had come in the past with nets and jars to collect them. At first light I counted two with several smooth newts. All was quiet but for the occasional plop of water as one briefly surfaced, the soft cooing of a turtle dove and the breeze pattering the aspen leaves nearby. I discovered a dead rabbit nestling that Meg and Bess had dug up with its litter-mates that night. Whether they had been too full to bother with them all, or merely overlooked that one, I couldn't say. I photographed it by the side of a well-defined badger print in the damp earth to give an indication of the rabbit's size, then dropped it down an entrance of Colts Farm sett.

A pair of great spotted woodpeckers were feeding their young housed in the trunk of a rotten birch. The parents were bringing them nestling birds. The mortality amongst young birds is very high. That June I had seen a confrontation between a pair of blackbirds, a squirrel and a weasel high up in another birch. The mustelid had either a nestling bird in its mouth or a very young squirrel. The blackbirds eventually flew away, but the squirrel continued its 'chuck-chucking' and foot stamping whilst the weasel calmly ate its prey. Then it darted at the noisy squirrel who rushed almost to the top of the birch where it clung perilously. This tree overtopped any near to it; a tactical error on the part of the squirrel. I couldn't see the weasel for some time though most certainly it was still there as the squirrel remained perched high up. Perhaps seven minutes later, the weasel emerged from a deep hole in the trunk (was there a squirrel's drey or blackbird's nest inside?) and descended with great speed to the ground near me, where it disappeared amongst the foxgloves and stitchwort. I always marvel at the speed with which a tree-climbing (or perhaps I should say, a tree-running) weasel moves, be it up or down. They make squirrels appear awkward and ungainly for although the latter ascend with great agility, they descend in a jerky, spread-eagled fashion. Weasels, however, cannot jump from tree to tree which is where the squirrel has the advantage.

I was finding many dead toads in the woods now. The excessive coppicing and removal of the undergrowth, had destroyed their habitat for the unusually hot weather of the previous month had dried the exposed ground out, turning it to dust. The vegetation would grow again of course, but too late for these dehydrated amphibians. Without intimate knowledge of a particular site, creating favourable conditions to encourage one species may well be the death knell of another. Altering any habitat should always be done slowly and with care. Ashcroft Woods has evolved over millennia and in spite of modern man with his destruction, pollution, motorways and sheer numbers, its complex ecology had survived. Man coppiced here for generations, but in such a way as to have a perpetual crop. Wood was the life-blood of his buildings, utensils, cooking and winter warmth. Remove too much one year and he suffered the next. He knew nothing of ecology and his concern for flora and fauna was purely material, but for that very reason, he husbanded with care.

Now, in spite of the hurricane devastation and the excess coppicing already done, the County Trust here were determined to carry out their plans to create five 30 metre-wide rides for wildlife throughout Ashcroft Woods. The Trust's conservation corps would cut down trees in the way at ground level and chain-flail them annually till they died. The only concession to the objections of the owners and local people, was that these new rides would not necessarily be a rigid 30 metres for all their length. Our woods have no great depth in any part and grow along the top of a hill ridge. Even without these proposed rides, the motorway could be seen and heard from the midst of the remaining trees. The noise was continuous by day and by night and habitat polluted. Ashcroft Woods will endure long after we are dust, but in us lies its future and the quality of that future depends very much on what we do now. It will be good next century to read what lived and grew in our woods, but better surely, to see it living and growing there still?

The tawny owlets were becoming venturesome and after much stationary wing-flapping to strengthen their muscles, would take off from their home branch on short journeys. Both adult birds were hunting for themselves and their offspring, so for long periods the fledglings were left to themselves. I was standing by the foxgloves watching these practice flights one night, when the hen owl came kewiking to fly round me and back. It had been a long time since she last perched on me, but on impulse I contact called, she came gliding round and, next moment, was there on my hand!

The badgers were out under the sprays. Above the click, click, click as the water jets turned I could hear the tawnies calling. Susie, Crisp, Lucy, Meg, Bess and Missy's newest litter, were all there. The sprays turned and they were soaked, their bodies glistening. Badgers are not very beautiful when they are wet, with their podgy, thickset bodies. How the cubs loved the mud! They were playing in the wettest area of the field edge. My badgers were very lucky; no lack of water, so no lack of worms. They would not starve.

After the Cook Report on badger abuse was televised I had several anonymous phone calls, one of which actually referred to the programme and my part in it. I knew who the callers were and how they had come by my ex-directory number. I wasn't afraid of the threats of physical violence, but was very glad my son and daughter had moved away. I was worried about the house though; it was empty at night and these local lampers knew that. There had been no threats of vandalism to the house, but it would have been easy to do and easier still to get away with it. I told my immediate neighbours who promised to keep on alert. It seemed pointless letting the police know for, after all, what could they do? I had been threatened before and it is part of the risks one runs. I also felt by agreeing to take part in the programme, I had brought it upon myself.

Watcher's youngsters were beginning to wander from the den to find insects and beetles for themselves as their parents hunted less for them. The fragrance of honeysuckle at night pervaded the woods attracting hawkmoths in abundance. Honey bees don't visit its blossoms as their one-sided tubes made up of two lobes of united petals are too long for their tongues to reach the nectar. Many insects, however, force their way down the tubes, including the white admiral butterfly's larvae. A pair of nightjars were catching the moths attracted to the honeysuckle one night. The field and woodland tracks were dry and dusty from the recent strong winds.

At 4.20 a.m. I walked out of the woods and started down the farm track towards Maddon Lane. My thoughts elsewhere, I noted a van travelling along the lane in the High Ridge direction (unusual for the time of morning), then my mind turned to the field bank I was passing that had once contained the evening primrose, sadly no more. At Maddon Lane I too turned towards High Ridge, looking up and right over the barley where already, a skylark was tumultuously singing from on high. To my left, the motorway was busy with traffic, when suddenly and directly in front, a grubby, white van was nearly on top of me. A blurred impression of tyres on the gritty surface and I was rolling over the bank onto which I had jumped, the nearside of the vehicle just brushing me. By the time I picked myself out of the barley, it had disappeared. Not an accident I knew only too well. I had not registered the driver, though I had a very good idea who had been behind the incident, if not actually behind the wheel. Had he been cruising round Maddon and Holmoak Lanes on the look out, knowing I would have to cross both at some time? I imagine on sighting a figure walking towards the lane, he had turned at the metal gate of High Ridge and waited in the little lay-by for me to walk up. Sure enough, half-way through the morning there came another phone call with the promise that next time he wouldn't miss!

That afternoon I returned to warden and at 5 p.m. was sitting quietly by myself on the Old Cherry, now overgrown and therefore neglected by humans. In one way, the hurricane had helped the remaining badgers here who were greater protected within the tangle of trunks. Those fallen trees, now in full leaf, hid me too from the path below.

The grey, cold morning had turned to sunshine with vivid blue skies. There were many gnats and butterflies about with the shaded grass below the Old Cherry a rich, moist green. These fallen geans were all in mature leaf and lay over their great parent, the Old Cherry, but by next summer these also would be dead. Nonetheless, life had come out of the old tree's death and so it would be again.

The sun disappeared behind a cloud and far below, hidden amongst the greenery, my bare arms felt chill in the sudden wind. I decided I would go and photograph the honeysuckle bower where recently I watched the nightjars and dormice feed. Completing my photography, I walked into the Chantry to be met by four youths who told me a companion had broken his arm and was deep amongst the giant, prone beeches. Together, we went into the very heart of this fastness, sometimes climbing over, sometimes crawling under, and sure enough, a very frightened lad about 14 or 15 years old was there with the skin of his upper arm pierced through in three places with splintered bone. Recent winds had toppled more trees, some already dead and others undermined in last year's storm. I went first to find the least painful route, then returned to help the youth surmount each obstacle. The hanging arm was an extra nuisance, so one of his friends took his sweater off for a sling to ease the weight and thereby the pain. They had been playing on the horizontal trunks when one had shifted and the lad was hurled off. He was fortunate it hadn't rolled and crushed him as he lay. We walked together down the hillside, all, including the injured boy, quite cheerful by now and I left them at the main road to go to their homes in Warby.

That night was cloudy and mild with excellent visibility. Three of Watcher's cubs, now well grown, played on the dusty trackway. They were two dogs and a vixen; the fourth cub, another vixen, I believed to be dead. When food was dropped by a parent, they were aggressive and fought for their share, but now they were gekkering, high-pouncing on each other and mutually grooming for a few moments, before another game of chase began.

One night I left home later than usual. As I crossed the main road, now silent and deserted, a car without headlights parked amongst others farther along, slipped out and came towards me at speed. Mindful of danger, I moved quickly into the street opposite, keeping the line of cars parked alongside the pavement between me and the road. The car with headlights now on was gaining fast on me heading for a vacant parking space! It reached it, stopped and the driver sprung out just as I turned to run. Relief, he was in uniform! 'You're out late

and moving a bit, we thought you were a burglar. Live far away then?'
Well, that's one way of getting a lift I suppose!

I told them of the phone calls and the van incident and I found it was this constable I had phoned about the theft of the gates. He queried whether it would help if they spoke to the lampers, but on finding who they were, agreed it would probably only aggravate the situation. I would soon be moving anyway which would solve the problem. We discussed how difficult it was for the police to catch thieves at night on the land and I said it was hard enough for me though I was sometimes in the vicinity, but it must be well-nigh impossible for them. He stressed that unless I could get a vehicle number, it was best to stay well clear. I agreed, but added that the people on the farms had been marvellous to me and the badgers and I *would* like to repay their kindness in a small way by helping. We said goodbye and I went onto Colts Farm to be greeted by Crisp and Lucy covered in mud and eager for a game!

The June day Warwick Reynolds, from the Surrey Badger Protection Society, came to cement the badger reflectors in was the hottest of the year. It was a job well done and my task now would be to regularly maintain them. I checked the posts before dark to see they hadn't been moved out of true before the cement hardened and continued on to watch the badgers at Weldon. The dominant sow had only produced one cub, a young boar who was made much of by his sisters of the previous year. Their father, could also be prevailed upon for a game. I enjoyed the challenge of following this little family without them being aware of my presence. My pleasure made me determined they wouldn't be disturbed by terriermen any more. Wherever I moved, I would continue to regularly check their setts; they deserved to live out their lives in peace.

Meg was missing and, very worried, I checked the Colts Farm sett and then the woods. None of the other badgers seemed in any way concerned so I doubted any human disturbance. Could she have been runover on one of the lanes? But all was clear. Eventually, I discovered a little grey figure moving slowly along the neat rows of strawberries and taking the ripe ones as she went like through a vacuum cleaner. The badgers had never found them as a food source before in the two previous years when strawberries had been grown here. Meg would not leave them and become quite aggressive till I retaliated with a hard smack to her snout. Then I shouted and, turning, she galloped away and under the gate, offended, affronted outrage in every line of her bouncing, shaggy figure. I fervently hoped she wouldn't bring the others or there would be no ripe strawberries left to sell! When I told the farm-manager's wife, however, she was very amused, commenting that maybe Meg had read the PYO sign and taken the hint! Fortunately, neither Missy's daughter nor any of the others repeated this and the strawberries were left for the humans to pick their own.

The orange sphere of the full moon rode through streamers of creamy clouds rippling outwards across the night sky as the badgers gleaned the remaining grass on the newly baled hayfield. There were still a few bales to be carted away with the smell of the hay strong and fragrant. Mícheál scrambled onto one and barked to his sisters below. Rather a mistake on his part; he might have known Kate could never resist such a challenge. One moment he was peering down at the others and the next she had reached up and caught hold of his tail hanging over the edge and yanked him off! They who bark last, bark longest! Farther over by the wood edge, Watcher was scavenging; a dead hedgehog and a bird – a skylark, I think. Her wet body seemed thin where her moulting fur showed her whippet-like contours. The three foxcubs by contrast, appeared stocky with their coats thickening and their brushes well formed.

The damson trees lining Briarmead were hung with strands of hay from the bales the tractor took down the winding lane. I spoke to Watcher as the first birds began singing and turned to walk out onto the farmland by Maddon Lane. She stood on hindlegs, forepaws at my waist and, all unknowing, I said goodbye for the last time as I put my face into hers. Walking on I saw the barley's whiskered heads were drooping and already bronze, ready for the harvest. Red drops of blood amongst the gold, the poppies moved on wind-stroked stalks.

Later that morning I returned to warden and was met by a man from Crosshampton. I knew he was police but not one of ours, merely living in the village. He was aware of the situation here and, like several others living locally, would walk round when he could. That morning he had found a freshly shot fox, dead near the Wildflower Path. 'I'm almost certain it's your fox, you know, the vixen you call Watcher, but you best come and see.' My poor Watcher indeed, her body nearly severed from the closeness of the shotgun; mercifully, death must have been instantaneous, her eyes and mouth wide open in that frightful moment when pain ceased her life. I couldn't leave her there. How silly I must have seemed, but somehow he understood. An old plastic binliner was torn open and laid across the back seat of his car and

Watcher laid on top as we drove home to Oakley. 'Going to bury her then?' my companion asked and I nodded. It was he who dug the hole and I who laid her to rest. He asked if I had any more threats or attempts to harm me. As I shook my head he said, 'The fox wasn't an accident. There's been no shooting for weeks in Ashcroft Woods and I didn't find her on the ground. Her body had been hung over the no shooting sign with the by-law notice deliberately smeared with her guts, but I didn't want you to find her like that. The best way to get at you is through the badgers and foxes here. When you move, my advice is don't tell *anybody* apart from us, where you're going. You've got a good opportunity to make a fresh start and keep your whereabouts secret. Make the most of it – and good luck.' I stood a long while after he had left, looking down at the fresh, clean earth. 'Make the most of it and good luck.' Oh, Watcher, Doppelgänger, my other self, the shadow in my shade.

Sett Destruction

In July I had spoken to the head of Oakley police saying I would no longer be able to warden Ashcroft Woods once I moved. I asked if copies of some of the monthly reports could be sent to the council officer responsible for our woods to illustrate the problems there and, hopefully, reinforce the necessity for an official, paid warden. True, both parish and district councils knew the problems full well, but the report might add some weight to this, my last request for a warden. The Inspector gave his permission, only asking that I make it clear the reports were confidential to Oakley police. I promised that whatever happened and wherever I moved to, I would somehow continue to map the badger setts in his police area. Temporarily, I would be staying with friends on the far edge of Oakley. I would let him know where I finally found a permanent home even if it was not within his area; we had all worked together for so long and so well to stop now.

I walked round to the badger setts at Weldon that same afternoon. No signs of human interference with the main sett well occupied. There was a clear badger trail showing through the freshly sprouted grass and weeds leading from the sett to the trees and undergrowth beyond the bulldozed area. There, under an elder was a very large, full dungpit with fresh snuffle holes nearby where the sow, her cub and yearling had foraged the previous night.

How strange to sleep on the floor of a house completely devoid of furniture; even stranger to have lived there for 27 years and borne two children in the main bedroom. I laid my sleeping-bag and pillow on the floor for the last time and went downstairs to make myself a mug of tea. The little black cat with the flattened tail, pushed against the front door as I passed, so opening it, I let her in. Very rarely was she allowed admittance as she had a home of her own, though the other cats also living there tormented her so. I carefully carried my hot drink upstairs with a small, dark shadow following on. She snuggled down against me in the sleeping-bag. Drifting off to sleep, I imagined she was Watcher, her neat furry shape cradled within mine, both taking companionship from one another.

Rain, rain, rain, but how the badgers thrived. Foliage and pasture seemed to engulf all else, whilst in the sunny moments, insects competed in a busyness from which swifts, martins, swallows and others partook of an easy meal. No more wardening; a great load seemed to slip off my shoulders. These woods were no longer my responsibility – my sole responsibility – with no one to care unless things went wrong. I could *enjoy* this place and whilst I would continue to care for and love it, the onus was no more on me. The anxiety and worry faded away and I enjoyed the rain-drenched woods as never before.

At first light, the Canada geese preened and groomed on the wide, grassy space above Cliffords Bank. They made soft noises and pecked the short blades that had been nibbled down by the rabbits. Crisp and Lucy regarded them uneasily from the sheltering elmbrush, but the geese showed no inclination to move and still the badgers waited. Slowly, I began to return to Briarmead and the Old Cherry Sett. Would they go the long way round and meet me from the farther side of the bank or might they pluck up courage to come *with* me as they normally did, foraging as they went?

Lucy saw me move away unbothered by the geese. Slowly, slowly she emerged and stole silently round the great birds. She was nearly clear of them when one, larger than the others, looked up and saw her. Its long neck snaked out in curiosity and the little sow fluffed up, but badger-like, stayed facing it. The neck retreated and, as if undecided what action to take, the goose plucked a few more blades of grass as it deliberated. Still the badger stayed, her fur now smooth. She, too, was curious as she stretched her head forward to scent the air, one forepaw raised. Then the long neck came down almost to her level and in the still-poor light, badger's mask and Canada's face-flash seemed vivid against their body colouring. Inspection over, both lost interest and Lucy trotted over to me with a *very* daring Crisp stealing after!

In the wood there was a great commotion of birds around an old holly tree. I went up to it and discovered one of the tawnies asleep on a branch against the great trunk and being mobbed. Probably a foraging bird had seen it and given the alarm, so bringing other small birds to scold away the danger. I made the contact call and the owl came to my hand. Then I walked gently to the Sand Pit with him, speaking softly all the while and feeling rather sorry for this sleepy-looking bird. I left him on the branch of an ivy-clad ash tree, hoping he would find some peace there!

At the field edge of the Sand Pit, there was a triangular area of broken wheat stalks. Farther along were little heaps of unripe and still green husks with the grain removed. Badgers do not take a head of wheat to a specific spot to eat, and then repeat the procedure over and over again. Neither, for that matter, do foxes, so I had felt it must be squirrels. When I walked that morning with the tawny, sure enough, a grey squirrel descended from a chestnut tree to the very spot. It ran up a wheat stalk which then snapped a third of a metre from the ground under its weight. (This accounted for the broken stalks.) It bit off the head and took it to a pile of husks already lying there; then removed the grain. Soon there were 11 squirrels doing this, so the mystery was solved.

Later that month we had a mild, misty night with the mist filling the woodland paths. But deep within the woods themselves, all was clear.

It was a strange first light. Looking over the farms, the trees in the landscape loomed like mournful ghosts – shapes without substance. Behind me birds were singing and in the dark dampness, flew many insects that the flitting bats were catching with quick ease. But on the farmland all was silence; no skylarks called, nor quail from the greyness of the fields.

The mist was fast clearing and the sun's pale wraith stealing through, looked for all the world like the full moon. Briarmead's banks were a mass of wild flowers and, surprisingly, a few bees still inhabiting the nest Susie had dugout earlier, were crawling back and forth amongst the grass lying in the hole entrance. White spots of slime fungus showed like markers on the tracks and paths of the woods. The chestnut tree near the Old Cherry Sett in which a nuthatch was nesting, had privet growing round its bole, sweetly smothered in white blossom. Enchanter's nightshade competed with honeysuckle to lighten up the dark places of the undergrowth. This first-named is a delicate, fairy plant and well deserves its fey title.

Round the field edge I disturbed three young squirrels that ran from the standing wheat, each with a head of grain in its mouth. They raced across my path and up the nearest tree. There they sat like the three wise monkeys far up on a branch and extracted the grain carefully, so allowing the husks to fall . . . on me standing below!

Later in the morning, I watched the bees renovating their home. They clearly hadn't given up in spite of a certain badger! As I sat on the Old Cherry writing these notes, I had a wren and three of her fledglings for company. This great trunk was a mossy causeway with bramble, grass, foxgloves and a tiny cherry tree growing from its decaying bark. At its earthy, roots end was a patch of wood sage with greenish-yellow flowers; the living dead. The wren family were hardly two metres away as they begged for food which their busy mother was endlessly supplying. Back and forth she flew searching for insects amongst the bramble leaves around the sett entrances closeby.

I was now looking for somewhere permanent to live whilst staying with friends at Hadley Close, Oakley. I could still go to my area at night though it was farther away, but had ceased to use the radio. There seemed little reason to continue to carry one and it would also give my radio contact a rest. One night I saw Watcher's daughter hunting on the cut hayfield of Newby, behind the woods. What a meandering, weaving path, foxes make in their search for voles and other small creatures in the grass! Along the edge of this field the long, pollen-laden sweet chestnut catkins cloyed the night air.

Walking back to Hadley Close a police car drove up and we stopped to talk. Had I left my home and where was I living now? He mentioned how good the badger reflector posts looked along the lanes. Later that morning I took shears and cleaning rags and cut the verges that overhung the reflectors outside Oakley; the officer's words had reminded me this was the next job that needed doing! The dimples on the stainless steel reflect back most of the oncoming vehicles' lights, so these need to be carefully washed and then polished with a soft cloth.

At 7.45 a.m. the following day I set out for the remaining reflectors by the Bourne; I could go the long way round via Ashcroft Woods. It was a lovely morning with a gentle breeze and birds flying, darting and twisting above my head in the insect-filled air. The PYO strawberries off Maddon Lane would soon be over. Already the gate was open with cars parked inside as I passed. Further in, pickers were being directed to the best spots and the thought that a certain badger had needed no such directions made me smile! I sat on the Old Cherry tree, now surrounded by cherries hanging over it from the hurricane-felled geans and ate some ripe ones to quench my thirst. Then checked the sett entrances slumbering amongst the sheltering greenery and continued down into Warby. The birds were moulting now with a jay's striped feathers and the soft browns of a tawny, lying nearby. The rowan berries were beginning to turn and at the wood edge of the Colts Farm bank, the pink's bright five-petalled flowers, like tiny stars, were drops of colour on the dark foliage. Some of these plants had invaded the farm track.

The old houses of Warby were bathed in sunshine as I passed through. In the meadow between lane and river the highland cattle and their calves grazed hot and uncomfortable in their shaggy coats. Cleaning the reflectors there and cutting back the thick vegetation, I noticed that more of the spoil heap from one of the sett entrances was beginning to drop onto the tarmac. It had until recently, been screened with a metal sheet preventing this, but the vandals had been busy again! I walked uphill onto the farmland looking back several times to enjoy the view, and so on to Weldon (taking the opportunity to check the setts there as I passed) and thus, full circle, home.

One rainy night, I left the badgers to walk amongst the wind-tossed trees enjoying the solitude, feeling the drop, drop, drop of moisture on my head and upturned face and thinking of Watcher. No longer was there bitterness in the memory. I had been granted some magic years with a wonderful companion. Well as I knew her, I never knew all, for part of her was wild, mysterious and unknown. She chose to seek me out, not I her, and I was privileged with her company. She will remain in the memories I hold and in her offspring too. Her older daughter has Watcher's way of turning and, of all her progeny, most resembles her mother.

That morning I returned to Oakley through Colts Farm early. At 3.45 a.m. the last rain was light in the air and very warm. Skylarks called from the barley and suddenly, there on the path ahead, a family of young weasels played. Jumping over one another, rolling and bounding to and fro with one chasing its own tail in circles! They continued for a few moments with loud squeaks, yelps and gutteral noises, then just as abruptly, disappeared into the standing corn. Five weasels I think, but so fast had they twisted and turned that I couldn't be sure. They reminded me that early this same month I had watched a weasel intimidating a very young squirrel in the damson trees of Briarmead. The youngster backed as far along a slender branch as its weight would permit, calling repeatedly. Other squirrels appeared on hearing its cries and the weasel had ran down the trunk and disappeared into the grass below.

Nearly home when I thought to look in at the Yew Tree Sett by the old farmhouse where once Wendy and I had seen the young sow playing ball with an apple many years ago. A housing estate had been built during the intervening years and children came to play under the sheltering trees, so usually now the sett was empty. I hadn't checked it recently and had an unexpected surprise; there were fresh dungpits. I stood looking across the wheat towards the distant road with my back to the houses. Nothing stirred, all quiet and still, when a movement at a sett entrance by the field caught my eye. First one badger cub looked out, then another jostled for a place. All clear, so out they scampered up the bank. They were at least a month younger than Missy's cubs. One backed onto and used a pit, then turned and saw me standing almost at touching distance. It fluffed up and, followed by its sibling, galloped headlong down the bank again into the safety of their entrance.

The new village policeman for Warby and Weldon had asked me to acquaint him with Ashcroft Woods, so that early evening we spent nearly two hours looking at the problem areas. He regards our woods as part of his beat and promised to help me. His enthusiasm and interest made me thoughtful. I explained that although no longer officially wardening here, I would try to do so at weekends and holiday times – the most vulnerable periods – if this was possible, and would let him know when problems arose. He said that every day on duty, he tried at least once to drive up Briarmead to check round the woods and had in fact, already met the farmers whilst doing so. He asked about the badgers and the siting of their setts and, as we crossed the fields to Cliffords Bank, told me he had seen a light on this meadow recently and gone to investigate, whereupon the light had abruptly gone out! There had been no shooting, but he had the impression they had dogs. I suddenly recalled when I had last met this constable; he and another had taken me to hospital after a lamper had lunged at me with his 'gutting' knife. It all seemed a long time ago now! He asked me if I heard of the councils or Trust appointing a warden officially for our woods, would I let him know? He would like to get some of the outstanding problems, that is shooting, snaring and camping, mopped up. Would I! We discussed the copies of the monthly reports I had sent to the council and I asked him to keep quiet the fact that I was still about. Perhaps, if the powers that be thought the place was no longer patrolled, who knows, we might get a proper warden at last! He looked at me with a grin and raised eyebrows, and I had to admit this was probably a case of wishful thinking. That day I found a real friend and ally in my struggle to care for Ashcroft Woods; he and the new rural sergeant have helped me ever since.

It was a dry, cool night when Missy and her cubs, Kate, Kirsty and Mícheál moved house to Cliffords Bank. They all helped to digout the old entrances in the sandy earth beneath the elmbrush and Mícheál was still at work when the red-eyed sun climbed the sky behind him. The oilseed rape had been cut in the field below with flocks of pigeons on the gleanings.

That evening I had a message to say that the main sett at Weldon had been bulldozed during the day whilst the caller (a neighbour) was out. I could scarcely believe it; surely there have been some mistake? An hour later I stood on the site. It was difficult to imagine that a sett had ever been there. The whole area had been bulldozed again; the shelter-belt grubbed up, the main sett itself completely flattened and the residue earth left from this final bulldozing, formed into a bank between that property and the next. The neighbour who had phoned, came out, saw me there and advised that I get off the land quickly. A civil action had already been brought against him for trespass; there was no point in the same happening to me.

I phoned Oakley police station to let them know. To describe this constable's reaction as incredulous was an understatement. 'What – but they can't do that Chris!' I had to say 'They can and they have and I don't think there's a thing we can do about it.' He replied 'But the badger is protected' and I pointed out that the badger is, but its habitat or sett is not. He groaned, 'Of course, I had forgotten.' Oakley police have been terrific over the badgers in their area and this officer had co-ordinated his force's first ever badger-digging case at this very sett, 13 months earlier. Then the two men were convicted of *attempting* to take a badger, but no one had ever been convicted of killing badgers when destroying an occupied sett! I told him of the sow, her little male cub and the yearling I had watched at this sett. I think he felt as sick as I.

Talking things over with the RSPCA Inspector later, the whole affair seemed hopeless. Habitat protection in Britain is granted only to endangered species and though badgers are very scarce in some counties, in others they are not. So habitat protection for the badger will have to wait until we have dug them out, bulldozed and run them over on our roads sufficiently to reduce their numbers to 'endangered'.

When a landowner or developer demolishes a sett, he is not going to allow anyone to dig and find if it was badger occupied; all the more so, if he has a very good idea that it was! He has the right to insist you be escorted off his land, by the police if necessary. A body decomposes very quickly, especially when not too far below the surface where beetles and maggots can get at it. If you can't dig and retrieve your crushed badger within three weeks at the outside (after that the fur will have come away), then you have nothing tangible as evidence. Many badgers die in their sett and later, other badgers will extend the sett and bring out badger bones onto their spoil heaps. This is very common but it would be impossible to convincingly prove the age of bones in court. Forensic tests are far too expensive to be used except in cases of serious crime. Therefore, one would have to prove a badger was present at the time of the bulldozing, without a body to back it up. The only clause in the Badger Act that might be used in such a case is that under Offences of Cruelty – 'if any person shall cruelly ill-treat any badger'. I had kept a written record of the three badgers there, but how much good was that? It didn't help either to be told that the RSPCA knew of many similar cases countrywide, especially with big building developments. If we had a choice of death: to be dugout and baited, or crushed and suffocated, might not the latter be slow and agonizing too?

By August the barley of Long Field was cut and the bales of straw stood in piles across the stubble. Lapwings returned to cry mournfully over the land once more and to search for insects where the harvest had been. Mist snaked along the valley. It was the coldest time of the dark hours, this brief period before first light. It had been a bright, clear night with excellent visibility and a sharp, sparkling crescent moon. I passed Crisp and Lucy unobserved as they drank from the Main Pond. The water was low now and they paddled well in before lapping. Young foxes were vocal with Watcher's offspring quarrelling over Newby farmland.

Some of the hot days were followed by thick early morning mist and foliage dripping from above. In one such first light I watched two young tawnies exploring their parents' territory within the woods. This learning of territory is vitally important to the fledglings; in another few weeks they would be finding their own and learning to defend it. Meanwhile, they made little attempt to hunt for themselves and the adults still returned with food. As the year advanced, so the tawnies exploited the changing seasons. To the list of mice, voles and worms were added the young of rabbits, moles and hedgehogs. Insects were a plentiful food source, too. For me, the more unusual tawny prey was a slow-worm one night and a pipistrelle bat that had alighted to feast on a moth another! Like badgers and foxes, the owls, too, gleaned from the harvested fields. Tawnies will take carrion, though they like it fresh.

How sweet the blackberries were now! Missy's cubs thought so too as they tried to beat me to the juiciest ones! In a weak moment I picked Kirsty some which was a mistake. Three chunky cubs instead of one, descended on me to get their share, with Mícheál climbing my leg to get closer to the food source. His sisters chittered their indignation, then, holding round my legs with their front paws and scrabbling frantically

with their back, they too made the ascent, adding a painful tooth and claw hold when they felt in danger of falling! I ended up on the ground with three bouncing busters on top and a faintly disapproving Missy giving me an 'I told you so' look! *She* wasn't so silly. Wrinkling back her moist snout to allow her teeth to come close to the fruit, she bit off each ripe berry carefully, detecting by smell, as well as ease of picking, which were sweet and ready to eat. Ignoring the youngsters' demands, they quickly learnt to pick their own by her example. Four badgers blackberrying silenced even the motorway traffic – they were not quiet eaters!

The grass in the meadow surrounding Colts Farm badger sett, was now cut and lay in sweet-smelling swathes to dry. Walking by homeward bound, I surprised a little owl sitting in a birch tree by the sett. It bobbed up and down as they always do when alarmed, so I stayed quite still and it began to preen its feathers. The eyes of tawnies are soft and brown; little owls have 'angry' yellow orbs. As usual on my homeward walk, I noticed that each lane had its pair of busy blackbirds along its length, already searching for an early breakfast on the silent tarmac. At my approach, they moved a little farther along and still a little more, then stood aside to let me pass and so continued feeding as I went my way. Each pair kept together with no other birds about and none sounding yet – Briarmead, Maddon, Sleet and Holmoak Lanes all had their busy blackbirds. The cut hayfield of Holmoak, where the gates were stolen, was grazed by a flock of sheep. It was 5.20 a.m. with mist hugging the land. Grey shapes 'baaed' as I passed – it was great to be alive.

Our RSPCA Inspector had discovered an active badger sett when out on a call the previous winter. It was in the side of a steep, quarry-like bank within a large area of neglected garden behind high chain-link fencing. Stopping his van in the quiet lane to write up his notes, he had chanced to look up. There, dug amongst the exposed roots of giant trees overhanging the cutting, was fresh sandy soil from the entrances. He made enquiries and was told the whole site was owned by property developers whom he contacted. They assured him that although a house was due to be built on the site, it would be nowhere near the quarry and the badgers would not be affected. We had been granted permission to go on the site and, together, carefully looked over it. Badger trails were evident, through the little wood at the back and in the overgrown garden. The latter intrigued me for many of the plants weren't native and though I recognized the species to which they belonged, I couldn't identify them. The mystery garden tantalized and after several letters and many dead ends, I discovered the place had once been planted as a botanical garden for a famous college. Travelling to and fro from the city had proved difficult for the students and eventually, land was acquired nearer the faculty itself. The person responsible for the planting was now an old man, long since retired. He had lovingly transported as many of the rarer species as was possible, to create the new garden. I have never had any wish to own property or land, but the desire to protect this overgrown wonderland was something different.

The RSPCA Inspector continued to check the sett whenever he was passing and with the tragedy of the Weldon badgers fresh in mind, he had been doing so more frequently. On one visit he had found wooden stakes hammered into the ground on the lower part of the sett, with one actually on a spoil heap and almost into the entrance. Together, we went to view it. Almost immediately, my companion spied a fresh hole not there on his previous visit, tucked away beneath a fallen tree and overhung with vegetation. I crept round the dead branches on my knees, the camera held carefully in front of me and steadying myself with my free hand. A bird flew up startled from the depths of the greenness beyond and looking above the hole I saw a 'day-nest' – the soft grass compressed into a smooth hollow where a badger had lain enjoying the summer warmth, yet shielded from the light. These day-nests are only found where badgers have little, if any, disturbance. Now the day's hot sunshine was gone, leaving the heavy air laden with musk. Where I knelt on the raw earth of the new spoil heap, short, neatly bitten-off grass blades and occasional bi-coloured hairs lay amongst the moist particles of soil, the owner's pawprints sharply outlined.

Again I was struck with the beauty of the flowers. The native species were easy – fritillaries, lords-and-ladies, the tall, stately spires of dark mullein, foxgloves and purple loosestrife rising from the lush grass, the loosestrife's purple flowers set in their whorls of green leaves. Then came a darkly-red cousin of our familiar bistort, but with flowers in a long, slender spike and with broader leaves. A profusion of what appeared to be three-cornered leek, but the flower umbels were a harebell blue not white and the stem smoothly rounded like that of ramsons. Then one not identifiable – a spray of lilac-coloured, bell-shaped flowers on a single stem, their six-petals veined, their stamens protruding and white markings visible within the flowers themselves.

Once more I had the feeling of timelessness. Standing gazing that summer's evening, the thought came to me that however absorbed with animals I might become, all paths lead me back to flowers, trees and the plant world. How barren would life be without them.

The Inspector was waiting patiently at the sett in the quarry. Workmen had recently trodden here with stout, wooden stakes hammered in marking out a curving route down to the chain-link gates onto the lane. There were other stakes, however, some apparently denoting an alternate route, with some not so easily understood. The 'curving route' passed over the lowest part of the badger sett and it was here that a stake had been hammered into the fresh spoil heap. If part of the sett wasn't actually destroyed, lorries and heavy equipment toiling up and down would certainly disturb them. Quite probably their tunnelling went beneath this route, so that vibration would be enormous. Another line of stakes stood in the steepest side of the quarry with, again, one actually in the spoil heap of the entrance I had so admired on my first visit. Why this was done we couldn't decide; for theodolites to take readings at these points? Too steep for a drive or roadway, but there seemed too many posts to account merely for readings. Was this sheer bank eventually to be landscaped to enhance the selling price; an attempt made to reduce the incline? With permission to build only one four-bedroom house on all this land, landscaping might be the explanation. What would become of the badgers?

After some discussion, we decided that our letters to the developers and their replies, really wouldn't count for anything in court. Could we get the police here interested? Oakley police would have helped, but these city police were unknown to me. As is often the case, at first we had a flat refusal and were told by the busy sergeant on duty to obtain a court injunction. Pointing out the Wildlife and Countryside Act incorporating the Badger Act and the onus of the police on its enforcement, didn't help much either. 'We do proper policing here, not this wildlife stuff,' he retorted. Thank heavens this force has a Wildlife Officer. On contacting her office, our irritating request for help took on a more positive meaning. Police from this station spoke to the workmen as well as the owners and have enthusiastically helped to keep an eye on the site too.

Now the chestnut catkins hid the dusty paths like dead leaves in autumn; they felt like carpet underfoot. The tawnies called and answered an hour before first light and though everywhere was still so dry, the badgers were digging out at the Old Cherry Sett and on Colts Farm. I noticed at the former, that the County Trust had been marking the trees ready for coppicing in the autumn. It was a poor year for the few ripening cobnuts; squirrels and the dormice were eating them.

Marjoram and bellflowers bloomed by the Wildflower Path with the berries of the wayfaring trees beginning to redden.

Then came a period in hospital, but on my return to Hadley Close, I was offered a new home in which I could live as long as I should want. It was twice as far from there to Ashcroft Woods, but still within Oakley police area. It proved everything I could have wished for, tucked away as it was amongst the trees. The owners lived further off on the edge of the property and that first morning I had one of their dogs for company. I took the winding path through the leafyness with the big dog following. The track meandered back and forth between the trees, crossed an open space, curved round as if looking for the way out and wandered some more. 'If the rolling English drunkard made the rolling English road, who made this one?' I asked my tail-waving companion. 'The strolling English dog perhaps?' I stood looking at the green door of my new home, opened it and together we went inside. To the left was the sitting-room, this was the kitchen/dining area and the farthest little room would make a wonderful office. Windows on two sides, one with ash and briar rose pressing against it; the blank wall could take my books. A phone, typewriter – I stroked a smooth, sleek head. 'Definitely a one person only place' I told her. She dropped her head sadly and leaned heavily against my leg breathing deeply. 'I'd be forever falling over you' and she heaved a sigh as her tail lowered to keep her head company. 'Cheer up, you can always come and see me,' I promised as she mouched back mournfully along the path. At the curve, she turned and saw me watching, her tail moved again and her head raised. 'Yes,' she seemed to answer 'I'll be back'... and she was!

Right from the beginning, the children of the family at Hadley Close, said my new home should be called The Sett. Seeing how many badgers were to come up to and through its green door, the name couldn't have been more apt! Those September mornings were wonderful, but probably the evenings were my favourite for birdlife. Then the late sun caught the bright red berries on the hawthorns and every tree was alive with birds. The finches and tits took the insects, but mistle and song thrush, a pair of bullfinches, blackbird and already, the occasional fieldfare, were feasting on berries. As the sun died in slow splendour and dusk stole through, the backcloth of aspens beyond the hawthorns, trembled in the slightest breeze. Flecks of light, a multi-coloured movement, danced on the feasters busy there. Soon the day was gone, the twittering subdued and the night sounds took over. The quavering call of a male tawny proclaiming his boundary rights, prelude to a night's hunting. He hooted and listened, flew as a dark shadow to his next perch and called again. But no one challenged his absolute possession to this stretch of wildness and presently satisfied, he joined his mate already hunting along the margins of the lake.

At first it seemed impossible to walk to Ashcroft Woods, but as I became stronger and the Indian Summer continued, I finally made it! A half-way house was at Hadley Close where I could stop and rest if tired or thirsty; this made a great difference to the frequency of my visits to the badgers. There were many lapwings on the land now as well as seagulls. The stubble had been burned off and some fields already turned under. Newby Farm was still sadly untended with only the grass of the long meadow behind Ashcroft Woods taken for hay. Briarmead had been re-tarmacked, the first time in 12 years!

The badgers were fine, knocking me down in their excitement that first night and quarrelling as to who should be fussed the first. However, they were certainly well and thriving! Later they came to accept that I would return in spite of my absences. Then there was pleasure and affection in their greeting of me, but no longer aggression amongst themselves.

In Ashcroft Woods there was rubbish everywhere; it looked uncared for and forlorn. Yet as I approached from Maddon Lane, the trees seemed to loom towards me and I had a feeling of warmth and welcome. I could never leave this place for good; part of me will always be there.

The first morning of my return, everything was very still as I sat alone on the Old Cherry, now surrounded at ground level by sprouting greenery from the hurricane-felled trees; even the traffic was muted. Looking up the slope, I could see the two entrances that Missy and her cubs had dugout; there were three more on my right. All the other entrances were disused as Crisp and Lucy were on Colts Farm and Susie, Meg and Bess denned on Cliffords Bank. Though we humans mourn our trees, I think on balance the fauna had benefited, except for the two badgers that had died in this sett – Sis, daughter of Lesley, and her cub Little Joe. It would soon be a year since that fateful night; how time flies and how much had happened since!

Sitting there that early morning, the wind seemed to whisper reassuringly in the trees ... time solves most problems and this place will endure. Far below, I still sat on the old tree I had known so long; how I had missed these ancient woods. My hand rested on the Cherry's bark. The years of dust, seeds, grass, fungi, lichen and moss have given its bark the soft pile of a luxurious carpet with many tiny foxgloves emerging from it now, ready to flower next year. The subtle scent of decay was not unpleasant as the ageing trunk disappeared more deeply into its earthy bed. 'Man to dust and trees to timber fall.' But this tree in death was greater than timber and rich as the life-giving earth itself. Trees form the essence of all that is here; eternity grows in these woods.

Late one evening, a teenager found a dead badger runover on the lane by the river. As his mother drove us there to see it, I wondered why the reflectors had failed to save it, or had it crossed beyond their range? A young boar lay on the tarmac, not yet cold, but where *were* the reflectors. Pieces of their red glass prisms lay strewn along the lane, yet the reflectors themselves and their posts had vanished! The picturesque village was popular with crowds of youths from the city who liked to drive out in the summer evenings to drink at the local pubs. Vandalism, abuse and dangerous driving amongst them was common. The previous weekend, a police cordon had caught the mainstream offenders, but others had escaped by driving along this quiet lane. With nothing better to do, I was told, they had ripped out the reflectors, posts and all. Some I later found broken in the field below, but most had disappeared. The badger had come from its sett directly in the path of two reflectors, which should have prevented the accident if they had still been in place. The boy and I, laid the body beyond the hedge to be collected the next day, before driving back. By now it was nearly midnight with an orange moon hung in a silken sky. Such a lovely night – such a wasteful end.

The couple left me near my new home and, deep in thought, I slowly walked round the curve of the path to The Sett. A heron stood there preening; had it been fishing in the lake? Carefully, it ran the long bill through its plumage and 'clicked' it once or twice, then flew into one of the nearby trees. With just the top of its head poking out, the heron looked very odd, before it slowly flapped away. What ungainly birds they seem in flight, long legs held backwards, long neck stretching and those slow, slow sweeps of their wings. The bird passed across the face of the moon and disappeared from my sight.

Some nights at first I found the journey to Ashcroft Woods imposs-ible and would get as far as the Embankment badgers off Holmoak Lane and stay to watch them for awhile, before returning slowly home. Though I missed my own badgers, I was finding out more about the wildlife round The Sett. Many animal trails wound through the undergrowth and there were two small badger setts not far away. A large sett had apparently been destroyed some years ago when four houses were built along the lane. There was now no way of telling, but I suspect that it had been the main sett. From the occasional dungpit and a freshly dugout entrance at one site, there were certainly still badgers in the area, though not many by the signs.

A wild service grew near The Sett and returning from Ashcroft Woods one morning, I picked up two bird pellets regurgitated nearby. They were too large and the wrong colour for a tawny and soaking them to take apart, I found they contained chitin from insects, small rodents' fur, tiny bones and . . . two sloe stones! It wasn't till I saw herons at this spot, that the mystery was solved. This proved a popular preening and resting place and their pellets usually contained no sign of the fish they most commonly fed upon.

Everywhere the leaves were turning and the hawthorns, particularly, were of every shade. The wild service had a fiery beauty and the yellowing field maples stood out conspicuously from the other trees. At my office window a pair of chiffchaffs were busy in the rain, occasionally shaking themselves as they searched for insects just beyond my typewriter. At times I did more gazing than typing, but justified my laziness with the thought that soon they would be gone! These chiffchaffs were quite unbothered, though aware of me, as they continuously flittered from branch to branch, up and down, turning sometimes to face me and lean slightly forward with just the glass between us, then hopping to a higher level in the ash and presenting their backs, before turning round again.

That evening a tawny came gliding above my home, causing the magpies to clatter one to another. The owl didn't call, only the magpies full of foreboding made the air harsh with their cries. A friendly dog lay patiently waiting outside, head upon paws. Each time I passed the kitchen window, her head raised and tail moved. Now I can take a hint like anyone else, so together we went for a walk! The western sky was blood-streaked on its horizon, overhead it was black, whilst to the east the moon rode higher as if to avoid the little clouds scudding by. Candy is a hunter at dusk, so I have to watch her. Through Ninepenny Wood and into the meadow, then back to her home at the big house and I returned for a while to mine. There were great gusts of wind that night, although it was by then quite dry. Out on the bare expanse of the farmland, the gusts took my breath away and tried to pluck me up. I stayed in Ninepenny Wood where it sighed and moaned and bent down the trees' crowns, but was surprisingly mild and pleasant. Too windy to hear noise nearby, I was suddenly aware I had three badgers rooting near me where I stood against the small holly sett in the wood. One badger's snout nearly touched my boot, but didn't seem to register a foreign presence. Finally they disappeared out to the sheltered side of the fields (the wood narrows almost to a point here), and I saw them no more that night.

The following evening I stayed to watch the full moon rising in front of my sitting-room window, an awe-inspiring sight. As dusk settled into darkness, the hawthorns' green became a black silhouetted foreground till the moon rose high enough to spread its light. Faint rustles and movement, then a fox stepped daintily by. Somewhere an owl called and was silent. A towering mountain of cloud reached the moon and temporarily eclipsed it. I noted its position as lunar light slipped briefly through, was again obscured, then finally triumphed and the vanquished cloud passed away. Now the moon rode higher and an incandescence streamed down. Never can the countryside appear more wonderfully mysterious than when seen by this soft radiance. I sat astride a chair, my chin resting on its back, gazing out at its majesty for two hours as the great white disc rose ever higher, leaving clouds and stars behind in its journey across the sky.

Later that night, I found my badgers foraging on Long Field. I rested on Briarmead's bank before returning home and watched the rabbits on the verge. It was another misty first light with the soft drip, drip of moisture from the overhanging trees. A small figure appeared through the greyness, snout to tarmac and coming my way. It was Susie. She had probably come onto the lane from the up-and-over path further along. She lifted her head and looked at me sitting quietly there. Then she sniffed the air, but though the sunken lane was less misty than the fields, there was little scent. I spoke gently and she came slowly up the bank. I was smelt thoroughly – jeans, hand, then boots; the last named she took her time over. The sow backed onto them, raising her tail and musked my left foot. Then examined her musking, turned and repeated the action, the smell static on the damp air. I like it, but suppose some people might not. (I've never forgotten the night that a patrol gave me a lift and the driver suddenly remarked in a puzzled voice, 'Funny, there's an odd smell in here'!) Then Susie yawned showing a neat set of teeth very clear and white in the greyness and scrambled past me up the bank.

A slight breeze sprang up and the first birds began twittering. In spite of the sodden countryside, I had a great pleasure in this new day just beginning. A fieldmouse foraged at the laneside, its whiskers twitching and I watched it disappear into the bracken, feeling at peace with myself and my world. From the farmland a quail began its lingering, lisping call. Again and again came the softly liquid sound as six of these small birds crept across the faintly lit soil. I watched them spellbound as they pecked, looked around cautiously and pecked, so moving slowly away from me with the call becoming ever more faint. So this family had survived and would soon be flying to warmer lands. Truly the autumn had come and I wouldn't see these secretive birds again this year.

= 8 =

Warden Wanted

One afternoon a friend drove me to Colts Farm and left me to walk through the woods in the sunshine. I spoke to a young Norwegian rough-riding amongst the trees. He was living for a year with a local family who had told him Ashcroft Woods was a good place to practise on his trials bike! His grasp of our language magically improved as I mentioned there was a local 'scrambling' group that held races for its members and promised to send him details of where and how to join, if he was interested. However, his English didn't seem to extend to him translating the relevant by-laws on the notice-board by which we were standing, so I pointed it out and explained. He was a charming young man in his early twenties, but charming people can be very persistent. I felt we hadn't seen the last of him and events were to prove me right.

I checked the Old Cherry Sett and took photos of the ancient tree itself. There were three tractors busy on Newby Farm. A landrover came up the lane and I spoke to the son of the new tenant, a farmer I had already met through mapping badger setts. It was good to see the land in use again. He gave me permission to be on Newby by day or night. A shooting syndicate operated on all their farms including this one; it was up to the individual members whether they shot at night or not. 'They are only allowed to shoot rabbit or woodpigeon,' said the son. 'Nothing else.' I made a mental note to tell the constable who patrolled here that anyone now shooting on Newby would probably have permission.

Then a slow walk home through the woods. Some leaves had fallen, but most were still green on the trees. The Main Pond was very low and the smaller ones quite dried up in spite of the earlier rain. This rain had brought forth a good crop of fungi. There were parasol mushrooms and earth stars with the white-spotted, scarlet caps of fly agaric pushing out of the grassy places beneath the birches. This last-named is a beautiful, fairytale fungus that causes hallucinations, convulsions leading to comas if eaten, though it is unlikely to be mistaken for another species. These fly agaric brought to mind that other fungi can cause strange symptoms too – and a headache for the police! One of their Wildlife Officers wrote to me: 'There are, as you know, varieties of mushrooms which when prepared in a certain way can produce hallucinogenic reactions similar to LSD. Well, it appears that a farmer's field in my area grew, or at least was reputed to grow these mushrooms and as a result, at the appointed time, numbers of people would appear out of the early morning mists to avail themselves of these fungal delights. The police problem was one of keeping the peace, for the farmer was less than happy at the intrusion. Following police advice and local publicity, the problem appeared to go away – perhaps the mushrooms were not what they were thought to be.' Certainly the problems that come a Wildlife Officer's way can be diverse!

At 5 p.m. the air was chilling; there would be a frost this night. I called in to the family at Hadley Close, my other home, to see them and to rest. I am very fortunate with my friends.

Sometimes that autumn I was given a lift to Ashcroft Woods in the evening and, in that way, was able to be with the badgers more often. One clear, cold, sparkling night with a crescent moon, the visibility was remarkable; it was a good 'scent' night too. My badgers were full of energy, spending more and more time foraging on the ploughed farmland in preparation for the coming winter. Kate, Kirsty and Mícheál were nearly the size of their mother now, though Missy was never over-large for a badger. Lucy, Crisp and Susie had all moved onto the Old Cherry Sett slope, but not near Missy and her youngsters who were living at the far end, the annexe sett. Meg and Bess appeared to be settled enough on Cliffords Bank. My badgers are always more vulnerable from diggers and lamping in this sett on the open farmland, but wild animals choose their own homes and lack our ability to reason.

The great autumnal cleaning-out was on hand; the place was a hive of activity! Lucy and Crisp seemed to vie with each other as to who was the most industrious. As usual, they denned together with holes adjoining and the two houseproud ladies bustling to and fro would have seemed comic, but for their earnest dedication. Each would disappear into her hole accompanied underground by grunts, bumps and shufflings clearly heard from where I sat in the moonlight that sifted through the tall trees. The noises grew louder as a grey rump appeared. Lucy's neat white tail and trim, smooth back arched, as her hind legs received the loose earth from her front ones. Then with strong kicks the dirt was pushed out onto the spoil heap. Small stones and debris splayed over the terraced platform to plummet clattering down the steep slope. Lucy turned round as if watching it go, then scented the air. All quiet, but for Crisp backing out to repeat her companion's action. Rumps are very distinctive. I could never mistake her shaggy, long-haired back and straggling tail for Mistress Lucy's!

By 3 a.m. that night a stiff breeze had sprung up, whipping the leaves off the woodland trees. I stood on one of the wider paths and watched this 'dance of the leaves'. There was a peace, a sense of belonging, impossible to describe. Watcher's cubs were young adults now, fine-boned and beautiful. She was born again in their image.

There were still some toads in these woods, though sadly, not in any great numbers. On mild, autumn nights they were most active and, like other creatures, had a territory. Toads are easy to trace since they rustle the leaves that they search amongst in their quest for food. One, I regularly watched, rested up in the mossy side of a boundary ditch; humidity, rather than day or night, seemed to regulate its foraging. If I went to Ashcroft Woods during the day and it rained, there was a good chance it would be active and had vacated its hollow, but on a dry day it would be there. The dampness collecting along the ancient earthwork made a fine habitat for the amphibian. They take any live, moving prey they can cram into their mouths, though they may watch it intently for some while before the long tongue flicks out to capture it. A toad's appetite seems insatiable. Woodlice, worms, beetles, may be taken one after another and I once watched a toad eating ants continuously for over an hour. In the autumn there are many insects still about and all hibernating creatures need to eat well before their winter sleep.

I suspect barring loss of habitat as here, toads are very long-lived. Many of course, are runover on the roads they cross during their mating migrations. If the days are sunny, these movements will occur more at night. Just one car on a country lane can squash scores of their massed bodies, but, fortunately, those of Ashcroft Woods have no such roads to cross.

That autumn brought a spate of badger road casualties either found by the police as they patrolled or reported to them by local residents. Early in the year many badgers nationally are runover. This is a time of intense activity after the winter when food is of paramount importance and the animals may forage further afield. It is also a peak mating period when boars may be searching for sows. Again in the autumn, badgers will be 'stocking up' for the winter and youngsters are increasingly adventurous. These casualties gave me more contacts with local people, many of whom were seeing a badger for the first time. Invariably, they were surprised at the size of the animal and saddened at the waste of life. Residents helped me to map nearby setts, taking an interest in 'their' badgers' welfare. At least some good was coming from the casualties which we carefully recorded for the National Survey. Age, sex, locality, time of year, were all adding to our knowledge of *Meles meles*, with more people wishing to be involved.

A fine-edged moon rose at 4 a.m. The tawny pair were in sole possession of their area now the young owls had flown in search of their own territories. Watcher's sons quarrelled behind me as I sat against one of the few living beeches in the Chantry, facing the headland of Great Chantry Field. How mysterious was this field with its sweeping curves and undulating furrows smoothly stretching down and outwards from the height of that age-old lookout post – the Chantry itself!

First light here is an unforgettable experience. Darkly-etched beech leaves framing the landscape; pinpoints of light from the stirring villages in the valley; a pink blush on the horizon preceding the rising sun; and above that a streamer of rippling cloud. Topping all in the clear sky beyond, the sickle moon rose higher to join the morning star.

All was silent and timeless. Light shafts crossed the land, seeking entrance with prying fingers to the secret depths of the still-leafy wood. A first twitter of birds from the far hedgerow to my left and a bickering of badgers – Meg and Bess passing by on their homeward way through the wood. In the far fields the autumn-sown barley was already well sprouted and the Jerusalem artichokes stood in shaggy rows of darkest green. It was a lovely, slow, colourful autumn. The leaves seemed reluctant to fall after the earlier rain. Many of the holly berries in Ashcroft Woods were a deep red. It had been a poor hazelnut and acorn year, sweet chestnuts were fair, but horse chestnuts, abundant. There were more conkers than the children wanted that season; a most unusual state of affairs!

One night the cubs and Missy seemed very disquieted. Anxiety is infectious; soon the other badgers, as well as myself, were uneasy too. At the Old Cherry Sett I found the cause; part of it had been coppiced sometime the previous day. The over-mature sweet chestnut not coppiced for many years, had grown as tall as normal trees. Originally, I had asked the County Trust not to have the trees over the sett cut down as the badgers here had been so persecuted in the past from digging, lamping and snaring. At first the Reserve Officer had agreed they should be left, but later went back on this; no reason was given. He had allowed me to take his private telephone number, however, as he said he was in charge of all the work here. Coppicing over active badger setts has always worried me. As a patron of the National Federation of Badger Groups, I had several times discussed this at meetings with other members and the chairman. There is coppicing and coppicing of course. If you are clearing a small amount of scrub or undergrowth, the disturbance to the badgers living below may be minimal. Cutting down fully grown trees like this on a steep slope already undermined by a labyrinth of tunnelling, was something different.

The County Trust's argument had been that badgers always come back eventually and probably this was true. Perhaps I fretted too much? Over the years, the badgers here had suffered so and now were enjoying a period of peace. All I could get was the concession that the coppicing would be completed before the animals' vitally sensitive period – November onwards – which we know is necessary for the implantation of the fertilized blastocysts into the uterine wall of mated sows, which if successful, leads to pregnancy and birth. All this had been agreed by the Reserve Officer a few days before the hurricane last year. Ironically, this little colony of badgers had lost its only mature boar two months earlier when Jude was snared. The chance now of a sow becoming pregnant due to delayed implantation was remote, though not unknown. Nevertheless, to be frightened and disturbed in the depths of winter, away from the home you have so carefully prepared for yourself the previous autumn, was to my mind an unnecessary ordeal for the badgers here, so this concession was something worthwhile. That early morning I noted that Missy and her cubs went to earth with the long tree trunks straddling some of their entrances and I did my utmost to drag them clear. Really it needed two men to each tree; I hadn't the physical strength. When the trunks were split into rails they would be stacked out of the way. There were still many to be cut down and the vibration would be unbearable. Where would they move to I wondered?

Wardening later, I walked by the chestnut-paling of a large house on the main road. Its garden went right back to the bottom of the Chantry and Great Chantry Field. A gate had been made of the paling the previous spring, with a loop of wire fixing it to the fence. The trials bikes used by two young men came in and out of this gate to ride round Ashcroft Woods. Knowing this was one thing, catching them coming or going was another! To enter the woods here they had to pass a small by-law notice-board. There were fresh tyre marks on the damp path. The young Norwegian to whom I sent details of the scrambling club had given this house as his address.

That evening my friend drove me early to Ashcroft Woods as she and her husband were going out. This proved fortuitous for the cubs and their mother whom I found trapped inside the annexe part of the sett. The trunks had been split right enough and more mature trees felled, but for stacking the men had used the only flat surfaces on the slope, that is the spoil heaps outside the badgers' entrances that jutted out like balconies from high-rise flats!

However much the family might dig round the entrances of their home to get out, the length of the rails and the weight of the stacks, ensured their continued imprisonment. It took me more than an hour unaided to clear one pile, and then I could only lift the end of each rail and sent it crashing down the slope. Terrified and with moisture running from her snout, Missy appeared in the cleared entrance in answer to my calling, sniffed my filthy hands a moment and scrambled up the slope with her family trailing after. They didn't return. What must it have been like that day – the noise of the chain-saws, the crashing of trees, the burning of twigs and small branches and the gradual pile-up and mass blocking of their entrances? Badgers need to breathe below ground and their network of tunnels allows for a free passage of air. A terrier trapped underground in an earth-fall will suffocate before long if not rescued; so will a badger if all the holes are hard-stopped, unless it can dig its way free. This is the contention with hunts, of course, who hard-stop occupied badger setts to prevent fleeing foxes escape from their hounds. In theory, the holes are unstopped at the end of the day, but more often the sett is left blocked. A badger will try and dig out the stopping or dig round it. If he is a strong, powerful animal he may free himself, but all the time he is using up valuable air. When young cubs are present, as the weakest, they will be the first to suffer from lack of oxygen. It is known that stress can prevent implantation in sows, or if pregnant, they may abort. Working quickly that evening to free my badgers with these thoughts running through my mind, I recalled being told recently that the chairman of *our* County Trust was a keen foxhunting man who for some years had even been a Master of Foxhounds! Did that explain his organization's lack of sensitivity towards the badgers here? Small wonder they regarded my interest in foxes and badgers as a nuisance, and my concern for our woods, such an intrusion!

It said little for his hunt that one of its earth-stoppers had been convicted of badger-digging and illegally using badger-tongs. These tongs lift the terrified badger from its opened sett without danger to the handler; the metal ends gripping the animal are sharp and tear horribly.

Before first light I found Missy and family digging out on Cliffords Bank with an interested Meg and Bess looking on. If anything, the cubs' older sisters seemed pleased with the company, though they also sensed the nervousness of the evacuees. It is interesting how readily this communicates one to another. I am attuned to their moods as they are to mine. Just as Wendy, my dog, sensed when I was unwell, so did Watcher and these badgers.

Whilst I waited to speak to the coppicers, I tried unsuccessfully to retrieve the fallen rails. The men were horrified to realize that badgers had still been below ground. They always thought they vacated the night after the chain-saws moved in. No, the Reserve Officer didn't oversee the coppicing, but merely arranged with their boss, which cant or portion of the trees, was to be coppiced and in what order. They who had always been so enthusiastic about the badgers here, were genuinely upset at what, unwittingly, they had done. On a gentle incline, they stacked the rails behind stakes hammered into the ground. On such steep slopes where the public had access, this could be dangerous if children climbed onto the stacks. They were expected to coppice to a schedule and to carry the timber down by hand would not be practical. All this I understood.

Talking to them that morning, I thought once more that no one took badgers into consideration when coppicing. It is a traditional job, and in fairness, only someone who knew badgers intimately would be aware of their numbers and survival. I regularly do a head-count of mine and know them as individuals. Again, of course, badgers are protected but their setts are not, so neither Trust Officers nor coppicers, would really be obliged to be concerned. I was lucky with these woodmen for they were all country bred and were interested in the wildlife, but . . . they weren't obliged to be. How many badgers might suffer or die like this? It was a sobering thought. The chain-saws hadn't reached the main part of the Old Cherry Sett, home of Crisp, Lucy and Susie. The coppicers promised to be careful; I would let them know when the sows had moved.

One Saturday mid-morning I came to warden and, as all was quiet in Ashcroft Woods, took the opportunity to walk over the fields to Cliffords Bank. I stood amongst the elmbrush enjoying the cool semi-darkness and checking that all was well with the badgers' freshly dug entrances. I sat awhile on a broken stump, idly thinking of the affection between Crisp and Lucy now denning here and watching a bank vole searching the moist earth – then suddenly sensed I wasn't alone. Three men had come in further along and were inspecting the entrances as they moved closer. None spoke till they came to the area of the dungpits, when one hailed them with delight. 'Gawd, take a squint at that – there's brockies all right here!' The first all but walked into me before he was aware, his dark eyebrows and big, broad features drawing into a scowl. 'Want to be careful in here missus, there's rats about this time of year.' I resisted a terrible temptation to ask if they were human, just as the second, fair-haired with a bald crown and chubby features, demanded to know if I had permission to be on this land. I said yes, and had they? Whereupon the third spat and they walked out of the elmbrush, ducking to avoid the branches and so onto the field. They had come from the Briarmead direction and appeared to be continuing to High Ridge. I slipped through the elmbrush inside the hedge (how good it is to be small and not have to double in half like a man) and so out to the far field edge unseen. Sure enough, tucked away against the hedge was a van and I looked quickly through our suspect numbers. Yes, it was the same van parked till well after dark last April when Lucy was snared! I waited out of the way till they returned to their van, then checked the badgers' entrances for possible snares, but all was well. The men had not been accompanied by dogs, nor were they wearing bulky jackets that might conceal equipment. It would seem they had been walking round to suss out this autumn's active setts. It was only later reporting the incident, that I found the van's owner had recently been convicted with another for badger-digging. Somehow that didn't come as any surprise!

The men had finished their work at the Old Cherry Sett and were coppicing in another wood. It was a strange sight. They had been told to fell right up to the chestnut-bough entrance and the great tree itself, so the few old, long-disused entrances beyond with their tree-cover were untouched. It was the Great Divide – most of the sett slope was completely bare except for its neat, high stacks of rails dotted at intervals. There must have been many tonnes of timber waiting for the contractor to collect. The Reserve Officer was right; the badgers would return, especially here, to their main and annexe setts. This area was the hub of their territory and the mainspring of family life. It would be a frost-prone slope till the cover grew, but grow it would. I took photos to put with the others I had collected of my favourite badger place in Ashcroft Woods. Comparing them, however, it didn't appear as the same place for it looked so bizarre – more like a building site than a badger sett!

This was the month of misty mornings and shreds of dew-drenched lace adorning each bramble and hedgerow. Leaves were fast falling now; the slightest movement sent them earthwards. The trees were showing their skeletal limbs and crooked finger twig-ends. Here and there in perpetual motion, a leaf hanging by a gossamer thread, slow-twisted its way to eternity and splashes of blood-drenched hips, shattered each grey dawning. A goldcrest searched for insects in the tangled wilderness of briar and hawthorns. Such a miniscule bird; its double white wing-bar and high-pitched 'zit-zit-zit' more noticeable at first than the orange head with its black border. I gazed fascinated as it deftly flitted between the sharp thorns of the lichened branches. There was a 'charm' of goldfinches one afternoon feeding from a stand of teasels. Their slight weight scarcely bent the stems as their calls filled the air. I was sitting drawing the teasel seed heads surrounded by the flock who knew I was there.

There was one mild night with a shrouded moon that will remain with me forever. It was the time of 'soft fall' in Ashcroft Woods with the last leaves drifting fast. There were so many different fungi that I left the badgers to walk round and make a note of them. The white spots of slime-fungus trailed along many of the small paths again that autumn and I still wasn't sure which one it was. In the grassy places, clusters of lawyers wigs reared their shaggy caps and common earth balls pushed up through the leaf-strewn woods. I sat on what remained of the chestnut-bough seat, all amongst the fresh coppicing and looked down the slope at the regimented piles of logs and the mud the vehicle had made crossing and recrossing the derelict sett. The tawnies came floating over the slope, calling on the quiet air and the male alighted close by me to run his curved beak through a wing and scratch his head with a taloned claw. His mate flew on calling and he followed. Now they hooted and quavered one to another from the depths of the wood and I was alone again with my thoughts. Midnight approached and the moon struggled forth, illuminating my notebook and casting a shadowy hand over the page. A snugglely snort and something reared a dirty snout. Missy, my gentlest of badgers – and my world was complete.

I returned to my home that morning, as the sun rose in molten splendour to glint in the windows of The Sett. It touched the many spider webs spread in smoky drapes on bracken, bramble and verge about my home; so many grey, lace handkerchiefs. There were redwings and fieldfares feeding on the berries, and three exotic waxwings taking the spindles' fruit. Like the woods I had earlier left, most of the trees here were now bare, but for the field maples. *Their* bright leaves were showers of shining gold. The badgers from Ninepenny Wood sometimes came to forage for snails and slugs hidden in the long grass opposite my kitchen window. Returning early from my badgers, I would steal along the path to watch them unseen. Already, I looked on my home with affection. It was placed back against the trees in the hollow of the curving path in such a way as to only be apparent when one was close by. In all these wild acres, The Sett was the only human habitation, apart from the big house by the road. Occasionally, the owners would pass this way or faithful Candy might patiently be lying outside. By day, she too had the freedom of this place to come and go as she pleased, but dog-like, she did enjoy being taken for a walk!

One afternoon I wardened and stayed over till nightfall to see my badgers. Then I walked slowly home enjoying the warmth and visibility of the quiet night. I made a habit of saying hello to the ponies and cat in the stables as I came home. Three heads appeared over their doors and three pairs of soft lips sought my face. The stable cat came round my legs and I picked her up and gazed skywards at the starry, starry heavens. Somewhere behind me and near my home, a tawny calling lingeringly and something rustling amongst the straw bales caused the cat's ears to turn. What a lovely place I had come to! I should have gone to bed on my return to The Sett, but merely took my hot coat off and with a mug of tea in one hand, sat on the step of my home, childishly swinging my legs and looking at my enchanted surroundings. Such a wonderful night – it would have been a blasphemy to go inside and shut the door against it. The moon rode high in a silky sky as a fox wandered out of the hawthorns to walk the path past my home. It never glanced my way, seeming more intent on something in the long grass beneath the trees.

Now we had nights of cold, deep frost that lingered well into the morning. I noticed the older badgers, Missy, Crisp and Susie, had grown thick, black fur on their necks and chests unlike the youngsters; cubs particularly, can be sparsely furred there. I enjoyed the night and the tawnies, one coming to perch on my hand as of old. First light crept over the land outside, unnoticed, as I called, answered and parleyed with the two owls.

I left the woods about 6.30 a.m. and stood on the part of Briarmead that permits a view of the hump of Cliffords Bank that houses the badgers' sett. Through the monocular there seemed to be a distant figure clad in an anorak gazing this way. I jumped down out of sight into the lane and sped along the Two Oak track where I couldn't be seen, though only too well aware that once I neared Cliffords Bank, I would be in full view again. Sure enough, three men were running across the meadow behind High Ridge and the woods with two lurchers and at least three little dogs. The latter were almost certainly terriers and there could have been more as the long grass conceals so. I ran down to Maddon Lane, but any vehicle parked there had probably left, nor was there anything parked round Ashcroft Woods. Walking back I carefully checked the sett. Everything was undisturbed except for the fresh, trainer-type footprints in the soft earth of the spoil heaps. With the three men and their van in mind, I stayed around as the sun rose, then returned to Hadley Close and phoned the police from there.

That morning I showed the village policeman exactly where I had first seen the men. He found he could drive the patrol car right round to the top of the bank directly above the badger sett itself, though he wouldn't be able to do this if the ground became waterlogged. He promised to drive up like this on Sunday and walk into the elmbrush to see all was well. I could stay here tomorrow – Saturday – but couldn't the following day. Driving back, he mentioned he had spoken to the District Council and attended a Parish Council meeting recently, but they seemed to be no nearer to employing a warden for the woods. 'I want to meet him when they do get one, then perhaps we can round up a few of the odd characters here,' said the constable. I fervently seconded that!

The barley I had watched being sown three weeks ago when I was given permission to go on Newby farmland, was already several centimetres high. There were five spent shotgun cases lying on the tarmac of Briarmead just above the Wildflower Path. At 7.45 a.m. a vivid light broke through the early morning mist and flooded the land. I checked the occupied badger sett, but all was well; the men hadn't returned. Walking on top of the bank, my lengthening shadow led the way below on the growing corn. The weekend traffic was already noisy from the motorway hiding any birdsong. Passing the railway, the occupied entrances of the Embankment badgers showed clear on the opposite bank. A cider smell hung over the orchard that had attracted so many birds to its rotting fruit. The still leafy branches were alive with their movement and the air, tremulous with their cries. My foot gently tapped a bright red apple that burst at the slight impact. Thrushes, blackbirds, fieldfares and redwings were all competing for the sweet food. Such a glorious morning with a hazy distance.

It was a mild, damp night and I walked the quiet woods for the pleasure of it. The badgers on Cliffords Bank were crowded, but with no cubs to be born next year, they might be content to stay like this; we would see. The older animals, Missy and Susie, now denned together on the bank of Colts Farm. This pleased me since not only did it appear to suit them well, but was probably the safest sett in my area. Though cloudy and overcast, I could see well and the damp earth smelt wonderful. Leap-frog played by Mícheál and Lucy encouraged everyone to play too, so I hastily got out of the way! At midnight there commenced a fine but wetting rain and the badgers, with Watcher's daughter and a dogfox a short distance off, were all worming along the field edge. It was a steady, dedicated worming as if they were having a race to see who could eat the most in the shortest time!

Walking homewards very happily with all peaceful in my world, I stood awhile watching the raindrops pitting the surface of the Holmoak soakaway. The Great Storm had snapped the willows in half, effectively coppicing them. These had now all shooted and, earlier that year, the council had cleared the rubbish from the little stretch of water. It was amazing the difference this had made and I thought of next year's frog and toad migrations. I continued on my way through Oakley and decided to look at the reflectors in the lane beyond. This was quite deserted and the rain by now had ceased. There I spied a little figure busy lapping quite noisily from the rainwater running into a drain at the road edge. It was a badger and, I thought, a young sow at that. I stood watching her with interest and suddenly realized why badgers knocked down here are sometimes well off the positioning of their regular paths. They must know from experience that the gutters run with water after rain and that owing to the dip in the gutter before the drain, the water is deeper and, therefore, easier to lap there. So . . . you trot along leaving your usual trail to drink and become a road casualty. There is so much to learn about these reflectors and their positioning and it must be exact. Unless I had seen this little badger drinking, the reason wouldn't have occurred to me. I reached home rather thoughtfully.

One day I set out from Hadley Close at 9 a.m. to make a start checking for setts on a golf course situated amongst woods and parkland. It was a hazy morning with frost still crunching underfoot and a struggling sun sending long shadows across the fields. Such a tranquil beauty of dying leaves and bracken; views across the smooth green golf course itself with distant vistas of knoll and coppice. A great country house lay out of my sight in the farther valley. I wondered who had landscaped the place; Repton or Brown would have appreciated its beauties. I explored three of the four woods within its parkland; the main wood I'd leave for another occasion. Bearing in mind I had also been out in Ashcroft Woods most of the night, I needed a little energy to continue my circular homeward trail through Oakley!

All the setts were disused and difficult to find under their covering of leaves. This disuse was partly through past badger-digging (old and more recent crowning-down holes were numerous) and partly through coppicing and burning over the setts that had been going on that autumn. I guessed the remaining badgers had moved out onto the nearby farmland; hedgerows are less given to this type of disturbance.

138

At the side of the golf course was a sudden rise of land like a giant anthill called Summerhouse Knoll which as its name suggests, had once had a building on its summit, now long since disappeared. The knoll is picturesque as it rises out of the smooth grass with its top-knot of tall Scots pines. Elder, dogwood, nettles and woody burdock's clinging seedheads, tried in vain to conceal the well-used badger entrances and dungpits. There was old bedding recently turned out with entrances freshly dug by the occupants. It would be unwise to try digging-out a badger here with the golf course round about, but how idyllic for lamping with no human habitation in sight! This close-cropped turf would see the rise of many worms on a damp night or when it rained – a badgers' paradise! In whatever direction they left the sett, the animals here would have to cross acres of sward, even to enter the woods or move out to the surrounding fields. I would remember to ask the village constable if he ever had reports of lights here.

I followed the track down toward the great house in the valley, noting dungpits at neat intervals along the way. Then stopped to look over a farm dump; no badgers residing, but trails and dungpit evidence, then farther down valley, a coppice containing old yew and scrub elm. Inside its concealing cover had been a large main sett, but now it had crowning-down holes, many of them old and rubbish dumped. A small part was still badger-occupied with a dungpit and trails leading here and there. Then I continued down to the gate-house and the River Bourne threading its way through the valley.

I was in the lane where the reflectors had been vandalized. The sett in the long hedge bank still showed good use with the low winter sun shining on the river and a heron preening on the far bank that leisurely took off with easy, flapping flight. A quiet walk through my favourite woods and back to my Oakley home for tea, toast and talk before returning to The Sett. By now a chill had crept into the dying day.

Sunday 20th November was bitterly cold with sleet showers blown on the wind that by first light had turned to steady snow. Walking home, the motorway was muted (snow has certain advantages) and the lanes had a fragile beauty under their white shift. Later at home looking from the windows, I saw the birds were fluffed up with a pair of blackbirds almost staring at me as they huddled close together on the ash tree's branches on the other side of the glass. I felt I should have invited them in, but instead, put out food and they came gladly, to be joined by a wren and three partridges. The trees grow so very close to The Sett with each branch and twig a-pile with new snow. There was a young oak with brown leaves still clinging and an occasional splash of holly or yew with

glimpses of red hips and haws, but for the rest, a delicate white tracery outlined the dormant trees.

Rain had melted the snow by midday and the late afternoon sun tempted me out. Snow still lay on the fallen leaves of Ninepenny Wood and along the furrows of the farther farmland. I checked the setts here and found them still badger-occupied and undisturbed by man or dogs, but a wicked wind seared in spite of the sun and I was glad to return to The Sett once more.

I didn't leave home again till just before midnight with a near full moon shedding a fitful radiance as dark clouds scudded across its face. Yesterday's wet grass was now frozen stiff, making walking difficult and dangerous. The little lanes were treacherous for feet; how much more for tyres? On the land, puddles of ice mirrored the moon in their glassy depths. Of the badgers, only pretty Lucy was above ground to greet me. She reached up purring and I laid my face against her smooth one. I asked her gently where Crisp was, the questioning tone clear in my voice. Just as domestic animals know their names, so do these wild badgers recognize theirs. Lucy stared into my face as I repeated my question and put her head on one side still gazing. Then round she turned, trotted to her companion's entrance and whickered softly into its dark depths. No Crisp – the older sow liked her comforts and bitter nights she preferred to spend in bed! Lucy called again as I urged 'Where's Crisp?' whereupon the little sow disappeared underground. Time went by and I moved to go; a shadow in the entrance and there was Crisp! How warm was her body from where she had been curled up somewhere below. I put my arms round her, the badger's warmth like a hotwater bottle housed in a rough-haired cover! Speaking softly to Crisp, something hard bumped against my arm and there was Lucy, with what in her mouth? I could hardly believe my eyes; it was Wendy's old, red ball! Long ago I had brought it to Ashcroft Woods for the foxes and I to play with. In time, it had become lost until I had, literally, stumbled on it. Successive badgers had taken it into their setts over the years. Who had been the last badger I had seen with it? Crisp's sister Candy and their mother Lesley at the Crater Sett surely, in December 1985, almost three years ago! Badgers must have rediscovered it in the intervening years, but that was the last occasion I could recall seeing it. I put out my hand, rubbing the side of Lucy's face with the other. I purred to her and it dropped into my palm. I had forgotten how heavy it was as the memories came flooding back – Crisp, Candy and Curly, the three little cubs and their mother Lesley, daughter of Old Joe. All dead now and all had died violently, except my Crisp. Lesley's cubs, Little'un and Sis from the previous year, had been big sisters to Crisp. Little'un who bore Luke and Lucy was shot and Luke too was shot, soon after the hurricane. Of all those badgers that so many people had tried to help me protect here, only Crisp and Lucy remained. These two had formed a bond such as I had never encountered with quite the same strength and affection between any other badgers. I cupped the ball in both my hands, unconscious of the two sows chittering for my attention; the memories overwhelmed me. 'One can't go back, only forward,' I told the puzzled badgers that suddenly blurred beneath my gaze. From above, a rushing wind bowed the stiff trees and filled the air with its sighing. I left the sows to return to the warmth of their sett and watched the owls for a time before wandering slowly homewards.

9

Trees and Trust

I spent the late evening watching the badgers, two sows and a boar, snuffling up the food left by the birds around The Sett. The blue and great tits didn't like grain and pushed it out of the containers in their search for more favoured food. The bird-feeders I kept well topped-up and during the course of a day, quite a quantity of grain – mainly barley – lay on the ground under my windows. Whilst I was out at night with my badgers, those here were exploiting the situation! They drank too from the big bowl set into the verge of my path. I suspected the sows were sisters; one was more dominant and possessive, with the other easily hen-pecked!

The full moon was well risen in a clear sky with a deep frost. As I walked out through the stable yard, the ponies greeted me, heads over their doors and clouds of horsey vapour puffing my way. I stroked each soft velvety nose in turn. One would expect them to be lying down in their snug stables in such weather, but like the three ponies I met later in the Holmoak field that are out all night and browsing the frozen grass, these were wide awake and asking for a fuss too. The little cat appeared from a stable and ran up meowing, so I picked her up and cradled her warm body in my arms. A rough, warm tongue washed my cheek and ear. (The badger Kirsty did the same later that morning and stopped to sniff my cheek with interest; the cat's scent must have still been apparent.) On the ground once more, mistress cat decided to keep me company through the paddock. The long frozen grass was difficult for her to surmount, so she jumped here and there over the largest tussocks, her neat white paws making a loud crunch at each step. I wasn't the only one to have difficulty walking silently that night!

The lanes stretched before me shimmering in the moonlight with the frost glinting like mica on the tarmac and a tawny calling lingeringly over Sleet Farm. Only two of my badgers were above ground; Kirsty already mentioned and Mícheál, her brother, rooting in the unfrozen boundary ditches of Ashcroft Woods. They came to me playfully and I gently buffeted them with my gloved hands. This was great fun as they tried to grasp my woollen gloves. Tiring of this, they bumped one another, head-butting sideways on . . . charge! I recorded them playing, quarrelling and grooming there in the woods that night (though later at home I was disgusted to find I had more motorway noise than badger), then walked through the place enjoying the moonlight slanting amongst the trees. First light came gradually at 6.20 a.m. with everything in the grip of deep frost. These past cold nights had taken the last leaves from the trees.

At 7.30 a.m. I returned to collect the tape-recorder from its hiding place and spoke to the coppicers coming in to start work near the Maddon Lane car-park. Their orders were to fell this cant of mature trees, then continue up the hillside and over the top, eventually reaching a complete cant of hurricane-felled trees. This last was good news as virtually no tree remained upright there. The full force of the wind had funnelled down the hillside and trunks sprawled on trunks in such a way that no sprouting seed could ever grow to tree size – there wasn't the space. Taking the cant of living trees too, however, meant that the woods here would be shorn in half once those uphill trees were gone. The width of Ashcroft Woods was being opened up to the effects of deep frost. The badgers, particularly, were losing their autumn to spring foraging grounds when the farmland outside was rock-hard and the bitter north-east wind drove the animals to find sustaining food in the woods. Perhaps it was as well there were so few badgers left now. Walking back to Hadley Close and a welcome mug of tea, the sun was piercing the mist with clouds of vapour rising from the recently frozen grass as it melted in the warmth.

The weather continued cold and frosty by night and no longer sunny by day; rather the grey, miserable days so typical of November. Ashcroft Woods was searingly beautiful at night with a waning moon reflecting on the deep hoar-frost. It was well dark at 6 p.m. the last Sunday of the month, when I had a phone call from Oakley police. Mr Morris, a friend of the officer, had picked up a badger in Warby, but with no apparent external injury. Mr Morris was a police officer from the city who had driven to Everington that day to visit his mother. Returning towards Warby along Thrift Lane he saw the little body on the grass verge and, on investigating, discovered it was still breathing. He went back to his mother's house with the badger in the boot of his car, to phone first the RSPCA who were on an answering phone and the local vet. The vet refuses to touch badgers 'Nasty, snappy things, you be careful' he once warned me. The policeman was due on duty at 10 p.m. that same evening, so had to return home and change. He didn't want to leave the badger on the roadside, but, obviously, had to find someone to take it in.

Mr Morris drove into the forecourt of Oakley police station and I met him there. It was a sow, this year's cub, small and stocky with no external injuries, no bleeding from her snout or mouth. Hopefully, she had merely been knocked unconscious by the passing traffic and if kept warm and quiet, might recover. Together we drove as near to my home as we could and parked by the ponies' meadow. He carried the unconscious body to The Sett where I made coffee for us both. I felt the accident had probably happened when Bessie, as her rescuer named her, had emerged from her nearby sett that evening and crossed the lane to go into the meadow by the Bourne. I promised to keep her here and see how she progressed. If things got too complicated (I had no facilities for keeping, carrying or holding a strange, injured badger at that time) I would phone our RSPCA Inspector on his private number for assistance. It was a challenge, however, and I'd see what transpired. Mr Morris said he would be very happy to help return Bessie to the wild if she recovered and I promised, in any case, to keep him informed. When I had seen him across to his car, I sat down and looked at the invalid.

The little badger was still unconscious, so the main thing was to keep her warm. The cupboard under the fridge with its double doors and good ventilation was ideal and I made a dark, quiet bed with some old woollen pullovers and a candlewick bedspread for warmth. Hopefully, time would do the rest.

Sometime the following morning, Bessie opened her eyes in the half-light of her new home. I sat on the floor and laid her head on my thigh to more easily spoon glucosed water drop by drop into the side of her mouth. She was still in a dazed and shocked condition and most trickled out. I tried gently stroking her throat to stimulate her to swallow; this was successful. Every half-hour I repeated the process and by the afternoon she began to turn her head when she saw the spoon coming. There was a distinct gleam in the small dark eyes! I let her sniff me carefully and stroked her head making the badgers' contact sound as I cleaned her rear end. No blood in the urine, nor hours later in her faeces and she made no outcry when I gently felt her. I imagined a vehicle had given Bessie a glancing blow to the skull. The past night was −8°C and had she been left unconscious on the verge, most likely she would have frozen to death where she laid. Certainly Mr Morris' quick action, together with his friend at Oakley station, had saved her. She was well developed and well fed to go through the winter and, unless complications arose, I would not need to keep her long.

That evening a deepening depression brought heavy rain. The previous night I had stayed with Bessie, fearing she might take a turn for the worse and I wouldn't be there. Only one night spent indoors, but it seemed far longer! Now, I felt I could safely leave her for a few hours. I enjoyed the night walk in the rain; it was much milder. My badgers whickered around me, taking a great interest in my anorak and hands. I had checked the invalid before coming out, noting with pleasure that her snout passing over my hands and sleeve was cool and moist now, rather than dry. Unthinking, I had carried Bessie's scent to my own badgers who musked me thoroughly, then groomed my hair.

Watcher's daughter was attracting one of her brothers and a stranger fox, that the brother routed. A fox on its own territory is always more sure of itself and, therefore, more likely to hold sway over an interloper. Her other brother seemed to have left my area. There was a kewiking from the hen tawny on the bank of Long Field with her mate caterwauling from a gean above the Wildflower Path. Towards dawn came a distant calling as a formation of 32 Canada geese crossed the sky. How their formation alters as a different bird takes the lead; an ebb and flow of geese. They were heading for the Bourne.

It was cloudy at first light, clearing to blue skies at 9.30 a.m. Briarmead was covered in mud and debris flooding off the fields and woods. Everywhere smelt wonderful and from the hedge a lone wren chinked. The men getting ready for the day's coppicing called out in greeting. That autumn was a good one for berries of all kinds, but now the stock was fast diminishing. A mistlethrush had staked out a claim to a hawthorn bush, defending it against all comers. A large thrush often succeeds in this, except when the fieldfares and redwings turn up *en masse*. Such a tree will keep the mistlethrush in food all winter, but is speedily stripped in a few hours by the migrators.

Bessie was cautiously moving about when I returned, so speaking softly I opened the two little doors. She came out and investigated me, then lapped some warm milk. I have no secret formula with badgers, but have merely come to be known by my own. I sat on the floor just as I was and she thoroughly smelled my animals' musking. There was no fear in this scent of strange badgers; rather, an increasing excitement. Bessie was no baby; she must have been eight or nine months old. She had suffered fear, trauma and strange confinement with a human being. Bessie should be trying to bite me; growling and retreating in the badger way. This smell of strange badgers should be causing her apprehension and fear. Purring, she settled into my lap, lay back with hind legs outstretched exposing her chest and stomach and, still purring, began to run her long-clawed front paws alternately through her fur. Occasionally, this raking would stop whilst she nibbled at a tatty piece and a long, moist tongue carefully cleaned the rest.

A rustling above us caused her to suspend this grooming session. Silky, my daughter's gerbil, lived in the bedding-lined aquarium on the table above our heads. Karen had moved lodgings and only been allowed to take her Spanish terrapin with her, so old black Silky of the white-spotted chin had come to me. The badger rocked upright onto its four paws with a little heave and stood gazing upwards, snout aquiver, as the rustling continued . . . a quick bound and the gerbil found itself looking through the glass into the face of the unknown. As fast as Bessie had come out of shock, poor Silky went into it! One moment the tiny glossy ball of fur stood quaking, next it disappeared with one diminutive kangaroo leap into the safety of its nest. Slower Bessie blinked, but her nose and ears told her it was still there.

I changed the subject – temporarily – by offering her a little soaked terrier-meal mixed with dogmeat. Badgers always eat as if the meal is their last, but Bessie broke the record, then looked at me and chittered. No more forthcoming? She grasped the bowl in strong jaws and turned it upside down. Nothing on that side either, oh well! And she gazed thoughtfully tablewards again . . .

I kept Bessie till the Wednesday just to be on the safe side – safe, that is, for Bessie. Silky went into a steady decline. I couldn't place his aquarium outside for it was too cold, but neither was there anywhere else to put his home indoors. As I had told my friendly dog all those months ago, mine is a one person home. I finally put him in a shallow container with a makeshift wire roof and placed that on top of my cupboard which acts as a wardrobe, closing the sitting-room door. Unfortunately, Silky rustled. His entire existence had been spent rustling and he couldn't in advanced age be expected to change that lifestyle. Bessie badger would raise her head to listen. No door, except the outside one, has catches in The Sett. They shut – usually – if you push them to and open just as readily. Bessie excelled at pushing; it was one of her better accomplishments. I suspect she had generations of survivalist badgers in her genes.

I have mentioned somewhere before that badgers are good climbers. Bessie had the added advantage of determination coupled with time on her paws. I was outside The Sett for a few minutes that Wednesday morning and had left the convalescing sow, so I imagined, in the darkness of her cupboard, when I thought I heard a sharp click. I was cleaning out and refilling the birds' waterbowl on the verge and couldn't think what had caused the sound. Glancing through the sitting-room window, I had a shock. Something shaggy was stuck on the side of the wardrobe. Just as suddenly it dropped and I heard a bomp as it disappeared from view. Moments later, a badger's head came into sight as its owner tried the slippery ascent once more. Indoors, it was difficult to persuade Bessie to abandon her mountaineering till finally I scruffed her. I gripped her at the back of the neck with one hand and by the tail with the other, somewhat in the manner of the more intrepid badger-diggers who have left their badger-tongs at home. Bessie objected loudly to this cavalier treatment and told me so in the strongest possible terms. It was the only time we fell out. She was unceremoniously bundled back into her little cupboard with a stool wedged firmly against its closed doors. There was a long silence followed by a plaintive snuffling, then silence again. The plaintive snuffling bothered me little, it was her silences I found rather worrying. What *was* she hatching up in that striped head of hers? On the back wall of that cupboard was the plug and flex to the fridge; there were also two small water pipes. Whilst I didn't want an electrocuted badger, neither did I want a flooded home – it was The Sett after all, not The Ark. I decided to phone Bessie's rescuer and suggest a return home that evening. An unworthy thought crept into my mind. Would we last out till then?

It was Mrs Morris I spoke to; her husband would phone back when he came off duty. Meanwhile, Bessie had defecated neatly in a corner of the kitchen having first done her best to dig a dungpit. It was to her credit that she had been partially successful with two floor-tiles chewed up and a piece of wallpaper neatly removed. It's amazing what an enterprising badger can do during a short telephone conversation. Now

Bessie was digging through the carpet – dogfood was all right, but surely there must be worms somewhere below the surface? To take her outside I would need to pick her up. I was concerned too that she might suddenly run off. The area round The Sett was one of trees and undergrowth; ideal for badger foraging, but difficult for human following and retrieving. If she was lost and met up with the two sows and boar here, she would almost certainly be set upon and injured. Badgers do not take kindly to trespassers on their territory.

I went and found my badger 'sounds' tape and, sitting on the office floor with my back comfortably against the wall, played it to Bessie who scrambled contentedly onto my lap to listen and be groomed. Like my own badgers, she nibbled my arms and neck, inviting me to return the compliment. Out of doors with my anorak covering me, this isn't particularly painful. Bessie's teeth, however, were picking up pieces of me as well as my thin jersey. This didn't break the skin, but she certainly bruised. Badger skin is tough and rubbery, their fur coarse and strong. My badgers know from experience when they are hurting me, but this one had never groomed a human before. We compromised. Bessie groomed my hair whilst my fingers nibbled her neck, head and chest. After a time she curled round and went to sleep.

We woke to the phone ringing and, reaching up, I took the receiver in time to hear Mr Morris' voice before a smooth head got there first and Bessie snuffled sloppily into it. I removed her head firmly and explained. Wide awake now and playful, the little sow romped around me and chewed my jeans. We discussed how and when to release her when there was a tremendous crash. A slightly shattered caller asked 'What's she doing now?' 'Knocking all the books off the bottom shelf,' I shouted above the din. 'Right,' he laughed, 'time to return her home I think!' Still laughing, he promised to come that evening about 9 p.m. and we would return her from whence she came.

True to his word, the car turned into the drive at 9 p.m. and, walking to The Sett, we discussed how best to get her through the meadow to her transport. Sadly, but perhaps for the best, Bessie was nervous of her rescuer having, of course, no recollection of him and I being the only human who had any contact with her. I decided to try carrying her and, if that proved difficult, to make a 'sack' of her candlewick bedspread and carry her in that. However, the latter proved unnecessary for with the bedspread snugly round the little sow, I was able to have her in my arms not only across the field, but also in the back of the car. She was very uneasy about the ride, but fortunately, it wasn't far by vehicle. I knew she must come from the sett in the copse by the houses in Thrift Lane, so we parked just off the tarmac and I carried her through to the beginning of the trail leading to the sett. I put her on the ground, took the opened tin of dogmeat Mr Morris had been carrying and tipped the contents next to her. Bessie looked round, scented the air and clearly recognized her surroundings. With no hesitation and no looking back, she trotted off on the badger trail through the trees, in the direction of the sett.

This was something of an anticlimax for her rescuer left with a pile of dogmeat under a starry sky, so I suggested we wait for, say, half an hour. The visibility was excellent and the night not cold; the lane was unlit so there were no distracting lights. The time was nearly up, when our patience was rewarded and Bessie came back along the same trail, this time with company! It was another little sow almost identical in size though not in facial stripes – I would always know Bessie again. Bessie was the one who galloped up to the dogmeat and dared the other to come closer. She ate as if she hadn't done so for weeks and we heard them still bickering as they disappeared once more. We laughed at 'Bossie Bessie' as we scrambled down the bank. In the car going home, Mr Morris was very enthusiastic saying that was the first time he had seen badgers in the wild; one or two dead road casualties and on TV, of course, but so different for real! If ever I wanted any help to ring him and if he could do anything, he would. A really kind man and another friend for the badgers.

Why did Bessie accept me as she did? I have a theory that badgers 'see' scent as we do faces, thus a family-likeness to them is something that can be smelt. Although now cut in half by the motorway, the Thrift sett and another one nearby, were once part of the territory of my own badgers on the far hillside at Ashcroft Woods. Old Joe came from the Thrift area. The badger musk I was bringing back and forth from Bessie to my own badgers was therefore still a 'family' scent though not identical to theirs. Difficult to prove, of course, and maybe I'm wrong. Whatever the reason, Bessie was a good experience though I think Silky was glad to see her go!

December began mild and wet; good badger foraging weather and I hoped Bessie was all right. Before going to find my badgers, I walked down into Warby and left the contents of a can of dogmeat in the same place. I would do this the following night, then hopefully she would be fully recovered. There was no guarantee that Bessie herself would eat some of it, but having once seen her in action I suspected she would! The place smelt very musky and well-frequented by badgers though the sett itself was almost impossible to reach owing to the surrounding thickness of hawthorn and scrub. The people living in the house nearby would probably have better access from their garden. Hugh, a local man also living in Thrift Lane, had an outlying sett behind his garden. He was a member of the Ashcroft Woods Management Committee and helped whenever he could with the wardening.

It was a mild night with cloudy skies and a light wind. My badgers pottered above ground and wormed in the wet fields. Hazel and birch catkins were well formed and the grey-plumed seeds of old man's beard made beckoning ghosts of the trees. By 3 a.m. the clouds began to lift, revealing twinkling stars suspended from the leafless branches. There were squirrels running in the treetops, chasing and quarrelling. The mildness was confusing the seasons for these seemed to be mating chases. From above came a churring and angry chattering, whilst three were feeding on the ground. I have found the squirrels here and in Ninepenny Wood are often active at night.

Against my own instinct for not wanting to be hurt anymore, Watcher's daughter came to know me in her mother's image that dawn. I startled her from where she was denning in the crater left from a hurricane-felled tree. The roots gave wonderful cover, all overlaid with autumn leaves that exactly matched the colours of her coat. She made to run off as I passed by deep in my thoughts and, unthinking, I barked

her back as I squatted down. What made me do it, I don't know, but for the moment I forgot and thought her to be Watcher. She came right up and we touched noses in vulpine greeting.

> And your bright promise, withered long and sped,
> Is touched, stirs, rises, opens and grows sweet
> And blossoms and is you, when you are dead.

Now it was a mild, blustery day with intricate cloud patterns, sometimes white amongst the blue and scudding along, sometimes black, mauve and orange as the sun struggled for supremacy. A badger had dugout a single entrance just above and facing the Old Cherry itself. No dungpits; these were along the lane edge under the damson trees, together with snuffle holes. A badger wasn't at present living in this main sett, but who was responsible for the digging?

That same day I watched blue tits, great tits, a male goldcrest, greenfinches, a robin, wren and sparrow all feeding from the hanging food by my office window at The Sett. There was a heavily pregnant squirrel also coming to the birds' food. Their pregnancies usually occur between January and July with mature females having two litters a year. Gestation is 42 to 45 days with an average litter size of three.

It continued mild with many wild (and cultivated) flowers having an extended or early flowering season. The privet's leaves become darker before they fall in November or December, but these were to remain well into the New Year making unexpected splashes of green amongst the bareness of other trees. The badgers had no real interest in intensive feeding now, but such a mild month made long periods of sleep below ground uninviting. Playing was always an enjoyable pastime, but coming for walks with me became a full-time occupation on some nights. Seven were now denning on Cliffords Bank with a partly-filled dungpit or two close by the entrances there – Missy, Meg, Bess, Susie, Kirsty, Mícheál and Kate. Lucy and Crisp, those ever-faithful friends, were together at the uncoppiced part of the Old Cherry Sett, using three entrances amongst the tangle of dead branches directly above the old prone tree. The coppicing had left the rest of the sett in such a dreadful mess that the sheer weight of the vehicle and the piles of timber had probably damaged much of the interior chambers.

I spoke to the Chairman of the National Federation of Badger Groups about the problem of coppicing over active badger setts, and mentioned I had contacted the Woodland Trust. Their legal officer had promised they would co-operate over this and other badger problems on their many properties nationwide, adding: 'I think that in future we might certainly try to be more sensitive to the needs of the badgers.' What did the Chairman think about contacting the Royal Society for Nature Conservation over coppicing? He said it was difficult to even get an acknowledgement from this organization, recalling his letters and phone calls to them on the snaring issue, let alone an active response. He was at present very busy on other matters, so it was agreed that I should approach the RSNC on the Federation's behalf.

Lucy and Crisp were digging out in the coppiced area beyond the chestnut-bough entrance. It seemed to be unusually hard work till I realized they were actually re-digging the tunnelling, not just opening up the holes. My impression that much of the underground workings had collapsed, appeared to be right. That evening I phoned the Reserve Officer on his private number to warn him of the two sows there; he certainly had been right about the badgers returning! If the piles of rails covering the slope were now picked up by the logging vehicle and transported across the sett where the badgers were denning, they would probably be killed. The alternative was to clear that part of the slope by hand. Sadly, he was offhand to the point of rudeness and hung up on me. The rudeness didn't matter, but I hoped he *would* let the contactor know – that was the important thing!

That night I saw a big, fat hedgehog searching noisily amongst the leaf-litter of Ashcroft Woods. There were plenty of insects, beetles, worms and moths about. Indeed, I had many moths attracted to my windows at The Sett after dark too. Returning home I found a hedgehog run over in the lane, so this was probably just the tip of the 'urchin' iceberg for activity in the mild spell. I met a beautiful dogfox face-to-face as I walked across the farmland to Ninepenny Wood. How lovely their winter coats are; sadly, I can understand why people so covet them.

The 17th was a cold night with the moon in the first quarter, the temperature just below freezing and ice in the puddles. The foxes were very vocal and my badgers came above ground briefly, but the wind across-field was bitter. Watcher's daughter came to meet me on the Wildflower Path at first light. There was a vivid dawn sky by 8 a.m. Most of the berries had now been eaten, though there were still many rose hips on the bushes. The squirrels were busy at dawn in the treetops and on the ground. Memory may be used to locate caches, but their sense of smell is more important and mild, damp conditions aid this sense. The present morning's weather conditions made this more difficult.

I stayed to warden Ashcroft Woods for it was a Saturday. Recalling the Great Holly Grab and stolen yew trees in the run-up to last Christmas, I was dreading the whole business though the police had promised to come and look round in between their other duties. The lengths to which quite well-to-do people will go when trying to steal yew and holly from our Nature Reserve without being detected are, in the words of one constable who came to help that weekend, worthy of the SAS!

That night into Sunday 18th December we had a deep frost and a wild, bitter wind with no badgers at all above ground. Even the cubs decided it was just too cold. Strange to think that Kate, Kirsty and Mícheál would be yearlings soon. Again, I stayed over to warden and again had several difficult persons to deal with, this time including three adult rough-riders. Tired, cold and extremely thirsty by now (hunger rarely bothers me), I found my goodwill to all men steadily evaporating in the private hope that the rough-riders would fall foul of the holly-grabbers! At 4 p.m., and nearly dark, a patrol car came into the Briarmead car-park. The rural constable had been checking vehicles leaving the woods. He also took the number of the car and trailer used by the rough-riders, so with luck we wouldn't be bothered by them again.

The full moon shining from a clear sky creates dark shadows, but the same moon behind heavy clouds gives a visibility similar to daylight. The 23rd December was such a night and returning home at 3 a.m. I watched a kestrel on the ground of the winding path leading to The Sett. It was mild and worms were active on the surface; the bird was feeding on the worms. Nothing surprising about that really for I've watched kestrels take worms before, but not at night. The following spring, I was to see this again, this time with a pair of them.

Insects and birds were busy in the sunny warmth of that Christmas Day. A clump of red campion flowered in the depths of Ashcroft Woods with pipistrelles flying each dawn and dusk of the dying year. It was reported to be one of the three warmest Decembers this century. Badgers locally as well as those of my own area were preoccupied with digging their setts. Not normal practice this month, but as it was so unseasonally mild they were active rather than sluggish. Mícheál had used an elder tree for his scratching-post, the wood below the torn bark showed white and clear. He was this clan's only boar and though not yet an adult, it was *his* territory. Jude, his father, had been the last badger to mark a tree so. Lucy and Crisp at the Old Cherry Sett sent showers of bright, sandy earth spilling downwards. An old coke-tin was turned out and played with by my two silly sows. Lucy would scamper off with it in her mouth, whilst Crisp pounded after. When the older sow grew tired of the chase and barked in frustration at her nimble friend, Lucy obligingly waited for her to catch up! The old, broken skull of a badger lay on a spoil-heap and also a large, heavy block of sandstone with their claw-marks clear upon it.

Missy came to inspect this reconstruction work at the main family home on the last night of the year. I sat down with her head in my lap and stroked my gentle badger. There would be no cubs born here in 1989, but Missy and the others had survived and were healthy and content. So many local people were concerned and interested now in caring for their woods and the badgers too. There was much to be thankful for. Might the New Year bring continuing peace.

The New Year began as the old had ended; mild and warm. Some catkins of the common alder were open in all their mottled beauty. The long tassels and the little cones swung gently to and fro in a light breeze. My badgers were very skittish and eating! They shouldn't be at this time of year I kept telling them, but they took no notice! Lucy dugout two entrances slightly lower down the slope from Crisp and denned in the tunnelling there. It was interesting, but the significance didn't dawn on me till much later. Apart from this slight difference, they remained, as always, sociable and friendly both amongst themselves and towards me.

On several nights, the badgers startled the woodcock worming on Colts Farm. Our single pair of woodcock were already looking for a nest site, seeming to favour an area of woodland coppiced 12 months ago and now beginning to grow up a little. This sloped down to the farmland and if I sat waiting whilst it was still dark, I would be ready to see them at first light or soon after, fly in from their feeding grounds outside. I thought they had chosen a place beyond a great oak standard and away from the damp spot where the common rush grew a few metres lower down. One morning I memorized the spot where they dropped; then moved closer and verified the place. Would they finally nest here? I would have to wait and see.

It was on the 10th of the month that Oakley police told me a badger road casualty had been reported from Cleates. Before I set out that morning to check the dead animal, I phoned the head of the Ashcroft Woods Management Committee and arranged to call in to see him afterwards. There was a lot as chairman he could do to help and I

hadn't seen him for many months. Walking through the woods that seemed to glow in the sunshine my thoughts were on the badger. I hadn't met Susie last night; what if it was her? I began searching along the main road when a passing car turned in at the layby and a young woman hailed me. It was the wife of the head gardener at Cleates who had taken me round his badger sett and allowed me to explore the grounds a year ago. Since then I had moved and not thought to give them my new telephone number. She had taken her two little boys to school that morning (it was the first day of the new term), when they spotted the body as their car passed. Their mother couldn't stop then for the flow of traffic, but promised the troubled children she would return and collect it as soon as she left them at their school. 'I couldn't bear to see it lie there and other vehicles go over it again. Anyway, it's letting undesirables know there are badgers here.' With the gardener, we went to look at the body they had laid in one of the sheds. It was Susie. Next month she would have been five years old. We all commented on her size and obvious weight. On death, she had vomited an enormous pile of undigested worms. 'I thought it was spaghetti at first,' said the gardener. Together, we checked his sett, now disused. We stood discussing the replanting of trees and shrubs at Cleates and how frustratingly slow the grants were for this; also the unusually mild weather and the vixen and her cubs he had watched in these grounds last year. I thanked him and his wife for their interest and help, then phoned MAFF to collect Susie's body. Walking to Warby along the main road, I too came across the 'spaghetti pile' by the gutter. The traffic was quieter now it was mid-morning and taking a stick I did a worm count – 202! Then into the village to, hopefully, get a positive response from the chairman living there.

I spoke of that winter's coppicing, its escalation with loss of habitat for the dormice and others, Crisp and Lucy's return to the Old Cherry Sett, the piles of rails still there and the Trust's lack of concern. It was a futile visit. This chairman was far more interested in discussing himself than Ashcroft Woods. Finally, I stemmed his flow of rhetoric by rising to leave and asking what we all wanted to know. When would a warden be appointed? He shook his head; he had no idea. 'Would it be fair to say that nothing has moved regarding an official warden for our woods these last 12 months?' I asked. 'Indeed, indeed, that would be correct,' came the cheerful reply. Then seeing my exasperation, he waved an expansive hand. 'I will look into the matter for you and let you know.' He never did.

The next day saw a complete change in temperature. Gone were the mild nights of 5°C or more. Now it was bitterly cold with a clear sky, deep frost and strong wind. There were no badgers above ground. I walked through the moaning trees feeling sadness at Susie's loss and thinking of her past. I recalled the last night of May 1986 when she had been injured by a lamper's dog whilst defending her three young cubs. In spite of everything, Susie had a long life for a badger in these parts and, at least, her death must have been quick. The pair of woodcock hadn't chosen the coppiced area after all, but were sheltering together just inside Ashcroft Woods.

Sometimes that winter I walked home by the motorway. There was a 'lagoon' meant for drainage that never contained water and a large area of waste ground surrounded by a chain-link fence. Inside the fence and facing the motorway, the trees growing there were crowded with roosting birds at night. They were all small birds ranging from sparrows and redpolls to goldfinches and linnets. Once I had watched a pair of tawny owls circling round this roost in an apparently clumsy fashion, but with the deliberate intention of knocking the branches and causing the birds to fly up and outwards. Both tawnies caught a disturbed bird. Further along, the area is well lit from the overhead lamps. Blackbirds, thrushes and a robin commonly sing territorially during the dark hours. One blackbird perches above a light standard to sing!

Leaving Colts Farm before first light one morning, I happened to see a van parked against the side of the pedestrian walkway and hidden from the road. Idly, I wondered if it had been stolen and abandoned, but the engine was still warm and in our area such vehicles are usually left late evening. I walked round to the motorway and stood watching the roosting birds that seemed strangely uneasy. Had the tawnies been troubling them again? The traffic was steadily passing as I stood in the shade when a man's shadow, grotesqely misshapen, reared up through the chain-link, seeping over me and the tarmac in front. Another shadow crouched dog-like to one side holding something before it. I've never been quite sure what goes on here, but memories of other odd happenings came crowding back. I turned suddenly, a deliberately sharp movement, shouted repeatedly and clapped my hands. The birds rose up in an enormous rush and the two men were left staring. Why hadn't I taken the number of that van? I ran back round the way I had come, but too late. An engine started up before I turned the corner and the van was a distant blur along Maddon Lane! I walked slowly round the chain-link and found several places where it had been cut and later repaired. Another part had been recently cut and bent back with wire holding it in place.

I discussed this with a Wildlife Officer from another police force as I wondered how they would have caught the birds. He had become interested in the traffic of wild birds years ago when on patrol early one morning; these men had set up nets, but there are several other methods. He warned that dismantled traps are merely chicken wire stretched over light wooden frames and would be unrecognizable as such to the uninitiated. 'Warn your local police if they have cause to search outside premises, to take note of such wired frames stacked casually against shed walls and so on. Goldfinches are big business and fetch £80 or £85 a pair.' Not so long ago, his force had picked up a man trading in birds illegally taken from the wild and their tip-off had told them one such consignment of goldfinches had come from my county.

For every wild bird that lives to be sold in this way, many, many more die of their injuries, stress or cramped confinement.

It had turned warmer now, though the wind was strong. All the badgers kept close to the sheltering trees; those at Cliffords Bank were foraging either amongst the elmbrush or across the field just inside the woods. Crisp and Lucy had no protection around their sett, but were searching nearer Briarmead Lane where the trees were still untouched. Lucy, the cub that Crisp befriended, would be two years old next month and Crisp herself would be four. The relationship had done much for both and stabilized the older sow. Unlike her mother and two sisters, Crisp had survived the depredations of badger-diggers and lampers alike, but her stressed early life had made her a very nervous animal. She had never produced cubs and, if she had, would have been a poor mother. She was, however, a much calmer badger now and I lived in hope that perhaps one day when Missy's Mícheál was an adult . . . but only time would tell.

It was a mild, though grey, first light with the tawnies calling territorially. Walking along the Wildflower Path I saw three men at the gate off Briarmead. They were about to bring in the logging vehicle to drive up onto the Old Cherry Sett slope and collect the rails to be taken away. I was horrified after all my efforts with the County Trust and their Reserve Officer. It did strike me as strange that I didn't know these men; in the past, the man employing the coppicers has also been the contractor who removes the timber, but perhaps this had changed now. These men had the key to the gate, however, and referred to the Reserve Officer by name. I told them they couldn't take the vehicle up the slope because of the badgers, nor for a good way round the occupied sett entrances as the tunnelling goes a fair way and badgers don't sleep just inside their holes. I added that the rails would have to be removed by hand down to the bottom of the slope; no way was it passing over Crisp and Lucy whilst I was there. I stood in front of the vehicle that wasn't yet off the lane and refused to let it enter the gate. Understandably, I suppose, the men were very abusive.

Now they had been told that there were badgers present *they*, not their boss, would be liable; badgers are protected (though sometimes, I wonder!). I threatened to run down to the nearest house at the bottom of the lane and phone Oakley's rural sergeant from there. Knowing our police, a patrol would get here quickly unless called away on something more urgent. Fortunately, the three men decided to call it a day and took their vehicle up to the top of Briarmead to turn it round. Their spokesman (the man in the van) relocked the gate. I could scarcely believe what had happened. That they knew the Reserve Officer by name didn't mean a lot. Others taking wood here last year named him as giving them permission. Poachers (including badger-diggers and lampers) always seem good at getting the farmer's name and swearing he has given them permission to be on the land, when in reality he knows nothing about it! The key to the gate seemed conclusive that the Reserve Officer had indeed sent them in. Sometimes I despaired of that man! Back home I found the County Trust's office engaged, so later I rang the Reserve Officer at his home number. After nearly yawning behind his hand, he merely said, 'Is that all? Oh good,' and rang off. I couldn't understand what pleasure he derived from being so negative; had he not heard of mutual co-operation?

That night, gales swept over the countryside with gusts of wind 100 miles an hour. Badgers and foxes were below ground. Recalling the Great Storm of 1987, with its hurricane-force gusts that I merely took to be a severe gale at first, I made my way home also. Once inside The Sett, noise was muted, the approaching wind sounding like the torrent of a waterfall or distant traffic roar which grew louder till a savage buffet violently shook my home! It was the first real gale I had experienced here and my little home withstood it well. The wind was blowing from the east across the open farmland and catching the hawthorns in front of the lake before continuing on to me. Several of these, I found later, had come down, with parts of others broken off, but that was all the damage.

I phoned the Trust Office again, this time getting a woman who appeared as disinterested and off-hand as the Reserve Officer; obviously, the two had conferred. I felt so helpless. These people are conservationists after all and also had re-started their own badger group (which later I was to join). Surely they were concerned under their uncaring veneer? I spoke to Hugh from Thrift Lane about it. Unknown to me, he too was dissatisfied with several things the Trust were doing in Ashcroft Woods. Like me, he phoned their office to complain of these and also the badgers' vulnerability at the Old Cherry Sett. He, too, received the same off-hand response. We didn't realize till much later that the strangers with the logging vehicle had come to steal the stacked rails. True, when wardening the previous winter, I had encountered timber stealing and reported it to the police, but the sheer audacity of this early morning foray would have guaranteed its success had I not been there. How those men must have cursed my concern for the badgers! It *had* resulted in added phone calls to the County Trust, however, and not by me alone.

That Saturday dawned bright and fresh with the birds singing like a spring day. Earlier, the badgers had been playing 'Let's all bundle Chris', which tends to be rather wearing (for me!). Mícheál, Kate and Kirsty, my gentle Missy's cubs, had none of their mother's nice restrained ways. I had my legs head-butted – ouch! – and ended up on the ground being jumped on by three tough little horrors; you can go off badgers!

Primroses, hazel catkins and snowdrops were open with many of the birds nest-building. It was the same story at The Sett where the nest-box Karen had made to put outside my office window was in process of being accepted by a pair of great-tits. Throughout the spring and summer, the action at Karen's nest-box proved eventful. One early morning I saw and watched a great-tit come with moss to the entrance hole, but something was already in possession. Both tits alarmed as they perched on the briar rose and I saw it was a yellow-necked mouse that was contesting their new home! I suspect the mouse liked a quiet life, however, for soon the tits continued their nest building and in due course the eggs were laid. One night the stable cat came and explored. Unknown to me, she succeeded in dislodging the box. The baby birds survived, however, and I duly returned it to the same position. There they became fledglings and in the course of time, flew away. When I brought the box inside for the following winter, the nesting material proved a source of great interest. The cupped nest was made of the softest moss and rabbit fluff. It also contained the stable cat's fur, a few very long pony hairs, many distinctive badger hairs and some hair I recognized as my own!

One day we had heavy rain that by nightfall had ceased with a fast falling temperature. The resultant deep hoar was like snow that night and crunched underfoot. Every branch and twig-end had its thick, white covering; hazel and alder catkins were delicate glass ornaments that tinkled in the slight breeze. I stood at the Chantry's edge and watched the tawnies hunting over Great Chantry Field, one gliding over my head as I called. It landed on the very edge of my hand, thought better of it and flew off, only to glide round again and this time land true. It seemed to stare straight at me, ruffled its feathers and, using its beak as a third hand, climbed up the rough material of my anorak to my shoulder. It was a long time since either bird had done that.

Later I walked into the Chantry and sat on one of the dead beeches writing my notes when something damp touched my hand and made me jump – Lucy and Crisp! My jump made Crisp snort in surprise; Lucy stuck her snout down and played 'charge' through the leaves and we all had a silly half-hour. I ended up very hot, took my anorak off and left it on the beech. Lucy and I wandered out to where earlier the tawny had flown on my hand, when I happened to turn. Crisp was sneaking off with my anorak! Bedding again I supposed. I chased madly after her for that anorak was new (well, fairly!) and luckily she tripped herself. Lucy bundled her friend in the excitement and I grabbed my anorak and hastily put it on. I seemed to recall a certain other item, viz. a new lambswool jersey that went the same way!

The dawn was wonderful with a deep rosy sun climbing the sky speckled with vari-coloured clouds. The primoses' pale heads were flawless pearls amongst the undergrowth and golden lambs-tails hung from many trees. Melting frost shimmered in the sun before changing to water droplets that softly fell from each twig-end.

That morning I returned by the motorway and stopped to speak to the occupants of a patrol car parked near by. Inevitably, we discussed the badgers, then I pointed out the trees close to and mentioned the men and the roosting birds earlier that month with their van left discreetly off the farther lane. They were very interested in the Wildlife Officer's experiences and the profit to be made from wild birds and promised to keep a look out, not just here but elsewhere round the villages, when on early morning patrol.

10

The Old Cherry Sett

January 1989 was the blackest so far for the badgers of Ireland. It seemed that the Irish government was determined to repeat the same futile, expensive and tragic mistakes as our Ministry of Agriculture, Farming and Fisheries. MAFF has wasted more time and public money, been guilty of more bungling and cruelty towards the badger, than can ever be assessed. Yet it has still found *no scientific evidence to show how the disease TB can be transmitted from badger to bovine.* Whether badger control really reduces the incidence of TB in cattle has never been tested, yet this would be easy enough to do.

The sorry and shameful saga of bovine TB amongst cattle in Ireland is one of unclean and bad husbandry, tag-switching on cattle and a high volume of illegal cattle movements. The main source of infection of bovine TB in cows is other cows. The agricultural business press in Ireland is strong, wealthy and powerful, whilst the conservation side are few, scattered and have no funds. The World Wildlife Fund has never wanted to know about Ireland; America sees it as part of Europe and Europe ignores it. Twenty per cent of Irish badgers now carry bovine TB. Other wildlife does too, but as in Britain, this is ignored. Thus the badger, protected under its Wildlife Act of 1976, has become the scapegoat for past failures of the Irish government.

The previous year had seen an active campaign by farmers against badgers. The State chose to turn a blind eye to this and many vets encouraged and condoned their behaviour. In some areas, slaughtered badger carcases were dumped at roadsides and, when found, were listed as road casualties. That summer, its Department of Agriculture had ordered the use of improved high-tensile steel wire snares for the taking of badgers by district veterinary offices throughout the country in the department's on-going TB eradication programme. The results were appalling for the badger, though they did nothing for TB eradication. These 'body snares' were made so that the wire loop passing through a steel swivel, tightened round the body of the animal causing it a slow cruel death. (Although they were theoretically not self-locking, the swivel was set at a level where it still permitted the loop to severely constrict the badger.) This was bad enough, but often the animals pulled up the snares and escaped badly maimed and dying. Even if looked at daily, the 'protected' badgers were ensured slow hours of agony.

It was against this anti-badger background that Ireland's first four Badger Groups were formed, two of them with the assistance of the Irish Wildlife Federation and two independently.

One of the badgers of Ninepenny Wood was digging-out and taking down soft, dry grass for bedding. This dominant sow was almost certainly soon to cub and I spent two hours happily watching her that mild night. She went to ground as colour crept into the landscape and left a ball of grass at the mouth of her entrance. The freshly dug earth was scattered with dry wisps that a passing bank vole picked up and sampled one after another, then dropped, and went on his way. Not much nourishment there I'm afraid! The three badgers here had no main sett now. The boar occupied the subsidiary one where the Japanese knotweed grew between the open fields with the other sow living in the bank of the ponies' meadow. There were crowning-down holes of various ages at all these setts; the badgers were vulnerable to diggers and lampers, though the latter didn't appear to operate here. How I wished I could make an artificial main sett in the grounds near my own sett where they would be safe from intruders and also have plenty of room!

Karen came to stay with me. She was slowly recovering from an accident, though her memory had only partially returned. Her living quarters might be cramped, but there was peace and an abundance of space outside in which to relax.

The first Sunday in February I checked my badgers. All Missy's family were with her still at Cliffords Bank, whilst Crisp and Lucy remained at the Old Cherry Sett. Watching the latter that night, I was reminded that Crisp was Lesley's daughter and Lucy of course, her grand-daughter. I wardened the woods all morning having first checked we had no campers. The previous Sunday a shooter had tried for the woodcock, but there were no such problems that day. I met a family out walking the woods who commented sadly on the state of the place. Not only were acres denuded of trees, but undergrowth and main paths alike had disappeared under the mud created by the coppicers' vehicles. 'It gets worse and worse here, it scarcely looks like a wood now,' the father said sadly. One of the farm-managers had said the self-same thing to be echoed by several local people I met whilst wardening that day.

Early in February, Watcher's daughter allowed her mate back and no longer growled at his approach. I wondered when her pups would appear at the den entrance. The vixen stood tearing pieces off the rabbit hindquarters that her mate had left. I still saw Dusky sometimes coming or going from the grounds of a large house in Warby Hill Road. He frequented this area of private land so I had no way of finding more about him now. My badgers had been foraging in the dampness with pauses to go below ground and rest. This strange, mild winter had not required them to use up their autumn accumulation of fat so they still appeared stocky and rounded. Those three tearaways, Mícheal, Kate and Kirsty, had been playing 'tag' and 'hold-onto-your-neighbours'-tail' on the top meadow. Then, a mad, whirling of bodies weaving in and out. Missy looked at me as if to say 'Let them get on with it – *we* aren't like that are we?' I sat on the grass and she clambered into my lap. I rolled her over on her back and facing away from me so that she was leaning her back on my chest. There she groomed herself, licking the black fur of her legs and combing through her belly fur. Then twisting round she started grooming me. Human hair seems to interest badgers a great deal. I recalled Karen saying once that the elephants she looked after found her hair a source of curiosity; their trunks would reach out and touch her hair, pick up and feel it very gently (more so than badgers!), then they would softly blow through it and watch her long hair part. I don't think it would be advisable to have long hair with my lot; I'd end up with bald patches!

I went out late one evening with clear skies and a sparkling crescent moon. There were three hares bounding and boxing and walking tall; that curious up-on-hindlegs act of theirs. Their mating rituals and competition for dominance was in full swing. The rabbits, too, were establishing territories and their status within their communities with frequent skirmishes. Tufts of rabbit fur lay in patches on the sward. The Embankment badgers were rooting between the rows of leeks off the Sleet House Path with much snorting and snuffling. Leeks, like potatoes, are earthed up so that moisture is retained in the dampness there. I walked on to my own area to be greeted by the whole clan of badgers. Eight friendly badgers *en masse* are rather wearing and soon I was covered in mud as they, too, must have been worming! By now it was into the next morning and a vigorous game of chase was in full swing – except for Missy and me. She stretched up on hindlegs and I bent my face to meet hers. Recalling her injury caused by a lamper's lurcher on this very field and her subsequent recovery and birth of her cubs, Missy is one of my few success stories. Those who have owned dogs will have many happy memories of them, but some dogs are more special than others. Missy is such a special badger and her gentleness and affection mean much to me.

Play over, Míchéal and Missy began digging-out entrances on Cliffords Bank. The moist earth was very workable. I walked into the woods with Crisp and Lucy going ahead, foraging as they went. The favoured place behind the Main Pond was investigated and so on through these woods to that below the beeches near the Old Cherry Sett. I sat on one of the coppiced tree trunks writing my notes and watching two busy grey backs as their owners rooted beneath the dead leaves. Down below, a tawny was calling and a shape drifted silently over the raw stumps. An outstretching of taloned legs, the wings cupped above the bird's head and it dropped on some small prey hidden from me. The sows still rooted in the leaves as the stars twinkled through light clouds.

Crisp and Lucy were mutually grooming! I'll wash your neck, if you give mine a good clean. Then they both decided to sit back on their tails and groom themselves. All badgers do this, of course, using their tail and hind legs. The badger supports itself as on a three-legged stool and leaning back with forelegs dangling on each side, appears to contemplate its stomach for all the world like a little fat buddha! The badger rakes through its under-fur using the claws of its forelimbs alternatively, rather like combs. It does this with great vigour and enthusiasm, making a loud abrasive noise. Then a hindleg is raised, inspected and groomed before being returned to the ground and the other hindleg treated likewise. The badger then gives a little jump and lands on all fours to groom its back or to go in search of food. One dominant sow I watched some years ago, had no tail and the scar of a very bad bite above her rump where her tail had been. Perhaps an adult badger had attacked her when she was young, or a dominant sow chased and injured her before she became the dominant one. Who knows, another may have challenged *her* dominance. With no tail, however, she couldn't sit back on it to groom, so used to dig a small hole and put her rump into that. This gave her support, but not quite the same agility and a dedicated bout of frenzied grooming would leave her more or less stuck. A rather undignified puffing and pulling would then ensue!

That early morning, Crisp and Lucy re-dugout their entrances, the fresh, sandy earth had a wonderful smell. I sat on the stump and listened to the snorting and grunting; their tunnelling wasn't far below as the hurricane proved when trees were uprooted here exposing the inner chambers. A neat rump appeared at an entrance and Lucy dragged the excavated sand between her body and forepaws shuffling backwards on 'elbows' till she reached open air. Then a brief stop to get her breath and free her nasal passages of particles. Two or three powerful kicks backwards of her hindlegs and the dirt was sent flying onto the spoil heap. A few moments later and Crisp emerged to do the same. All this work was making me tired and I stroked each dirty badger head before walking home under the stars.

I reach The Sett as the sun's long fingers touched the frost-patterned windows. Karen was waiting for me and over mugs of hot tea we sat talking. Candy appeared outside with Leo and the other dogs, so we took them for an early morning walk. Poor Leo had fallen hopelessly in love with Karen and his drooling affection was doing her good. The pup on his spindle legs, had difficultly keeping up with the adults, so I gave him a carry with Leo his father looking down his long nose in disgust. We suspected *he* would have liked to be small and cuddly too! My daughter is great company and we laughed all the way into Ninepenny Wood. I missed her when she went back home.

I left late on Friday evening 10th February and arrived in my area by 2.30 a.m. on the Saturday to be greeted by a very distraught Crisp who kept up a continual crying as she wound herself round my legs. No Lucy. The other badgers – Missy, Meg and Bess with the yearlings Kate, Kirsty and Mícheál were all searching the undergrowth just inside the wood as it was deeply frosty on the exposed farmland. My first thought was that the young sow had been snared or runover, but though I searched Maddon Lane, Briarmead and the main road, there was nothing to be seen there. More significantly, perhaps, Crisp wasn't keen on accompanying me, either to search for a road casualty or on any of the animals' 'runs' in the woods or hedgerows. She only seemed to keep with me for the company unwilling to be left, and constantly got in the way as I tried to walk about. In the end I sat down tired and puzzled and she scrambled into my lap. Later we were met by Meg and Bess who would have normally groomed Crisp in friendship, but she would have none of it. The continual noise she was making was beginning to get to us all and at first light the two sisters left us to go to earth in Cliffords Bank.

It was only when I crossed the lane and walked over Sand Pit Field above the Old Cherry Sett, that Crisp left me to go ahead and I suddenly had a premonition of what had happened. As I reached the outskirts of the slope in the woods that lower down becomes part of the main sett, she went swaying down the trail to her home. The first thing I saw was that most of the huge piles of tree trunks had gone and I felt sick. Then I reached the deeply gouged out tracks left by the vehicle that had collected and transported the trunks down and over the occupied part of the sett where Crisp and Lucy had denned. One entrance that Lucy had freshly dugout as I watched two nights earlier had disappeared beneath the tread of the transporter. It had sunk nearly two metres below the normal soil level and been compacted. The chestnut-bough entrance was hard-blocked with a flurry of mud (and a cut-off from the trunks) as the vehicle had gone by. Other entrances, too, had been completely blocked by mud churned up in its wake. It had needed to avoid the chestnut-bough entrance as that is actually in the bole of the tree. In doing so it had also avoided Crisp's favourite entrance and her part of the tunnelling; it had undoubtedly saved her life. But not so, my Lucy.

I hadn't the folding spade here now that I used to keep hidden in case the badger-diggers hard-stopped the sett, so had only my hands and pieces of stick to dig with. But there were Crisp's claws of course. Lucy might still be alive, but with no free flow of air, would soon suffocate. The terrier-rescue services reckon that a dog may still be alive up to twenty minutes below ground after an earth fall. After that it just depends on luck and situation. My frantic digging stimulated Crisp and soon she had taken over, once I had removed the log cut-offs that were squashed into the hole. Piles of bright earth were pushed out and down the slope; at least one entrance was free. But Crisp had come up against a blank wall of earth and I realized with a sense of helplessness, that the entire tunnelling had collapsed under the great weight that had passed over it. Lucy could never have survived. That part of the sett might never have been; it resembled some grotesque demolition site. Why,

why had it been allowed to happen? Crisp had ceased her futile digging and whining, pushed a muddied snout into my face. Arms round her shaggy body, face against hers, I stared at the desolation trying to come to terms with what had happened. All I could see was Lucy as I last watched her alive; healthy and digging her home in the dampness.

I followed the deeply-gouged path of the logging vehicle along the Wildflower Path and walked up to the piles of tree trunks that had been removed from the sett slope. As well as these, there were two fully loaded trailers by the Briarmead gate waiting to be taken away. How many tonnes of timber had been carried over the occupied sett and how many such journeys had it taken? What it must have been like for the badger trapped below was unthinkable. I hoped and prayed that she had died instantly . . . or had she waited partly crushed, till the next shuddering, crunching journey made an end to her suffering?

By now it was 7.45 a.m. and Crisp had gone to earth. I saw there was a quantity of rails still to be brought down from the slope. What if the next time they killed Crisp? The quickest phone I could get to was at Colts Farm and I ran over to meet the farm-manager getting ready to take the family out for the day. Oakley police promised to send a constable if I waited at the junction of Maddon Lane. Soon a patrol car drove up and I found I was talking to the same man who had discussed the taking of wild birds. Together, we surveyed the damaged sett, noting the broken and blocked entrances, the difference in Crisp's freshly dug ones compared with those infilled and the deeply gouged out tracks made by the logging vehicle. Lastly, he inspected the piles of trunks stacked at the side of the path and the two full trailers awaiting transportation. I asked if *he* would phone the Reserve Officer to stop the rest of the trunks being brought down the slope. I hadn't the phone number with me, but would phone it in to him at the police station. The County Trust *must* take notice of the police, even if I was ignored. The constable gave me a lift half-way home (he had a series of calls to attend to) and promised to do so.

At home I phoned in the number and put down the receiver, when the phone rang. Hugh's voice to tell me that developers were demolishing the sett in Thrift Lane that was Bossie Bessie's home and please could I help? The man driving the vehicle had seemed reasonable when Hugh had asked him to wait whilst he phoned the police before he went further, but the owner of the plant, a Mr Peters, had been very unpleasant. I re-phoned Oakley police and explained the situation. Yes, someone would go immediately. Shortly after, Hugh phoned to say that two patrol cars had arrived. No more could be bulldozed, but the constables weren't sure of the actual wording of the Act. I phoned the station and explained that the only part of the Badgers Act that can be used in a case of demolishing an active sett is the section under 'Offences of cruelty – If any person shall – (a) cruelly ill-treat any badger.' The fact that no case had yet been brought under these circumstances was (as I was feeling at that moment) neither here nor there. I also apologized for all their time that morning taken up with badger incidents. 'That's all right m'dear,' came the answer. 'Some mornings it's break-ins, some it's car thefts and this morning, it's badgers. At least it makes a change!'

Taking the folding spade I returned to Ashcroft Woods and the forlorn and hopeless task of opening-up badger entrances. There was no one about (Saturday mornings in the winter are generally quiet), so I called and called quietly down the entrance I opened up. Oh for a whimper, a musky scent, anything, but she must have been dead long since. I had no way of knowing for how far the tunnelling was blocked or crushed, or indeed, of judging exactly where she might have been. The damaged sett slope looked so different, an alien landscape; who could say? Something wet touched my hand and there was Crisp, blinking in the light as I knelt there. I stroked the smooth fur of her face and told her to go to earth, just as a dog barked distantly and she disappeared.

A little later I was on the spare plot of land next to the houses in Thrift Lane, the scene of another devastated sett. It appeared that the owner had bought the plot some years ago and put in several unsuccessful applications for planning permission. If he cleared the land and lowered the roadside bank, it would more nearly resemble a building site at the end of the farmland and, who knows, the next planning application might be successful. The machine wasn't a JCB as I had expected, but a plant machine owned by Mr Peters – a Hitachi that swivelled on a caterpillar tread. In fairness, the landowner could never have known it was a badger sett when they started. The area had been a little wilderness and even I had no idea of its extent. The annexe sett had gone with one entrance crumbled and broken and one intact where two different-shaped scoops for the machine lay nearly obscuring it. I walked over the raw, levelled earth and instinctively felt that a large part of the sett had once been here below my feet. In the far right-hand corner were the remains of the sett with all but one of the eight entrances, well badger used.

Home once more; I seemed to have been walking back and forth for a very long while. I settled down to try and sleep for not only had I promised to watch at the Thrift Sett to see what badgers were there, but I also wanted to see Crisp that night. Part of me couldn't accept that Lucy was dead; perhaps she had got out somehow and gone to one of the other setts, perhaps she was still there and alive, perhaps ... The pretty cub I had taught to find food, who had survived her parents' and brother's deaths and was two years old last week; mischievous, engaging Lucy who made rings round her big friend Crisp ... hers seemed such a stupid, senseless end. And why?

170

Going out that night a police car caught up with me and in it was the constable who had attended the Old Cherry Sett. He had spoken to the Reserve Officer who maintained he knew nothing of any badgers at that sett, nor of Hugh's and my phone calls! 'I'm sorry,' he said, seeing my face. 'He *does* know nothing must happen to the remaining badger there.' I thanked him and continued on my way to wait at the Thrift Lane sett. Badgers came and went, but it was difficult to judge just who was who as the cleared land made it unwise to stay close. I did recognize Bossie Bessie though! There were three young badgers, Bessie, another sow and a boar. An adult boar and a much older sow disappeared out of sight at midnight, into the garden of the first house as it began to rain heavily.

I left then as I had still to find Lucy if she was alive. I would check all the outlying setts and anywhere a badger might den in the area, though in my heart of hearts, I knew that she and Crisp would have stayed together after their first fright with the logging vehicle. Poor, poor Crisp, how lost and lonely she was, like a shadow forlornly following after as I searched. Again I checked everywhere including the road, but no Lucy. It was a bright, mild night with a clear half moon. After dawn I returned to Thrift Lane and did a rough sketch showing the cleared land and the positioning of the remaining sett entrances. Here and

there on the cleared, raw earth were slight depressions and taking a stick, I dug into them and found more entrances. Like those of the Old Cherry Sett, however, the tunnelling beyond had collapsed. Once started on this I became absorbed and found 11 more! This must have been a main sett with the remaining eight holes merely a remnant of the original. How many badgers had been alive here when the Hitachi machine had cleared the land was impossible to say.

I was reminded of the time as a car passed along the lane. I was due to phone the RSPCA Chief Inspector at 10 a.m. I phoned from Hugh's house and met him at the Warby roundabout. The other times we had met had been in Steve Hammond's day, that first RSPCA Inspector who had helped me so much with the badgers. It all seemed a long, long time ago now.

The Chief Inspector was introduced to Hugh and his wife and we walked over to the Thrift Sett. A great pile of trees and brushwood had been piled up ready to set fire to and the RSPCA man suggested that Peters might try to stink the badgers out under a pretence of 'tidying up' when they returned to complete the job on Monday. It was a good point. The Smiths living in the last house who had first raised the alarm that their badgers were being bulldozed, came out and were introduced. None of us liked the plant machine parked there; somehow the little corner retaining part of the sett with its shelter of trees, looked so vulnerable. It wouldn't take more than a few minutes to destroy that. I said I would come at first light the next day and stay till nightfall or until the men took it away. The RSPCA man promised to leave a message for our Inspector to come here tomorrow, but it wouldn't be till he came back on duty. The Smiths were extremely worried about their badgers.

Saying goodbye, the two of us went on to the Old Cherry Sett. The Chief Inspector was staggered at the destruction here and by the County Trust at that! Comparing both sites he remarked that the damage here was far worse than the developer's site in the village and what were the Trust thinking of? Like myself, he felt it pointless to even consider bringing a case of 'cruelly ill-treating' against such a powerful organization as a Trust (amongst the other 47 County Trusts, this one is known as 'the Trust with the money' through several bequests), but he suggested I let the Superintendent at RSPCA headquarters have the details and see what he said.

He gave me a lift to The Sett for which I was truly thankful. Letters had to be written; to the Reserve Officer formally stating what had happened and asking that he didn't let the machine up anymore as a badger was still in residence; and to the owner of the land at Thrift Lane pointing out it was an occupied badger sett and these were protected animals. I had never heard from the RSNC regarding my earlier letter on coppicing over occupied badgers setts; the chairman of the National Federation of Badger Groups had been right. Now I sent a copy of the Reserve Officer's letter to the head of his organization the RSNC, for what it was worth. To this day, neither of these letters have ever been acknowledged. The chairman of the NFBG phoned me arranging to come on site to see the damage to the Old Cherry Sett for himself. I also sent copies of both letters with a covering explanation to the rural sergeant at Oakley.

Late that afternoon I walked round the Ninepenny setts. That at the Japanese knotweed was in good order and the well occupied Holly Sett had fresh dung in the nearby pits and neat badger spore on the wet earth of her spoil heap with more signs of bedding taken down. This mother-to-be was preparing for the big event! Much later I returned to my own area and continued my search for Lucy, but to no avail and by midnight of Monday 13th February I had to admit, even to myself, that she had died in the Old Cherry Sett. There were only seven badgers now in the entire 800 acres.

Later I watched at Thrift Lane. I discovered the adult sow *did* go to earth there, but away from the youngsters. She growled if they tried to include her in their games and turned on the boar when he smelled her. She continued aggressively, so that he hastily retreated and went on up the field edge and under the barbed wire. She must be expecting cubs surely? Bessie and her sister spent awhile at the plant scoops where the entrances had been. Later I looked at the ground there and found it covered with grain husks. I guessed they had at some time been helping themselves to the grain dropped by the rabbits and guinea pigs at the hutches in the Smiths' garden next door. The yearlings tried in vain to drag one of the great scoops away; later one of the workmen said it weighed several hundredweight!

First light was 6.20 a.m. with a sky that never saw the sun all day. I walked upfield to keep warm and noted paths under the wire and a small outlying sett the other side of the fence. Further still, a bright tawny tuft of hairs (Hugh's fox Patch!) caught on the route of another trail. Suddenly I heard men's voices near the lane and there were three men and the owner of Peters Plant. I ran down and explained that the fire should be moved away from the badgers and asked if any of them was the owner as I had a copy of a letter for him. No. Would they please move the fire? No. 'You have no authority and you're trespassing – – – – off,' said Peters and pushing by me he nearly knocked me down. I asked him not to light the fire till the police came to reinforce what I had said, but instead he picked up a large can and threw petrol over the piled brushwood. There was a tremendous whoosh as he lit it and close on the flames came a great cloud of thick, grey smoke that billowed in the strong breeze, straight into the sett entrances. I phoned the police from next door and they promised to send someone quickly. Ten minutes passed, then 15, whilst more and more smoke poured from the fire as the plant machine gathered great heaps of dead wood in its scoop and dropped them on top. I could hear the men laughing and I thought of the badgers cowering in the remains of their sett. I phoned the police back to find a patrol car on its way and nearly with us; it had been held up by the rush-hour traffic. The man that jumped out looked terribly young, but taking one of the copies I had of the owner's letter, he went up and spoke to the men on the site. All the time their chainsaw never stopped and the smoke and flames belched out. Then another patrol stopped with two men inside – the one I had called out on Saturday to the Old Cherry Sett and a companion. 'Don't worry, *we'll* soon stop them,' said the reinforcements grimly as they strode up the bank. Moments later the chainsaw ceased and the three officers returned. The workmen were moving the fire well away from the sett. 'Any more trouble and you just let us know,' and I thanked them with relief as they went.

I hadn't realized how easy it was to move such a large fire. The plant machine trundled forward, the scoop with its serrated jaw on a crane-like arm stretched out in front and simply pushed the flames, trees, branches and debris steadily down the slope and out of the way of the sett. Peters tramped down the slope glaring to his truck, saw me standing there quietly and spat. The strong breeze re-directed the spittle and he received it back. Swearing under his breath, he drove off. I fervently hoped he wouldn't return.

I carefully walked round the field edge and came out in front of the little tangle of remaining trees that housed the rest of the sett. I had no desire to upset the men, especially as I must stay here till they had finished to ensure the badgers' safety. It was going to be a long day and I would rather it be a friendly, than an anti one. Two uniformed men appeared from the road and came towards me there. The rural sergeant and our own RSPCA Inspector had met *en route*. The sergeant was going on duty to Oakley when he had seen the other parking his white van. As yet he knew nothing of the weekend's events and walking up together, the RSPCA Inspector enlightened him. The sergeant stood reading a copy of the owner's letter I still held, whilst the RSPCA man and I talked about Lucy in Ashcroft Woods. It was hopeless even considering taking a County Trust or its employed officer to court I maintained, they are too strong and powerful and, anyway, the chairman of *our* County Trust is on the Nature Conservancy Council. The Inspector argued that there shouldn't be one law for some and another for others; the Trust should set a good example to the public. Whether he liked it or not, I said, there was. I looked up to see the rural sergeant regarding me thoughtfully and I realized, not for the first time, how frustrating it must be sometimes for them. 'Anyway, it's a futile argument,' I said. 'Bet you whatever you like, they'll only get at most, a slapped-wrists-naughty-boy-and-don't-do-it-again letter from the RSPCA!' The two men laughed and told me to take care, by now it was raining as well as windy. 'Don't fill those chaps in down there, will you?' said the RSPCA Inspector with a grin. 'If they don't toe the line, phone us,' commented the rural sergeant as they went on their way.

All that day I stood just in the shelter of the trees round the remains of the badgers' home and watched the machine with the three men at work. No, not quite all day, for twice I went into the Smiths' house and was dried off and given sandwiches and coffee whilst one of the sons kept a lookout for trouble from an upstairs window. Refreshments were also brought out to me so I lacked neither food nor moral support and the latter warmed me more than anything else. Once that morning inside their house, the eldest called out from his window seat in the bedroom 'They're coming back' and I quickly put on my dried anorak and boots and shot out again next door to stand in front of the sett. The men had left at lunch-time and probably had a rendezvous too with their boss who was now standing there with them. The wind blew strong across the open fields and the rain continued. The workmen went on burning the remains of the copse they had destroyed, sometimes throwing petrol over it to make the flames leap high. Then one man came over and asked me to move as the Hitachi machine came near. I refused. Its scoop tore up a tree trunk close to me and trundled back to throw it on the pyre. Some time later the same thing happened. I refused and another tree was taken. Time passed and the machine began levelling the plot. Peters suddenly reappeared on the scene and I watched from the shelter of the trees by the sow badger's first spoil heap as the wind howled across field. Then I saw rather than heard above the noise, the machine crossing diagonally towards me. This was what I had dreaded, yet knew would come. Taking a deep breath, I stepped out to meet the wind and rain . . . and the mechanical monster with its jagged jaw held aloft. No more of this sett was going to whet its appetite. The earth shuddered a little below my feet at its slow advance and a picture crossed my mind fleetingly of the animals in their home behind me. And they all had the look of a badger called Lucy. The scooped jaw was way above my head and, looking up past its crane-like arm, I saw the fixed expression of the young man driving it. Much earlier that day, we had stood talking about badgers, badger-diggers and artificial setts to protect them and, instinctively, I had known he bore me no malice. But his job was his job and Peters his boss, after all. His face disappeared as the front of the machine loomed nearer and, watching fascinated, I saw the caterpillar tread was only half a metre away.

Then it stopped, the side door swung open and the young man jumped down. As he came round to the front where I stood, the relief on his face was indescribable and I knew he thought he had come too close. No, I was still standing upright and we stared at one another. 'I thought, I thought . . . you must be perished there, what with this wind and rain. Do you want to come by the fire?' I shook my head and he stammered, suddenly red-faced. 'Honest, we won't take any more trees; I promise we won't hurt the badgers. The police have our names and addresses after all.' But again I shook my head.

There's too much money involved. True, no case of this kind had ever been brought, but what is a possible court case and a fine of, at most, £2,000, when so much money is tied up in houses and land? If I had jumped out of the way, the machine would simply have ploughed on taking sett and all, then stopped at the top of the plot where it meets the farmland and come down over the sett again. No fine would have saved the badgers then. My Lucy had died a few days ago and nothing would bring her back. Doubtless, other inhabitants of this sett had been crushed before anyone realized it was a sett. Mrs Smith appeared anxiously at her garden fence. The machine trundled down the slope again as we stood and talked. It was all right. Peters went off in his truck and we watched the men nearer the road now, tending the fire. They wouldn't try again. It had been worth a try, but it had failed and the first round was ours, or rather, the badgers. I was given another welcome cup of tea, then the lady took dog and children for a walk (it was half-term) as the rain had eased. Time passed and I stood in the shelter belt of the copse and watched the men whittling sticks to toast their sandwiches over the remains of the fire. The Smiths were wonderful; they really cared about what happened here. I didn't need a fire to keep myself warm.

A big florid man in a beautiful white sports car then appeared and demanded of me his letter. 'You know you are on private land,' he said and I nodded. 'Will you get off my land?' he asked and I shook my head. He walked down to the workmen and spoke to them. They shook their heads as they looked my way.

The machine levelling the roadside bank was fascinating to watch. One man stood in the road to stop traffic along the lane as the jagged-jawed scoop gulped up loads of bright earth, turned and dropped them in neat piles at the hedge by the Smiths' garden. Soon it was 5 p.m. and Peters was in the lane, backing the transporter into the drive ready to load the plant machine. Traffic was halted as it was carefully driven down the bank and straight onto the transporter. Minutes passed with directions called, then at 5.15 p.m. it was driven towards Everington, followed by the build-up of traffic caused in its loading. I never saw men or machine again.

A quick word to Mrs Smith and then Hugh, now returned from work. We all felt the entrances might be stopped-up sometime to try and get rid of the badgers, or one of a number of poisons placed in their sett. Between them, the two families would check this sett morning and night. The Smith's dog was very good at barking if anyone was around and sounded formidable. In reality, she was far from such but that didn't matter; she was a good warning of prowlers. I was offered a lift home, but refused for the walk would warm me and my mind was alert with thoughts of Lucy.

It was nearly dark as cars passed close to me in the narrow lane, when I looked up to see a police car, lights flashing just ahead. It was the village constable who helped me so much with Ashcroft Woods; he had left some things at the station and would give me a lift to the church. There we parted, I to go in to The Sett and he to collect his gear. The pain in my back gnawed from so many hours standing. It was good to lie flat on the floor and rest.

A soft thud awoke me and for a confused moment I was still in the woods watching Crisp and Lucy dig out their home. There came a lovely wavering, quavering 'whoooooo', then an answering kewik. The tawnies were serenading on the roof above me. It was 10 p.m. and time I was out.

= 11 =
Ninepenny Wood

Crisp was calmer now and seemed to have accepted what had happened to her companion. I sat on one of the remaining tree trunks left by the loggers with Lesley's daughter and Meg came up too. I stroked both sows and pushed my face between them to find I was being groomed! Later I remembered the terriermen's shovel that had been left behind and using it, had another go at a blocked sett entrance. This seemed to stimulate Crisp who took over from me. Meg looked on and whickered, as an idea occurred to me. Why not encourage this sow to den at the Old Cherry with Crisp? Not too near and not on the coppiced part, but perhaps those holes above the old prone tree itself. No sooner the idea than the action and in no time at all an excited Meg was making a new home for herself. Give a badger the incentive and then stand back! Later Crisp came to view the work, climbing on my lap till Missy's daughter emerged dragging a load of sandy earth beneath her. She looked up from her labours to us sitting above and Crisp whickered softly. I left them to cement a new relationship in the ancient family sett.

The following night I found Meg *and* Crisp taking in bedding. I could understand why Meg was doing this for, after all, she was making a new home, but Crisp couldn't want any more surely? Crisp started to dig out one of the machine-crushed entrances that I had reopened with the shovel, but then abandoned the idea. Lying flat on the ground I saw that the inner chamber was blocked too. A badger would virtually have to re-dig the whole passage (was Lucy's crushed body beyond?) to use this entrance. It was not really worth it with such a large sett, so I could understand why Crisp had left it.

Walking back via Oakley, I checked the Embankment badgers' sett that was well occupied and there could soon be cubs; also the Yew Tree Sett that was still empty.

Crisp and Meg continued together. I was glad for Lesley's last daughter. Both sows would go up to the field edge above the Old Cherry Sett and collect bedding using the dead bracken and even some long bluebell leaves that the mild weather had encouraged to grow, as well as dry grass from beneath the thin line of trees. There was nothing like this now near their sett for the coppicing had not only cut down the tall chestnut trees, but temporarily churned up and destroyed the undergrowth there. The bedding-collectors were making a path in their energetic to-and-froing to the entrances as first one, then the other, appeared over the slope travelling backwards in a quick shuffle to their destination. Meg, resting briefly, was caught up by Crisp. A quick sniff, Meg backed onto and musked Crisp, who returned the compliment and then groomed Meg's ear briefly. I was still wondering at Crisp's insatiable desire for bedding.

The rest of Missy's offspring were with their mother on Cliffords Bank and foraging in the field below the sett. Their grey bodies dotted the field where the well grown corn stretched in neat rows. Further over there were rabbits galore that came from the warren in the corner of the bank where once the beehives had been. The elmbrush was growing up well since the hurricane damage was cleared the previous year and would soon make a good windbreak again for crop and beast. That morning one of the men from Newby Farm drew alongside on his tractor and we discussed the mild weather, crops and, inevitably, the badgers!

Watcher's daughter was now denning with her cubs on Cliffords Bank between the badger sett and the rabbit warren. Her suckling pups had worn sores round her teats and stroking her I could feel her ribcage under the thick coat; nevertheless, though thin, she was in perfect condition and the living reincarnation of her mother.

Crisp and Meg greeted me in the little beech grove above the Old Cherry Sett where they had been rooting for grubs and insects amongst

179

the leaf litter. How many generations of badgers have I recorded searching this area? Stroking Crisp I was amazed to see she was soon to cub! Like foxes, dogs, cats and, indeed, most other mammals, it is often not till the final days of gestation that this becomes apparent. Her belly was tight and hard beneath the sparse, black fur. She allowed me to examine her quite happily, only insisting on grooming my ears in the meanwhile! Meg looked on with some interest, then came to help in the general clean-up. I was delighted that Crisp was soon to cub and suspect, in retrospect, that this delayed implantation, from a mating with the now dead Jude, must be due to Lucy's calming influence. This explained Crisp's desire for bedding of course – and I had never guessed!

It started to rain at 6 a.m. with the tawnies calling in the Chantry. Wavering hoot, kewik reply and then two dark shapes flying low over Long Field on their way to roost. I thought I had found their chosen nest site, but could only verify this in the next few nights; I had been so involved with the badgers lately.

For the first time since Lucy's death, I met one of the farm managers that morning and, inevitably, we discussed what had occurred at the Old Cherry Sett. I was in the process of writing to RSPCA head-quarters as had been suggested by their Chief Inspector, over and above his own report. I had phoned the owners of the woods asking for confirmation of a detail, only to find the district council official concerned, unobtainable for an indefinite period. However, the chair-man of the Ashcroft Woods Committee was obtainable; moreover, he had been in a jovial mood, sure of his ground and confident. He knew about Lucy from her beginnings as a motherless cub and had borrowed a copy of an article I wrote for *Dog & Country* on teaching Lucy and Luke to find food. He knew, too, of Luke's death, my struggle to integrate the orphaned cub and Crisp's adoption of her. His laughing allusions to 'your unfortunate badger' left me stunned; was her death such a joke?

He then mentioned the letter from the National Federation of Badger Groups sent to the County Trust's chairman and warned, 'We will be conferring on an answer.' In the face of impending trouble, all ranks were drawing together to sweep the dead badger under the carpet. Those with a lifetime's experience of committees will, I dare say, be well versed in this. In one fell swoop, honesty and integrity vanish out of the door at the prospect of possible criticism. If this can happen in local conservation politics, what goes on in State affairs, I asked myself? I suspected, too, they had already met to discuss their plan of campaign. This man knew what hunts and developers know – the sett itself is not protected. He could afford to laugh.

It was raining heavily as we parted at the farm entrance, I walking despondently down into Warby to look at the Thrift Lane sett. The farm-manager and his family had helped me enormously with my badgers over the years and, from his words, I knew he wasn't at all surprised at this turn of events. I really was naive! The more I study badgers, the more I learn about my own kind. There are times, too, when I'm not very proud of my species! I was carefully checking the sett entrances with the rain pouring down, when a voice called asking if I would like to come in and have a cup of tea. There was Mrs Smith to restore my faith in human nature, her kindness as warming as the cup she offered!

That evening Hugh phoned to discuss the woods and when he could warden; between us we were still trying to keep the vital times covered and care for the place. He was pleased that Crisp was soon to cub for it was the one piece of good news amongst the bad. His pleasure put fresh heart in me. In all the years of struggle, this February was the nearest I had come to walking away from Ashcroft Woods. Was I really allowing the pettiness of a few to influence me so readily? We discussed the death of Lucy and events leading up to it at length. I had discovered that the real contractors who unwittingly brought the rails down, were the men I knew well and they had never been warned of the badgers' return. Earlier, I asked Hugh to find out, if possible, how many duplicate keys were in existence that opened the gate onto Briarmead. This he had done. Both the council and the County Trust had a quantity of these keys and the exact number wasn't known! There was no disagreement that January's men were unknown to any of us or that they must have been attempting to steal the timber. Nor had the Reserve Officer denied that he never let the contractors know the badgers were there. He merely denied any knowledge of my phone calls or Hugh's and therefore, any knowledge of it himself! That he should have monitored activity at the badger sett himself, rather than wait for others to inform him, had not escaped the owners' notice. The one thing that was obvious to us both was that responsibility for the incident was being shifted and there was little anyone could do.

That evening I had another phone call, this time from the RSPCA. They were prosecuting the owners in the Weldon badger case; it would be amongst the first of its kind.* I would be called as a witness for the

_____
* Unfortunately, this case was dropped.

prosecution and my records of this clan of badgers would be required. It was unlikely that such a case would be brought against the Reserve Officer or the County Trust, however, but I had already come to that conclusion myself!

It was a wind-tossed night with heavy showers, but still very mild. All the badgers were keeping close to home and foraging within the sett areas. There were plenty of grubs, worms and insects in the warm dampness, so much snorting and grunting ensued as their flexible snouts rooted down. A badger turns as it does so, which produces that smooth-sided conical pit so typical of the animal and totally unlike that of a rabbit or fox. No other British wild mammal has quite that length of flexible snout after all!

By mid-February the hawthorns were all in tiny leaf and turning into Thrift Lane, I found a frog full of spawn and another further along, both runover. Now the Ninepenny Wood sow who denned under the Holly Tree was lactating and of my own badgers, all but Crisp was above ground to greet me. Was she cubbing now? Meg did a snuffly snort down her friend's entrance, but there was no response and I wondered how Crisp would react to the other sow, when the cubs were born. The following night there was no Crisp again, but she had been out and strongly musked the entrance down which she had taken so much bedding – the nursery entrance. Meg came up to inspect, caught the scent of musking and abruptly moved away – the hint was taken! The tawnies chose to hunt over the coppiced part of the Old Cherry Sett and a bank vole was caught whilst I was with Meg.

It was on the third night that Crisp appeared and she was lactating. She made much of me, purring and whickering softly and was happy for Meg to come up too. Anyone who really knows their badgers will be aware that this last is unusual, but then Crisp has never been the most ordinary of badgers! I stayed well into that morning to try and track down a persistent shotgun enthusiast, whom I felt was a local man. There were no vehicles parked round the area whenever he was about, though this didn't rule out the possibility that he might be dropped by a friend and picked up later at a pre-arranged time. Somehow I didn't think so. Sure enough, about dawn I heard shooting from a coppiced area and trailed a young man with fair hair who moved off towards the Chantry, weaving in and out of the fallen trees. I reached the lower path too late to catch him, but in time to see him run into the back garden with the chestnut-paling gate, passing directly in front of the by-laws notice-board as he did so! Our persistent young Norwegian forsooth! It was much later that Hugh phoned to say he had caught a young man with a shotgun carried broken barrel across his arm, coming out of the Chantry into the garden with, yes, the chestnut-paling gate! The young man was fair haired and spoke with a strong foreign accent. Did I know him? Clearly it was time to enlist the help of the village policeman. Thus the problem was solved and the charming young foreigner hasn't graced Ashcroft Woods with his presence again.

One clear, mild night in late February, I sat on a tree stump with Crisp below me lapping from the water left in the deep ruts made by the logging vehicle. The moonlight made her look white rather than grey and her white mask with its two black stripes, showed up with startling clarity. Meg and Bess appeared from the Wildflower Path, but only Meg approached her. The two sows whickered softly and came up the slope towards me. The smell of sweet, warm milk from Crisp was so strong that I wondered if a dog could detect it when a badger is below ground? Each time a sow lactates, the smell reminds me of my bitch Wendy years ago when she had her pups. It seems stronger on badgers than vixens, I'm not sure why. Bess came up for a fuss when her sister and Crisp had gone to earth and almost 'asked' to play. A small round offcut of wood about two cms thick and 15 wide was fine when bowled down the steep slope to chase after. The only problem was that Bess was unwilling to give it back, yet she wanted it bowled down again!

Mícheál, the little Dublin lad, sent me a birthday card for his namesake. He had drawn a rainbow and the sun on it as he felt they were things a badger never sees. The words inside read 'To Mícheál Badger from Mícheál Tinney on your first birthday. Hope you find lots of worms.' I wondered what future lay in store for an Irish lad that loves badgers, in a country where on one hand they are protected and on the

other, their farmers were encouraged to dig them out to be checked for bovine TB. Farmers there were employing badger-diggers to take out the badgers and not bothering to send the animals for examination; after all, why should they? Tests for TB are only done on dead badgers. It was simpler to encourage the diggers and baiters to move in and clear the lot.

That month I discovered what appeared to be a flat-sided wooden paling pushed into the elmbrush of Cliffords Bank. The pointed end was splintered and broken with teeth-marks all along the sides. Caught on the sharpness were short, white hairs and long bi-coloured badger hairs. The paling didn't correspond with any on the farmland; that surrounding the soakaways was rounded rather than flat-sided, and green with lichen. This suggested it had been brought there specially. An animal would have difficultly gripping such a smooth, flat object. When I had met the village constable regarding our young foreigner, he had mentioned seeing a van one morning come quickly off the farmtrack and turn down Briarmead. He had been sitting in his vehicle in the car-park at the top of the lane catching up on some paperwork and couldn't have intercepted them before the van reached the main road. There it might have gone either right or left and speedily disappeared amongst the traffic. He checked the Bank and found a hole partly dug but not, he thought, near the badgers' part. Were my badgers all right? They were, but these happenings were the start of a series of events that proved what we already knew – the poaching, lamping and digging fraternity would always creep back eventually; it is merely a question of time.

Before first light on the last Sunday of February it began to snow. At The Sett I wandered about in the whiteness for some time, when a vixen came round the side of the lake. We stood still looking at one another and I did the soft 'mmmmmmmmmm' as she stealthily drew near. Later, making a cup of tea, I happened to look out of the window. There was the vixen sitting with brush neatly curled round and big ears turned forward, watching me watching her. I emptied the stew I had intended for that day's dinner into a shallow tin and, making the same soft noise, opened the door, placing the tin slightly to one side. She remained sitting for some time after I had gone back in. Her nose twitched and, gracefully gliding over, she bent her head. The fox ate a lot faster than I for her need was greater. Observing her side-on, I saw she was in milk like Crisp and Watcher's daughter. The snow was still falling heavily at 5 a.m., but wouldn't lay for long as it was barely freezing.

That afternoon, when the snow had cleared, I strolled through Ninepenny Wood and the adjoining farmland for the joy of it. Returning home, there was a yellowhammer, a cock pheasant and two redleg partridge, busy eating the wild bird food I had scattered earlier. I stood awhile watching, then gently walked round them and indoors. The chucka-chuckas barely glanced my way and the pheasant made his quiet little noise to himself. A blue-tit chose to land on the doormat a few moments later before I had a chance to close the door and I was minded to rename my home The Aviary!

Now it was March, the month of promise; rich, golden gorse gleamed bright in the rough places with pussy willow and damson adorning the winding lanes. One wet night there were toads mating in the Holmoak soakaway. The water was crowded with them, a bobbing, moving turbulence, incredible to witness. Further along, many lay squashed on the tarmac. By the time I reached Ashcroft Woods, the light rain had ceased and the temperature was dropping. It was cold enough for frost. I sat on a split tree trunk with Crisp warm and sleepy in my lap. Her grooming began on her own belly, then her moist tongue touched my sleeve and I was being washed too. Meg was a few metres away, trying to tip a trunk over with her shoulder. There was something living beneath it. She succeeded, but it was a woodmouse and much too quick for her as it leapt away – a flash of long tail and big ears and the tiny creature was gone. She snuffled where it had been, started digging and turned up its nest with the young still blind and naked. The rubbery snout passed over and they were gone in a few quick chews. Meanwhile, Crisp was still grooming me and had reached my neck. A tawny quavered somewhere behind us farther up the coppiced slope. These bare stumps were multi-shaped sores, open wounds under the clear sky. The Old Cherry Sett that the badgers and I had known for so long is no more. Even that curious chestnut-bough seat where I have sat and watched the family playing, has been mutilated and however it may re-grow, it will never contort like that again. With its trees gone, this eastern facing slope has no protection from the frost for the two sows and cubs denning there. The first birds twittered at 6 a.m. and a blush stole into the far horizon. The cold was beginning to gnaw at me and I rose to go as a green woodpecker laughed into the morning.

On the evening of 9th March as I went out there was a strong wind blowing though it was very mild and wet from the day's rain. There were four badgers, Missy, Mícheál, Kate and Kirsty worming on the cornfield below Cliffords Bank. Standing watching them I spied two Canada geese feeding further down. Bess found me gazing and advertised her presence in no uncertain terms by head-butting my legs! She had decided I was good for another game.

Sometime later, I came out of the woods near the old abandoned Tossy's Sett to find lampers on the field below the Bank! There seemed to be dogs everywhere. Three were lurchers, two a greyhound cross and a small, collie cross, six terriers, two being Jack Russells and the others, Fell or Lakeland. The three men were in their mid or late twenties and though one looked older because he was balding, he probably was much the age of his companions. The balding one held a long stick that he used as a walking stick, grasping it a third down its length. The whole scene with the uncontrolled dogs reminded me of a daytime incident a few weeks earlier with three roving men and their dogs on this land. These poachers had caught some rabbits and a pheasant when one of the dogs found Bess. Most likely she had been foraging a distance from the Bank and had been caught out in the open. My God, she was a very brave little badger. No fear here, but she was being overwhelmed by sheer numbers. I shouted at the men and dogs and kicked the latter as hard as I could, so making a path to the little sow's side. Next moment I was struck by the 'stick' to find it not wood at all, but a metal rod! Something jogged my memory and I recalled the wooden paling I had found tucked into the elmbrush of Cliffords Bank. You don't go a-lamping for rabbit and fox with something like that, but to jab at a badger? (This metal rod wasn't unlike the probing bar used by diggers to trace the direction of the sett tunnelling; it leaves small, round tell-tale holes in the ground above.) The lurchers were unsure of me and veered off which left us with the terriers. Bess grasped one and flung it high and it fell with a thin scream. The rod caught her on the side of the head. I kicked at first one small dog, then another with all my might, till I saw the rod swing and ducked. I had the most curious feeling that we were a partnership and I *knew* we would win. It was like something in slow motion, yet was probably over in minutes. I saw the rod swing down towards my badger and I head-butted the owner in his stomach. Not perhaps very wise from my head's point of view, but the man doubled-up with a grunt.

Then the men were gone leaving two terriers still sparring with brockie who seemed to know far more about fighting than they. She ducked her head between her front legs and a dog eagerly closed in. Next moment, Bess' head whipped out, her teeth fastening on the side of its face – a horrible scream as she twisted and flung and the dog landed yards away. Then all was still under the quiet sky and I knelt on the grass. The badger stopped licking her shoulder and licked my face

186

instead. There was blood on her breath; poor Bess, but somehow she didn't look poor. It occurred to me that she had fought dogs before; that would explain her quiet self-confidence. The village constable and I had been aware that lampers were around.

At 2.15 a.m. I left for home feeling stiff and exhausted. There I phoned Oakley police to tell them what had happened and had a rest and a mug of tea, but I could not settle and before long was walking back again. Colour was stealing into the countryside when I reached Cliffords Bank – no badgers, so I called softly by the sett. All the badgers, but no Bess. Ah, there she was, but in what a state! The bitten areas had swelled and distorted her face, the rod marks showing clear on her body. The others began to lick her as she stood quietly there. I stroked gently behind her ears, careful not to touch a swollen or bitten area. Tonight, I would return with something to speed the drying up of her wounds and prohibit infection. Light was diffusing the eastern sky as I walked slowly back through Ashcroft Woods.

It was two nights later when Bess opened up three entrances of Tossy's old sett, long ago abandoned, as well as one a short distance off under a tree and she started living there. Strange that she had chosen this new home. The lamping incident had affected her more than I thought. Each night I gave the young sow an antibiotic capsule wedged between two small pieces of cheese; her only complaint seemed to be that the cheese, was *so* small, as she snuffled first one hand and then the other looking for more! I dusted the worst of her bites with the antiseptic powder and hoped that nature would do the rest. She looked a very lop-sided little lady and was obviously in some discomfort. However, I think Bess was one of the tough ones!

The four foxcubs of Watcher's daughter were now growing fast and played around their den. Plump Crisp in motherhood had come into her own, busily foraging a short distance from the sett that housed her cubs and going into them three or four times to nurse. I wouldn't know for another five weeks how many she had and I fervently hoped one, at least, would be a boar. She didn't seem so dependent on Meg's company now she had others to care for and though both sows were friendly enough, I suspected that Meg might return to Bess her sister. The enormous pleasure I had from Crisp as a mother, eased the useless waste of Lucy's death, though at the time it made no sense.

At 7.15 a.m. the next day I caught up with a man firing a double-barrelled shotgun in the woods. He maintained he had no idea that shooting was prohibited. Yes, he had walked by a notice-board, but he never read that sort of thing. Oh well, at least he wasn't abusive!

I had arranged with the farm-manager to collect his spare office key at
8 a.m. but this incident, and another of a lone man lurking about by the
Main Pond, held me up for nearly an hour. The manager was still
waiting on Colts Farm, however, and gave me the key to use the phone
at night if I had another problem. He said that my description of the
recent lampers and their dogs coincided with those warned off Glebe
farmland about ten days before. The two farms now had the same
owner and although different men managed them, the rest of the

work-force went wherever they were needed so communications between them were excellent. For whatever reason they might be trespassing, poachers were definitely *not* wanted. Strangers wandering about by day often turned up at night having sussed out the land beforehand, and were extremely unpopular.

I reached home in a daze of tiredness longing to sleep, but the problem of the lamping worried me too much to rest. I was conscious that living a distance away from my area, I was often not around when terriermen or lampers were about. That coming weekend I would be away and the village constable didn't know where Bess was now denning. I hadn't thought to mention this long disused sett when I had shown him around the area last year. On impulse, I left a message at Oakley station and sat writing down for the constable exactly what had occurred in the last fortnight. I seemed to be so tired lately that I feared I might leave out something important if I left it till I saw him. Whilst doing this, the rural sergeant phoned, I mentioned about the message for his constable and he suggested I met him in the drive and he would relay the details. Sitting in his car a short time later, he read my notes and called the constable on the radio. He arranged we would meet up in the Briarmead car-park and visit the area together. We looked at the Cliffords Bank sett complete with dungpits and bedding turned out in the sunshine to air. The sergeant asked about the radio and commented on the lack of a person now to hold the contact. How often was I here at night and what part of the night? I now had access to the phone on Colts Farm, but that was nearly a half hour's run through Ashcroft Woods and over the farmland. He discussed possible parking places with the constable who said that with binoculars at dusk, standing just within the wood, one had a good view over this farmland and the tracks leading onto it. He had obviously done his homework! We walked over to Tossy's sett and I explained how the enormous old hole was in reality, a crowning-down hole dug before the event of radio locators on terriers' collars. This particular one had almost destroyed the outlying sett and was dug around 1973 or '74 with the sow and two of her cubs taken. 'Tossy' survived until late autumn, when he mysteriously disappeared. I called him that from his lonely game of tossing a pebble up and running after it. I was asked the badgers' most vulnerable time from digging and lamping, and replied, 'Right now when the sows have young cubs to care for and are at their most aggressive. Lamping here will cease from June to August when the crops grow too high and will begin again after the harvest.' On many Welsh hillsides, lamping is an on-going, all-season problem, often with locals involved so that vehicles are not required and detection is well-nigh impossible. Our few lamping incidents were child's play by comparison.

That Friday I went to Bristol to do some recording and stayed with friends overnight. Saturday morning I went over their area and was shown setts that had been recently dug or snared. There was a young dead sow roughly pushed, rump first, into her entrance with only a small mark above her snout to show how she had been killed – a strong blow from the sharp end of a terrierman's shovel. This young couple patrolled many setts regularly in their van, but it was impossible to be in the right place at the right time and the wife was near despairing. There are so many people caring for badgers against such great odds. I have no right to feel anything but fortunate in mine.

I returned home to find my badgers fine. I hate to be away overnight and the destruction in the Avon area had made me more uneasy than ever. Bess seemed finally recovered from her lamping injuries and Crisp – oh, she was beautiful! I was longing to see the cubs. Greater woodrush, woodspurge, bluebells, lesser celandine, cherry and damson blossom were bright in the sunshine. Our wayfaring trees had their flower-cluster buds well developed and dog violets nodded brightly from the grass. The reflectors would soon need cleaning again I noted. Best done before the Easter school-holidays. The fewer people seeing me clean them, the less likely they would be vandalized, or was that merely a case of wishful thinking? The homes of the Ninepenny badgers slumbered on in the warm air and the dull crimson balsam poplar catkins were beginning to fall over the spoil heaps like so many tassels. There appeared to be the undigested remains of some in the badgers' dung in the wood. I had a great deal of pleasure watching the boar and two sows so close to my own home and often saw them before I went to the Ashcroft area. One night the boar caught a partridge that had been unwise enough to roost within the furrows. I was aware that another partridge was contemplating the space below The Sett as a nest site; a most unwise one in view of foxes and badgers (to say nothing of Candy and Co.) that passed by, but I could scarcely tell her so! That nest was doomed from the start.

So many tragedies seemed to have befallen the Ninepenny badgers – their demolished main sett, digging at other setts and their reduction to three in such a wide area told its own tale. Though I didn't know this trio as I do my own animals, I felt for them deeply. They badly needed a safe main sett somewhere near me that no one could digout, then perhaps the lactating sow's cubs would survive and help increase the clan's numbers. Amongst the trees near the lake was an old abandoned oil tank perhaps three metres long and a metre wide. It had three 'portholes' into which I had scrambled one day and, though dirty, could so easily be cleaned. Sunk into the ground with tunnels curving outwards and up . . . we would have to see.

Good Friday is usually Bad Friday for wildlife locally, so after checking and observing my badgers that night, I stayed to warden both woods and farmland. That holiday weekend and the following week had the warmth and sunshine of midsummer and were a foretaste of the drought to come. It was a practical demonstration, too, of how badly Ashcroft Woods needed a warden for that weekend saw the activities of a wargames unit, three groups of campers, shotgun enthusiasts, an arsonist who tried to do his best (or worst) well into the Sunday night *and* lampers on the fields outside! My greatest fear for the place is fire, but fortunately we all survived, not only the wildlife, but the ancient woods themselves. It was only later talking to the rural sergeant that I found several woods in the area had also suffered fires, one seriously, though it was uncertain if they were due to campers not putting their fires out properly or arsonists. Walking home along a country lane I caught the unmistakable stench of rotting flesh and discovered a full, black bin-liner thrown over the hedge from a passing vehicle. Opening it with some trepidation (after all, there's no knowing whose remains you may find), it was with considerable relief that the contents yielded the bodies of two skinned foxes and one skinned badger. Perhaps it had been a busy weekend for the local DIY taxidermist industry too!

The living green seemed to vie with itself that spring. Short periods of rain interspersed with a sunny warmth was encouraging this growth. The wild gooseberry bushes near the Felled Logs Sett where the fox cubs now denned, had their tiny flowers purple-edged with the petals turned back; such attractive green, spiny little plants in the under-growth. The primroses and bluebells of Ninepenny Wood with yellow archangel were all in bloom together and also that curious plant the goldilocks buttercup with its different sized petals, one usually much larger than the others, which give it a deformed appearance. The wild flowers of Ashcroft Woods made a poor showing by comparison. The paths were just churned-up mud as was much of the undergrowth from the continual passage of the coppicing vehicles in the winter months. That year, too, the coppiced areas hadn't yielded the hoped for wild flowers because the soil varies a great deal and plants flourish according to habitat. The invasive bramble took over several such sites, whilst those consisting mainly of gravel remained bare.

Picnickers invaded the open Old Cherry slope; the stumps made good tables and seats, the sett entrances, excellent receptacles for their litter. Both sows were greatly disturbed. I removed the mess as soon as I found it, but their unease remained. The climax came when a pile of rails was thrown down the slope and lager was emptied into the nursery entrance with the can pushed down for good measure. Meg, Crisp and her cubs moved home, back to Cliffords Bank. This made them of course, more vulnerable to lampers – the badgers here just couldn't win. I missed seeing the mother actually move her family but by chance saw them a few nights later. There were tiny, peevish chirps and trills coming from inside the elmbrush and, gradually creeping nearer, I saw three lovely, snuffly, unsteady badgercubs, one very small. They were too young and unsteady to play as such, but were cautiously venturing over the sandy spoil heaps of their new home. One would bump into another myopically with a grunt and a chirrup, another nervously nosed over a leaf as if half-expecting it to bite. The smallest fell into a dungpit and immediately squawked frantically as it struggled to right itself and scramble out. Ugh, not the sweetest place in which to land. Just then Crisp herself appeared and, taking it by the scruff, hauled it out and down into the sett with the other two following after. Not a very good start in life! My badger hadn't noticed me and I had to smile as creeping back up the slope, I continued on my way.

Watcher's daughter (Watcher II) and her four cubs seemed settled now at the new den in the Felled Logs. Would they reach maturity without mishap I wondered? The remaining badgers were worming along the rows of young radishes. The polythene covers that bring the plants on early had been removed and the ground irrigated earlier that night. I followed the farm track down towards Maddon Lane at the side of the field called Pond Hollenden. As the name suggests, this place of the hollies once had a pond where the land dipped creating a natural watershed, but it had vanished years ago together with local springs and wells and the loss of water in the River Bourne. We had lost the lake by the motorway where I had planted trees and wild flowers, when the County Council spent 25 weeks cementing over it to create an artificial 'lagoon'. The geese and wildfowl had gone with the flora and, at present, its sterile concrete bed, walls and lookout tower surrounded by high chain-link fencing, more resembled a concentration camp, though hopefully, it would be recolonized one day. In the meanwhile, the farm-manager on Colts Farm had dugout a new pond for the place, hoping that aided by the irrigation it might replace our lost lake. It looked lovely that night with a half moon reflecting the shadowy trees

whispering around its margins and vegetation already growing on its banks.

Quite suddenly in all the mildness that April we had a period of snow, sleet and driving rain. In the early morning, during the sleet, I put out wild bird food, fat scraps and granary bread for the crowd sheltering under my home! I knew they were there from the occasional arguments I could hear beneath the floorboards. At the first hint of food, out came the redlegs, a pair of partridge, a pair of jays, a single robin and five dunnocks! No wonder it was getting crowded! Some time later, I happened to glance from the kitchen window to find the replete birds gone and a badger wolfing down the remains of the fat! Her wet fur clung to her body and the big snout was brown rather than black. Something flew down to feed, changed its mind and bounded over the hawthorns. Whether snow or shine, the resident green woodpecker here always 'yaffles' throughout the day from early until dusk and will take the scattered food though he prefers to feed alone.

At 6.30 p.m. with slight rain in the mist I stood in Ninepenny Wood. It was a vision of green with almost every tree seemingly covered in a haze of tiny leaves. The earlier snow had flattened the dog's mercury somewhat, but the bluebells stood tall and pliant amongst the yellow archangel, lesser celandine and wood anemones. Lords and ladies would soon be in bloom, but the flowers of the greater stitchwort, garlic mustard and perennial honesty were already open. The trees' bark was a lichened green, the woodland floor carpeted with colour through which the autumn-leaved paths wound back and forth. Drops of moisture hung suspended from every twig and growing thing and the grey mist accentuated this living world. Coming out of Ninepenny Wood, I saw a squirrel standing on one of the fallen trees that lie across the grassy path. It was eating something pale green which it then discarded before jumping off into the undergrowth. Coming forward to pick it up, I found it to be the closed sheath of lords and ladies. The squirrel had bitten straight through it, his teeth marks were clear, and extracted the spadix with its whorls of green flowers growing beneath. Friends tell me they have watched badgers eating these too, but from all my years of badger observation, I have never witnessed this beyond a doubt, though sometimes I have wondered. Rabbits I know will eat them, and now squirrels.

One afternoon a farmer living outside the Oakley police area phoned them regarding a badger incident that had occurred earlier in the day. Nothing had resulted from his phone call to his local police and he was aware that Oakley's couldn't attend another force area. His wife and I had known each other years ago before they sold their old farm. Would I please come and see the sett?

It was good to meet the Wilders again, though the circumstances were sad. The badgers had made their home in a bank between the field and a derelict nursery. They had recently dugout their entrances and taken fresh grass as bedding down two of them; it was likely that cubs were present. At 8.30 a.m. that morning, the ploughman coming on the field to start work, had noticed a freshly dug man-made hole. A footpath runs along that side, however, and he didn't think much of it as 'children often mess about there.' Later that morning he noticed a 'little puppy' running about and on his return to the farm at dinnertime, mentioned it to Mrs Wilder. She came, looked and decided the dog was not a puppy, but a scarred terrier with 'a nasty, mean look'. Inevitably, it was the old, old story of a brand new crowning-down hole and a dog left underground. Probably the badger-diggers had been there earlier, having driven up to the front of the nursery. John Wilder promptly disappeared, checked for fresh tyre marks and confirmed this. Presumably, they had dugout their badger, seen the ploughman arrive and abandoned the dog. All the signs were that a badger had been taken; we could only hope it hadn't been a lactating one.

We searched and whistled whilst Mrs Wilder returned to the farm-house to again phone her local police. There were plenty of badger signs everywhere; dungpits on the bank and the vacant land above, trails through the long grass and typical badger snuffle holes. There had once been other occupied setts too – a terriermen's paradise. I gave up counting the crowning-down holes. Anyone coming here would never be seen from the distant road or the farmland; nor would they be heard. Only when the remaining badgers had moved to the bank adjoining the farmland, had anything been noticed and, then, it was too late. Mrs Wilder was angry with herself for not taking the terrier and tying it up in one of the barns. It could have run off, of course, but more likely with the double set of tyre marks, the men had discreetly returned and whistled it. At that moment her husband appeared with a city police officer who introduced himself and who was very interested in what had happened. He had shooting rights on land with two Oakley officers and knew of the lamping and digging that went on. We exchanged telephone numbers and I was told to contact him if I ever felt he could help. The Wilders were especially pleased for it gave them someone in their own police station who was willing to help. It was no good fretting over lost opportunities; the terriermen would certainly return if the past was anything to go by. At least everyone was now aware and good had come out of bad. It usually does!

Driving me home, Mr Wilder mentioned there seemed to be a big increase in rats on his farm. I told him he would need to really start worrying about rats, when he had as many as Oakley town centre. For some years, I have seen a steady increase in rats at night as I walk through its streets, but living farther away now, I often take the route through the shopping precinct. A combination of mild winters and dirty human habits, made rats *en masse* a common sight now. We are a throwaway nation, dropping everything as we go – from our hands as we leave the shops, from car windows as we pass by. Rats will eat virtually anything including paper, but the sweet or ice-cream wrapper that smells or tastes of its contents, will be eagerly fought over. How much more so the take-away carton with some of the discarded food still inside? This winter had been particularly mild so the rat population explosion would continue to increase. As I walked past unemptied, over-flowing litter-bins aheave with searching bodies; from the darker recesses came squeakings and the scampering of rats. Those caught out in the open, won't move from a choice titbit, but continue to gorge.

There is safety in their very numbers and they know it. I'm sure other towns have the same problem.

With plentiful food and continuing mild winters, breeding can be at any season with an average litter size of seven or eight. Young rats are fair prey for predators, but the aggressive nature of adults, coupled with their size, means they have few enemies. It's a brave cat that will tackle a full-grown rat, though terriers it is true, have a love of ratting. Wendy was no terrier, but her habit of catching outhouse rats and leaving them on the farmhouse door-step, endeared her to the farmer – though not to his wife!

I told Mr Wilder I had written to the town council three years ago about the rat population by their prestigious Civic Centre and had had the silliest reply. It stated their Inspector had checked the area, found no evidence of rats and inferred I was scare-mongering. A case of what the eye doesn't see, the town council wasn't going to grieve over! Now they seemed common in many other locations and I noticed three had been recently runover in the High Street by the Bank. The road-sweeper must see evidence of rats, if the Pest Inspector cannot. Rats like the proximity of water, since they swim and dive proficiently. 'Whatever you do,' I said to Mr Wilder, 'Be careful of water, especially lying water on your farm, be it a small puddle or a pond, for rat urine will quickly contaminate it. Use protective gloves and never allow a cut or graze to become wet. Of several unpleasant diseases rats carry, Weils or leptospirosis, is unquestionably one of the most horrible, but until a few locals catch it around Oakley, we haven't a rat problem!'

That evening a spokesman for the National Federation of Badger Groups contacted me saying he had received a phone call from the chairman of our County Trust in response to the NFBG letter on the devastation at the Old Cherry Sett and Lucy's death. It had been a far from satisfactory conversation since the head of the Trust had merely said how hardworked his Reserve Officer was and refused to discuss the badger. He *had* promised, however, as a direct result of the incident, that an official warden was about to be appointed for Ashcroft Woods for four days each week. He was to be paid for by the owners, but employed by his Trust, 'thus increasing our ability to monitor the activities of the contractors.' He also promised, regarding the con-troversial tree-felling and its speed, that coppicing would be halted for three years allowing for the present situation to be assessed. Thus 'we hope the measures we have taken will increase the protection not only for the badgers of Ashcroft but all its flora and fauna.' It was, of course, far too late to do anything about the badgers of Ashcroft and much of its other fauna. But, at last, we were to have a warden. Hopefully, he would not be merely a cosmetic exercise to promote the Trust, but someone genuinely willing to care for our woods!

= 12 =

Harry

The badgercub, Harry, was brought to me at three months old and he is now living back in the wild. A success story due to the co-operation of the two BR electricians who found him, our RSPCA Inspector and an unfulfilled sow!

The Inspector came to The Sett one Friday evening with the cub amongst straw in a tea-chest and some packets of dried baby milk. He and the BR workmen had walked along the side of the railway line that day and caught the young badger with a grasper, for his companions had already found it could bite. It appeared to have come from a small sett in the steep chalk bank. If I would check to see if that was a sett, perhaps the cub could be returned on the Monday. When he had gone, I had a good look at the new arrival. He was stocky, aggressive and a good month ahead of the cubs of the Ninepenny sow and Crisp. He rejected the baby bottle and teat that the Inspector had thoughtfully provided, but thoroughly enjoyed lapping glucose and out of date human baby milk. Given the opportunity, this cub was old enough to inflict a strong bite, but was easily scruffed with my left palm under his stomach to support his weight.

The tea-chest with plenty of straw placed in the sitting-room was his bed during the day. The base of my shower in the washroom was his eating place and a change of scene indoors. I made the sides higher by fixing boards around the base. He became used to this as his dining-room and looked forward to going there. His deep-throated 'foghorn' growl, chittering and snort were similar to that of an adult badger and he already had the cheek tufts of the boar. That he didn't need a bottle meant he was easier to feed and required less handling. At first, Harry merely lapped the liquid, but with wholemeal bread well soaked and crusts removed, he was soon coping with that too. I massaged his abdomen after each meal, just as his mother would have done, to help him defecate. He always objected to this at first, but inevitably after a few minutes would begin to doze off! Harry's protests were predictable and instinctive; to the uninitiated, he must have seemed a dangerous young animal. He fluffed up, growled with his legs well apart and, successfully, tried looking mean. I've twice seen badgers kill foxcubs when the vixen is away and, occasionally, an adult fox will kill badgercubs above ground at an early age. Not many foxes would attempt to try this with Harry or a cub of his size; not because he was particularly fierce, but ... he looked and sounded it. His best defence was an appearance of aggression and his striking black and white face said, 'Watch out – I'm a badger!' His only real enemies at that age would be his enemies for all time – man and his dogs. I admired his guts and was determined not to soften him. His aggro was necessary if he was to survive after his temporary fostering.

Well before first light that Saturday morning, I carried him the few metres to the grass by the unfinished lake to enable him to get some exercise, whilst I stayed nearby till he was tired. (It was to be a far larger lake than the first and its base had still to be completed.) The turf here is wiry, but he persevered and dug small scrapes. His instinct to dig was strong and obsessive, far more so than other cubs of that age and I didn't immediately understand the reason. Baby-like, his concentration would go after a few intensive minutes as he moved on through the grass and dug again. When tired, he settled into his last scrape and chittered. If approached, he fluffed up and growled with facial colours 'warning'. When I came on to pick him up, he tucked his head between his front legs, then brought it round quickly and tried to bite my hand.

Badger mothers have several contact sounds, two of which are easy for us to copy. One is the noise we make when we try to speak with mouth tightly closed. The other is an open-mouthed 'hhhhhhhhhhhhh' like the beginning of Harry, which is how he came by his name. The times I approached him to lift him out to feed or exercise or change his bedding, were times of emotional stress for the cub. I found that saying

'Hhhhhhhhhhhhharry' softly under my breath when first going to him soon made him relax.

He enjoyed playing in the shower area indoors. A small piece of a birch branch was nosed about, chewed and carried a short way. He had a Cox apple as a ball, a large dogchew shaped like a bone and an old jersey to ill-treat. His snout rolled the apple which he chased after. It was big, but he found he could bite into it and it tasted good – all part of weaning. The jersey he shook dog-like, growling as he did so. He scraped it up under himself, carried it along and tripped over it, finally going to sleep on, over or under it. The jersey and straw lining the tea-chest he would push first his snout, then head and the rest of him under if he was cold, so that it covered him. Harry spent much of the daytime in his tea-chest sett, grooming himself. He kept himself very clean, wet paws going over and behind his ears. He nibbled out tangles in his fur like an adult.

Sometime after midnight I fed Harry again, massaged his tum and put him on the same stretch of grassland. He commenced to dig. Occasionally, he would set off on a relatively straight course, only to find something like a minute wild briar seedling in the way. After threatening it to no effect, he attempted to barge straight through. Not quite as easy as the long grass though. After several such attempts and some rather bad language, he decided to go round. By then, however, his infant mind had forgotten where or why he was going, so he turned round and trotted back. A quick snort at the wild briar (oh yes, I think I swore at that before) and after a little hesitation, he would sway round it and come back to his latest little hole. Backing onto it he used it as a dungpit and then moved further along. More digging, stopping, sometimes to look up and scent the air. As with other badgers, distant noises, however loud, like aircraft or a car back-firing, had no effect on his activities. The crack of a twig nearby or the squeak of a mouse, would make him break off his digging with a quick snort of intaken air. Harry would freeze a space, decide all was well and continue. If he came upon anything unknown (like my boots!) he kept quite still and fluffed up, then approached a short distance and uttered a growl, before backing away again. This was repeated several times and if the object stayed still and didn't attack, he would eventually get so close that his snout would touch it before he backed away. Again, this is typical of the badger's approach to something suspicious. The maxim seems to be, *never* turn your back on the unknown. After the nose-touching, if the object hadn't moved, Harry generally ignored it. Till the next time, of course! During this outdoor session, he came in contact with my boots several times; not surprising since I was standing around keeping a safe eye on him!

I went to my area briefly to see all was well with my badgers. Again I saw Crisp's cubs unnoticed by them, though their mother came to me as I was leaving, so she had been aware I was there. It was interesting to note the contrast in their nine weeks of age to Harry. His extra month gave him an enormous increase in co-ordination and self-confidence. Crisp's three came and went so quickly from their entrance that I couldn't be sure of their sex and privately wished they would keep still a moment! The little runt was lively enough, though it inevitably came off worse in any rough play. I thought it was a boar when I briefly saw it head-on. Come really adverse conditions, the runt would be the first to succumb.

Walking through Ashcroft Woods, I saw that much of the rubbish had been cleared and every gate was padlocked! These three gates had been provided with padlocks and chains for many months, but to find all on and locked at any one time was something of an event. The new warden must have started work! The deep ruts in the woodland paths had been removed by a JCB scoop and levelled off. Those going up and over the damaged Old Cherry Sett were partially cut, their depth reduced by two-thirds.

With my promise to the RSPCA Inspector in mind, I set off to view the length of railway track in the cutting where the badger cub had been found. It was a miracle Harry had survived. The double track and conductor rails ran far below between nearly sheer chalk embankments and standing on the field above, I could see three entrances nearly at the top of the opposite bank. There was scarcely any undergrowth growing on the chalk, but here and there some bushes or a rugged tree clung tenaciously to its incline. Had he really come from there?

The land above this sett was owned by a warehouse complex. The security guard at the main gate allowed me to go through and look. I pushed under the hawthorns directly above the sett and found two more entrances, dungpits and several, well-worn animal trails. Long distance lorries, many from the Continent, had their cargoes loaded and unloaded here. There was the usual litter associated with such places and food lying about – much of the latter seemed deliberately left. I returned to the guard in his office who immediately mentioned the food and the family of foxes he and the drivers fed. Then he pointed to the closed-circuit television on which he had been watching my movements! This struck me as rather amusing, especially as I had asked if I could look round for an injured fox (you never *ever* mention badger) and, watching me, he hadn't believed the story for one moment! He brought out two books on birds and asked if I had read David Macdonald's *Running with the Fox* which we discussed with great enthusiasm. Then, 'You're really interested in the badgers here, aren't you?' he asked. Nights can be long and boring for security guards, but not for this one. He could sit in comfort and watch his badgers and foxes on the screen! He was very interested in birds, regularly frequenting the reserves to see migrating arrivals. He hadn't been aware of any badgercubs; perhaps not so surprising as the television only encompassed the immediate area. We both felt the badgers had been there before the warehouses and offices were built and had gradually found themselves blocked in with these buildings, the motorway and the far older railway. The only route out of this man-made triangle was across the electrified line. A suicidal sett by any standards, but really this sow had little choice. Was it right to put Harry back with his mother or would history repeat itself and this time have a fatal end? He would still need a mother at least till the autumn. What was in the cub's best interest?

That afternoon I went out to stretch my legs after writing my notes and checked the Holly Tree Sett in Ninepenny Wood where the sow and her cubs denned. All was so peaceful with a gentle breeze blowing the green corn. Then I walked over the field to where her sister, the cubless sow, denned with the boar. Standing there silently in the sunshine, I saw the nettles and cleavers move further along and there were the vixen's three cubs playing in the entrance to their earth. So now I knew where she kennelled them; they would be about six weeks old. Their red coat colour was developing and their ears were more upright. Even as I watched, one with his back to me crouched, waiting to jump on another lower down. He misjudged his timing and his litter-mate moved away before he landed! It was an unexpected pleasure watching their play. I am so lucky in the place where I live now.

It rained that Sunday evening, but by 11 p.m. had stopped. I fed the badgercub and put him on the grass. It was during one of his digging sessions, that I was aware of much snuffling in the undergrowth beneath the hawthorns. The cubless sow was rooting amongst the moss for beetles and larvae. Gradually she worked her way through to the open and snorted at sight of me. Harry till now, hadn't heard her approach. She looked at the young cub and forgetful of me, advanced purring loudly. Harry responded and galloped forward ... to snuffle underneath her for milk! His disappointment was comic. Disappointment

202

gave way to renewed exercise as he got down to his excavations, but the sow was still very excited and backed onto and musked him twice. This made him growl, so she rolled him over and washed his stomach – squawk, chitter, squawk – he made a lot less noise now when I did that! She tried to pick him up and carry him off. However, he was not only too big and heavy, but struggling frantically! (At this age, cubs follow their mother if she moves home, rather than being carried.) She finally settled for a game with him and they ran round and round, Harry becoming tired first. She found one of his dungpits and used it herself, musked him once more, gave his ears a quick wash and swayed back under the hawthorns. All this while, she appeared to have forgotten about me.

Harry, obviously, decided that a milkless foster-mother was hopeless, but it struck me that he hadn't, apparently, pined for his real mother. Cubs up to a few weeks old will keep up a continuous 'trilling' for their dam; he was too old to make that noise. If he had been left hungry or cold, he probably would have shown signs of distress, but as it was, he seemed remarkably adaptable.

That Monday, the RSPCA Inspector and I went to view the railway cutting to decide if the badger cub should be returned. We stood looking over at the sett entrances high up on the chalk escarpment. If Harry had come from there, he would have slid from grass tussock to bush all the way down. (He wouldn't have directly fallen as he was unharmed apart from a smutty mark above his snout.) He could never have climbed up. There was trails leading from entrance to entrance, but none going down and on the near-vertical slope it was doubtful whether an adult badger would descend from choice. There was one curious factor against his coming from here. In order to get to where he

was found, that is on our side of the line and under the motorway bridge, he would have had to cross the electrified line. This would involve him climbing *over* the rails and over or under the electrified conductors. If any part of him had touched the ground as he negotiated the conductors, however, the BR electricians wouldn't have found a live cub. Was the current on? We had no way of knowing, but maintenance of the line here is carried out at weekends, not during the busy week.

Walking back towards the lane, the RSPCA Inspector pointed out another sett near the bridge, this time on the opposite bank. This was much lower down the chalk cutting, sleepers held the earth back from the rails below and it was the same side on which Harry was found. It was a very long way indeed for such a young animal to travel, especially bearing in mind, that at this age they still tend to go 'back and forth' rather than keep going. (Perhaps an in-born safety mechanism to stop them from straying too far when the mother is away foraging.) So from which sett did he come? If he was to be replaced in a sett, it might be the wrong one and he could be badly bitten and rejected. Also, he might fall down the bank again and at any time when he was older, he might attempt to cross the rails and be electrocuted.

If I reared him, he could help to re-establish the badger clan in Ninepenny Wood and bring in new blood. At present, there were the two sows (one with two cubs of nine weeks) and the boar. The cubless sow had already come across Harry and musked him. His own dungpits told the others he was there and the sow had used his dungpit. I couldn't integrate him with the younger, smaller cubs; that would be like placing a cuckoo in the nest. Once I had properly weaned him, however, there seemed no reason why, when he was ready and in his own time, he shouldn't become part of this family, too. However, I left it to the RSPCA to decide.

For the first time, Mrs Ellis from the big house was due to come and watch him for a few minutes. But that evening, Harry acted quite out of character. Up to then he had dug his holes and taken little notice of me quietly standing there, except if he came in contact with my boots. As usual I put the badgercub on the grass and stood away watching him. Then feeling cold, I went off to put an anorak on quickly over my jersey. I had done this before, but always returned immediately. This time, however, Harry must have registered my going for he followed chittering loudly in distress. I stopped, turned and came back. In moments he had clambered up one of my wellington boots with his paws round it bear-like and his teeth grasping the top of the boot to more easily pull himself up. From there he continued up my trouser-leg in the same manner, grasping the material as he went and so up to my waist and me. There he lay pressed against the wool of my jersey with his chittering now changed to a soft purr. So Harry now connected my boots with me. I never 'cuddled' him even though badgers love laps and warmth because I didn't want him to lose his aggression. However, he would grab at my wool jersey if he could when I picked him up.

Now I set him down and walked slowly round the empty lake, careful not to trip over him. His nose anxiously touched each boot as it came earthwards. We walked slowly back for I felt he must get some exercise and since he was cold and refused to dig, hurrying after wellies was as good. He chittered loudly all the while and we stopped in the vicinity of his holes and dungpits. I think he might have started digging, but Mrs Ellis who had meanwhile come along and was standing quietly a short distance away began to talk to me. Immediately, he tried to run off. He had never done that before.

However, following my boots was what Lucy and Luke her brother used to do to me in Ashcroft Woods when their mother Little'un was shot. I picked Harry up and brought him back into his tea-chest home. There was no point upsetting him further.

The next day proved a cold one with heavy showers. At The Sett, I stopped typing for a moment on hearing the cuckoo just outside my office window, and, looking out, saw it displaying in the briar rose. Later the RSPCA Inspector came with a bale of straw for it had been decided I should retain Harry. As he pushed the bale safely under cover, the Inspector said 'I've just heard the cuckoo – first time this year – and look, there it goes!'

We walked out to see a cage in the grounds, once used to house injured birds. It had no floor, but upended and with the floor side wired, would make an ideal badger-holding cage. The Ellises had said we could have it, but being immensely heavy, it would need to be loaded onto a lorry and somehow brought along the winding path to a position near The Sett. It would need a solid, rather than a wire floor too, or dung and urine would soak through and be impossible to remove. There was also a smaller one we were welcome to use as a 'recovery' cage for sick badgers. For the first time, I had the opportunity and space to do this with the active encouragement of the family who owned the land. The Inspector promised to help.

We discussed the letter I had received that morning. A report called *Badgers and Bovine tuberculosis in Ireland* was being prepared for their Eradication of Animal Disease Board by two economists (later known as the O'Connor Report). Selected parts of it had been leaked to the Irish agricultural business press whilst it was still in draft form. Amidst the anti-badger furore that followed, had come requests for total clear-out licences for some areas and East Offaly in Central Ireland was already dealt with. Now farming groups had put in applications for several other areas including the Burren in County Clare, a unique habitat, and it was feared that many would be granted. A tragic aspect of this was the call for a badger gassing campaign on 'humane' grounds. Whatever type of gas is used to exterminate badgers, the labyrinth of tunnelling in which they live, ensures a slow death. Even MAFF established it was an inhumane method, though only after they had despatched thousands of our badgers in this way over a period of seven years with hydrogen cyanide gas. We humans seem incapable of learning from each other's mistakes! Many concerned individuals, as well as organizations in and out of Ireland, wrote condemning these developments and pointing to the British experience. Would their letters be heeded?

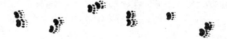

All of us were enjoying a spring that seemed like summer, with dew-laden nights and hot, sunny days. This was the start of a drought that would continue well into the autumn. Now, however, we rejoiced in the unusual weather and the rush of early growth that it brought.

One such morning I spent cleaning the reflectors and cutting back the thick vegetation that threatened to engulf them. Returning at midday, I heard quiet 'talking' sounds and looking into the tea-chest, saw Harry lying on his back on top of the straw, his giant rawhide chew balanced on his four brown-padded paws! Some badgers' pads, like their snouts, are black and some are brown. Some like Harry's have tiny marks on them. He had a dark area on the lowest part of each pad; all four paws were identical. He often groomed himself during the day in this position, or played with his paws, patting the front ones together as if silently clapping. He would sometimes take a hind paw in his front one and draw it into his mouth to suck. He didn't appear lonely, though at such times I regretted he hadn't siblings with which to play. On many a summer's day I have heard cubs playing below ground at the Old Cherry Sett as they scampered along its tunnels.

As I continued to watch him, Harry was suddenly aware and bounded upright on all fours whickering eagerly. I noticed that the white hairs on the edges of his ears were growing into tufts as I placed him in the shower-base to play till I was ready to leave again. I had taken some new photos of him and was surprised to realize how much he had altered. He no longer dug dungpits or defecated when we were outside, mainly I felt, because he was frightened I would disappear. He used one corner of the shower-base particularly and never fouled his tea-chest, though he occasionally urinated in it. He was very, very clean and always grooming. Now he lapped water noisily from a small dish in the corner, then turned it upside down and bomped it about. He appeared to like the sound! He burrowed under the newspaper that lined the area and came up the other side. Typically, everything was touched first with his nose, before he played or continued on his way. Scent is far, far more important to badgers than sight. Their sight is useful for distinguishing between light and dark and perceiving movement. The area of their sight is limited, though movement against a lighter background is often noticed even at a distance. If you keep still with strange badgers, they may come very close to inspect. If they can't scent you, if you are up-wind, and you stay quite still, chances are they will be unconcerned.

An hour later, Harry was fast asleep again and I was walking to Everington to clean the remaining reflectors there and check the setts. It was hot work in the sunshine. By my return in the evening, I had checked all setts in the locality and noted that activity at each was greatly reduced, almost certainly due to the unaccustomed dryness and the extra time needed for the badgers to forage farther afield. Walking in, I saw it was 7.30 p.m. and after feeding the cub, I brought him out onto the grass where he cried and began climbing my leg. Forestalling him, I sat on the grass and lay back. He climbed aboard and crept whimpering against my wool jersey. I spoke softly, repeating his name over and over again, till he ceased his cries and lay silent against my warmth. After a while I stood up, placed him on the grass and still repeating his name, slowly walked home with him touching each boot as I walked.

That night I thought hard about Harry and the change in his behaviour. When he was found, he was lying in a little scrape he had dug for himself by the side of the railway line. I am sure by his exhausted state and great hunger when I was first given him, that Harry had been lost for more than a few daylight hours. The moment I had put him on the ground, his instinct to make a safe hole in which to crouch was the same. As time past, however, he came to know that if I placed him outside, I would, nevertheless, return him – there was no need to dig. We had a routine and he, a new home. He found my boots were part of me and if he climbed high enough, he found my wool jersey. I held him against that tatty old jersey, I spoke, so my boots and jersey were me; they were safety, food and home. They were comfort, for his play area and sleeping quarters were never left fouled and badgers hate to be dirty. I didn't think my face registered, usually, it was too far away. My voice came from somewhere above my jersey. I must remember to speak more to him; I live on my own, so rarely speak. I found this the case with Karen's gerbil. He too was a sociable animal and loved company. When I spoke, he would rush out of his nest and be up on his vantage point – a piece of log – whiskers aquiver. He loved to be stroked. If I forgot to speak, I rarely saw the gerbil, so Silky taught me to speak more. Harry was still a baby and this I tended to forget as in many ways he was so independent. In my desire that he should keep his independence and revert to wildness, in a sense, I was avoiding contact. However, the reverse was happening and he was losing confidence and, thereby, his independent ways. Confidence and security breed independence and I must strive to steer a middle course. When he was old enough, confident and mature, Harry would go his own way in his own time. The adult sow might well accelerate this. In the meantime, he was only three months old, still being weaned and needing some stability in his life. I would take him out for a short walk each night, talking to him quietly and speaking his name. If at any time he should run off or briefly become lost, the calling of his name should help to establish contact again. I had found the previous night that when he went to run off, I approached closely and he had swung round growling and fluffed up. I then turned and walked slowly away from him and he followed as before. It was one thing for Harry to decide to go from me; it was quite another for me to leave Harry.

Now that official permission had been given for me to have the cub, I discussed his future with the RSPCA Inspector. In the last few years, many people including these Inspectors and badger group members have cared for motherless cubs with a strict view to returning them to a life in the wild. It is rightly an offence now to keep badgers as pets. One important fact that has emerged from this is that lone cubs do need a certain amount of contact and affection, otherwise they have difficulty 'socializing' later with their own kind and may become loners. So, a careful balance is necessary to avoid imprinting of the young wild animal, whilst at the same time satisfying its need for social contact. However, two or more cubs can generally give each other the mutual grooming and contact so necessary to the well-adjusted adult. I had never had such close contact with a badger as young as this. Lesley was eight months when her family were dugout and taken; Luke and Lucy were five months and had one another. Harry was three months and had no one. I was learning too.

One warm, sultry night returning early from Ashcroft Woods, I stood by the reflectors outside Oakley, listening to the blood-curdling sounds of a badger fight! Suddenly, a grey figure almost brushed by me as it bounded down the bank, hotly pursued by another. In the middle of the road on the cat's-eyes they fought, rushing round and round in a tight circle, as each tried to get behind the other to bite it above the tail. The noise they made masked anything else and, horrified at the danger from possible traffic, I went down too and stood over their whirling bodies, shouting loudly – with no response whatsoever! Next I tried kicking, at first not too hard but, in desperation, some hefty blows. Once a badger did look round briefly, then continued into the fray. At last, a well-aimed kick apparently broke up the contestants as one ran behind my legs and tried attacking the other through them. And I wasn't wearing boots that night! I tried my angry-badger-growling-act and that may have worked, for the badger in front of me dashed to the far gutter where the fight continued unabated! I stood by anxiously as a taxi approached, returning to the station and, as usual at night, well exceeding the speed limit. However, it slowed down as it reached me, the driver leaning out to peer blearily into the night. 'What's that?' he asked uncertainly. 'Only cats fighting – surely you've heard that before?' I stared at him disapprovingly. 'You should be ashamed of yourself, drink driving.' His eyes avoided mine as he muttered 'My God, they look big from here, but I guess she's right' and striking the side of his head with an open palm, he drove off.

It was true, the more subdued noise the two were making now was not unlike a cat fight. Eventually, one badger broke away, swayed up the far bank and disappeared into the field above with the other following. The noise of their quarrel gradually faded and I was left with the rising moon and a sense of unreality!

One Sunday morning we made a determined start on cleaning the empty oil tank for use as an artificial main sett for the Ninepenny badgers. Mrs Ellis placed a clean dustbin half-full of nearly boiling water on a wheelborrow and trundled it along the winding path to the clearing by the empty lake. There I transferred some of the water into a pail and climbing inside, feet first, carried it through. The blazing sun on the metal tank, coupled with my efforts and the hot water, soon made it feel like the inside of a sauna, rather than a sett. But we both enjoyed the work for at last we were to give the badgers here a safe, impregnable haven. It was something the owners of the land and myself had discussed many times, but now it was becoming a reality. Mid-morning I happened to look out of a 'porthole' for some more water, as my companion came round the corner labouring under the weight of yet another burden carefully wheeled along the rough, uneven path. I thought she looked hot, but she assured me I looked hotter! Deep in my iron cavern, I was conscious only of the increasingly clean surface all about me. It wasn't till I felt the earth tremble, that I looked out to see the JCB pass by.

That day its sharp-edged scoop dug deep into the pure chalk and a pit large enough to bury the tank was made. Then it returned to the cleaned container and pushed it the length of the clearing to the edge of the new hole. The most difficult part of the whole operation was, undoubtedly, the need to drop it in at the right angle, so that trenches could be cut in the chalk leading from the three entrances. Mr Ellis successfully did this and with a smaller scoop formed trenches on curving paths to prevent the wind blowing in whilst still allowing a free flow of air – just as the badger digs its own tunnels. The trench leading to the bank below where the hawthorns grew was too short to curve, but it sloped down more sharply than the others and, hopefully this would suffice.

The completion of the sett took several weekends. During the intervals I collected earth by the bucketful, walked along one of the trenches and crawled with it through an entrance. These entrances reminded me of portholes at the side of a ship and were set half-way up the tank's sides, so the floor level would need to be raised. When enough earth was inside, I carried in the turfs torn up by the JCB and laid them evenly on top. Next, the ponies were deprived of a bale of their hay which was dropped into the chalk pit by an entrance. From there I carried it in armfuls, by necessity, backwards! This badger-action isn't as idiosyncratic as it appears, though till now I had never practised it myself. It is far easier on four legs (or on all fours) to carry backwards something like hay that disintegrates easily. I did come in for some teasing though, from the men cutting through the thick sheets of metal that were to top the tunnels before the whole area was infilled, to the RSPCA Inspector who just happened to turn up in time to photograph the strange badger head protruding from the tank!

The tunnel walls would never collapse, dug as they are through the solid chalk. I recalled the far deeper deneholes, dug centuries earlier on the land around Ashcroft Woods, that had and always should, stand the test of time. Raising the floor level within the tank had successfully reduced its overall volume and, therefore, its echo – something that had bothered me greatly from the start. Sitting comfortably on the hay inside, my voice had little reverberation now when I called. Someone from outside, however, hearing the experiment, enquired unkindly if I had permanently moved home? It was indeed, good enough to live in oneself! Soon the metal strips were laid about half a metre above the base of the trenches. Breezeblocks were put round the entrances to stop excess chalk falling in. The metal strips were laid right up to them and metal rings fixed into the entrance of each trench. Then the entire area was covered with the chalk again and smoothed over. All that could be seen was an area of white and looking closely round the edges, the three holes, but they weren't at all obvious. Later, grass and weeds invaded the surface till it was impossible to tell it had ever been disturbed.

Everything was growing fast with heavy dews at night and the sun hot by day. Walking between the side of Ashcroft Woods and the wheat my trousers were soaked above my wellingtons. The ash trees' leaves, some of the last to open, were unfurling and the flowers of the oilseed rape were a golden glow. Watcher II's cubs, sharp-faced young foxes now, explored well beyond their den. Already they caught insects with a high pounce that practice would perfect, though their mother still left food in the area for them to find. The badgers, too, were spending long periods in search of insects, due to the unusual dryness. A paw would descend on a beetle pinning it to the ground for a probing snout to snuffle up. A few weeks later, this turned to grasshoppers and crickets, so easy for predators to detect from their penetrating stridulations.

Harry and I walked regularly at night now, either before or after I left for Ashcroft Woods. Sometimes the cubless sow appeared a short way off, but in his desire not to lose me, he scarcely registered her watching us. We would walk along the winding path and through into the ponies' meadow. Harry relaxed and investigated, before hurrying back to my boots. We past worms feeding above ground and many slugs venturing out across the dewiness, but all these the cub ignored. I picked up a worm one night and gave it to him indoors in his play area, but though instinctively he knew they were good to eat, he made a hopeless mess of that first one, pawing and chewing it and ... his usual sign of defeat, hiding it under the newspaper! The next was dangled in front of him. He took the end and eagerly chewed it, dropped it a couple of times and finished it up. I offered a small, white slug which just as eagerly he snuffled over, but pawed at its stickiness on his mouth. He rolled it over several times and I thought it was eaten. Renewing the newspaper later, however, I discovered it rather battered and squashed, tucked away in the folds! Harry found it easier to hide this prey, than go to the trouble of rubbing them back and forth before eating. However, several practical demonstrations almost under his snout and plenty of patience prevailed; soon he was coping with these too. If I turned over the ponies' manure he would snuffle up the grubs beneath. At first, he decided that beetles were too hard and chewy! Whilst Harry debated whether to eat them or not, they would scurry off. Beetles do not hang around to be eaten!

Sometimes we took the other path into Ninepenny Wood, he padding under the hurricane-felled poplars and I jumping over. He loved playing in the rustling dead leaves, mainly I think for the sound they made as he pushed his snout through them. How many generations of cubs have I seen doing that in the leaves of Ashcroft Woods? He bit bluebell greenery off near the ground and gathering a tiny bundle, backed along the path from which we had come for a few metres, before dropping it. Returning, we startled a bank vole. This excited the young badger who hunted about in the long grass, unaware the tiny creature had escaped long since. By now he was finding worms for himself and coping with them proficiently. One morning as we returned to The Sett, we came upon a heron in the process of swallowing a frog. Immediately the cub fluffed up, legs apart and growled a warning. Monsieur heron saw me standing just behind Harry, choked on its meal and striding away a few paces, took off with strong flaps of great wings. The badger gave chase and reared upright on hind legs for a moment to see it off; then returned to me whickering and climbed my boot up to my jersey with the air of a job well done. Clearly he felt his frightening appearance had sent it rushing away!

The Ninepenny mother's two sow cubs were growing fast and would come with their mother to the bowl of water I left below the great beeches there. Sometimes Harry used the others' dungpits; sometimes he dug his own. Whenever he came across evidence of the resident badgers, he musked the area also. Twice going out across the farmland near The Sett on my journey to Ashcroft Woods, I saw the cubless sow musking where Harry had played.

Then, one early morning Harry and I saw this lone sow and, on our return to the green door of my home, found she was waiting there. I squatted down small, well out of the way and for once, he was pleased to see her. She backed onto and musked him and he tried to return the compliment on her so much larger flank! Gently she nuzzled the side of his face, making a soft contact sound. Then slowly she moved off with him beside her, foraging in the moss beneath the hawthorns as they went. I tried to keep them in sight, but the sow quickened her pace knowing I was behind and, of course, Harry did too. Thus, I let them get well ahead and in doing so, lost them.

At The Sett I was left with the most appalling sense of loss – how ridiculous! This was the best thing that could have happened; I had hoped and prayed that it would. But was he really ready to go? What might happen when the other sow and boar met him. Would her sister protect him from any attack? Full of self-doubts for his well-being, I laid the tea-chest complete with his old bedding, chew and

jersey, on its side by the winding path that lead into Ninepenny Wood. If he came back, he would find security there when he scrambled inside.

Daybreak found me at the Holly Tree Sett staring in amazement at the digging-out in progress. The spoil from an entrance farther round from that of the two little sowcubs, was piled high with bright earth. The solitary sow backed out with a fresh load that she kicked backwards with gusto, but there were other sounds too. Now a familiar face with dirtied snout and tufted ears was framed in the hole. Helpful Harry had found a natural mother and the sow was solitary no more!

I left the tea-chest there for a few nights, till the stable cat found it and Candy ran off with the chew. My first doubts had given way to great pleasure at the thought of how painless his adoption had been.

One evening I walked round after dark and sometime before midnight came across the family foraging between the rows of wheat – the big boar, the sow with her two cubs and Harry with his new mother. He looked so much bigger than the little sows. I stood there happily enjoying the scene, when the boar scented the air, raising his snout as he turned slowly in my direction. He gave a sharp snorting bark of alarm as he caught my scent and the family made off through the corn. I called 'Hhhhhhhhhhhhhhharry' softly and squatted down. A few moments hesitation and Harry came up to my boots, touching them with his snout and leaving on each a tiny damp mark. His mother had returned and watched us anxiously; the others had disappeared. I slowly stood up and walked away in a daze of relief, knowing Harry was truly accepted and in his right place. At the curve of the wood I turned round to see they had gone. A crescent moon was rising over the land and shining on the rustling wheat. I would keep clear of these badgers now, just checking their setts by day. May Harry and his kind prosper in peace.

The O'Connor Report, *Badgers and Bovine Tuberculosis in Ireland*, was published. Whereas the earlier 'leaked' parts of it appeared to condemn the badger outright, and the badger only, the whole document told a very different story. A government spokesman admitted the badger was well down the list of difficulties and defects in the TB eradication scheme and advised farmers, 'If you pin all your hopes on the badger, you will not get rid of bovine TB.' He added that his department would only co-operate with scientifically conducted and organized disease investigation. The flood of letters from people concerned at the suggested gassing of occupied setts, halted the go-ahead for this. Officially, at least, there was an uneasy truce.

The damage had been done, however, as the perpetrators of the leaking had intended. In TB blackspots such as County Clare, farmers renewed their invitations to the diggers and baiters to move in. In theory, it is still an offence to digout and take a badger without a licence, but, in fact, officialdom doesn't want to know. Powerless to stop the atrocities all around their villages, people can only stand by and record.

Vets gain more than half their income from bovine TB which is a thriving industry in Ireland with many millions of pounds spent on it in the last 20 years. An Irish bovine changes its farm three or four times during its life and there is a huge trade in cattle transportation. Many farmers don't want TB to go away; it brings money into the industry. So what is the point of cleaning up your farming practices and thereby the spread of the disease?

Our English summer saw a complete absence of thunderstorms and so dry did the air become, that the dark hours ceased to be dew-laden as the drought intensified. Thus the close, airless nights guaranteed that I would find the Ashcroft badgers dotted about the fields of Colts Farm as they searched for food. Missy and her family, Meg, Bess, Kate, Kirsty and Mícheál, together with Crisp, were finding very few worms now in spite of the irrigation, for the constant heat had sent them far underground. Slugs and snails could still be found and insects were plentiful, but it required many hours foraging to take their fill of these.

Crisp still hadn't weaned her cubs: two sows and the smaller boar. The journey to this farm and back from Cliffords Bank on the far side of the woods was too great a distance, so for most of the night they were left on their own. Whenever I could, I stole over the hayfield between the wood edge and their home, drawn by the sounds of cub play. In and out the elmbrush of the Bank they would scramble, whickering and squeaking their excitement. Tiring of chase, one would tuck its head between its front legs and gripping its tail, bounce down the soft earth of a spoil heap to the field below. The others, calling and snuffling, promptly followed suit – Geronimo, or the badger equivalent! The spoil heaps of their home were enormous and the dry, dugout earth, wonderfully soft. Once at the bottom, they raced up to have another go. The scent of their musk lay heavy on the air and clouds of dust hung over their playground. At 3.40 a.m. the eastern sky was lightening, and ten minutes later, it was first light.

Now they were silent, tired and hungry. A quail called hauntingly from the growing barley as one cub began to wash herself, to be joined by another till all three mutually groomed. Suddenly a sound closeby halted them – a tableau of three small figures. Then a soft, reassuring whicker from a tired and muddy Crisp. She lay on her back in the meadow grass as they suckled. All too soon it seemed, she rolled over onto her feet and shook them off. I suspected her milk was drying up in spite of her continued efforts to nurse. As I watched, Crisp coughed twice, then regurgitated and her three still-hungry offspring, filled themselves on their mother's foraging.

One morning I walked through Ashcroft Woods waiting for the new warden to arrive. There was a wide patch of Solomon's-seal in bloom, the pendulous bells very delicate and fine. Fluffy aspen catkins lay thickly on the Main Pond, hiding what little water remained. Foxgloves, red campion and mallow were all in bloom with the dainty spindle tree and elder flowers. Soon the warden's van drew up and together we looked at the problem areas of Ashcroft Woods. I realized I had seen him working here the previous year, when he had been employed to clear some of the paths of the hurricane-blown trees. He had already met the rural sergeant and was hoping to speak to the village constable and the farm-managers soon. He was interested and caring and privately I prayed that at last this place might come into its own.

Leaving woods and warden, I crossed Colts Farm. The hot sun already scorching the baked earth, felt unbearable on my head and neck. I stood under the jets to get cool whilst the farm-manager saw to the spraying heads farther along. Then we stood discussing the oncoming water privatization and what it would mean for his boss. He enquired about the badgers and I mentioned that these irrigated fields were too far for Crisp to bring her cubs. It was a pity the Old Cherry Sett had been so disturbed for it was much nearer. Any benefit gained from the better foraging here for the youngsters would be burned up in the effort required to journey to and from Cliffords Bank.

Crisp's three cubs, Harry and the Ninepenny youngsters, were to successfully survive the drought that summer, mainly through human intervention, though their mothers repeated regurgitation of food for them undoubtedly helped. I have witnessed this before, but never on such a scale and members of Badger Groups in some of the worst drought-afflicted counties, reported this too. One of the joys of being in touch with these Groups is this pooling of information and the discussion that springs from it. Another unusual behaviour pattern observed that summer was the regular (rather than occasional) depositing of dung without the use of pits. Sometimes this appeared to be randomly left in open places – perhaps in the middle of a field, but also on objects, much in the way of foxes when scat-marking. The obvious answer to the lack of dungpits seemed the hardness of the earth for digging and the badgers need to spend all their waking hours searching for food to survive. Hungry adults and their cubs were wandering unusually far, with heavier road casualties for the time of year as a result. Possibly, this territory marking was also a desire to warn off these intruders from feeding grounds where food was already scarce. Young animals tend to suffer first from the effects of starvation and dehydration. Of the nine cubs in distress I was called to that summer, only two survived to be returned to their parents. How many died unseen in the fastness of their setts, was impossible to guess. It could be argued that in well populated areas the drought was a natural culling. But in areas such as ours, the badgers have suffered so many man-made cullings, that their numbers could ill afford nature's equalizer.

The Ninepenny badgers discovered the artificial sett when they left the dust of the open fields to forage in the long grass and wildness of the Ellises' land. One night I heard a commotion as I returned home along The Sett path. The adult boar appeared to be pushing over my heavy cast-iron door-scraper with his powerful long-clawed forepaws – I'm not sure why! A hissing, not unlike that of an angry cat, was coming from the recovery-cage; the temporary home of Vicky, a half-grown vixen given to me by the RSPCA Inspector till she was old enough to be released. Harry peered with interest at the arched back and forward turned ears of the outraged foxcub. He probably smelt the surplus food she had tupped over in the corner of her 'den'. Then he sneezed, lost interest and padded after the swaying figures of boar and sow.

Through the binoculars, I enjoyed watching Harry play with the other cubs. He was the leader in their games, as they chased through a chalk entrance of the 'tank' sett, out another and back again. One night his play was too rough for the little sows, who ganged up on their boisterous friend and ran whimpering to their mother. Sows are handy with their paws as he found to his cost when she came over to Harry and cuffed the young boar. Then it was his turn to cry and run to his mother – that's how family rows can start!

At the Old Cherry Sett it was slowly becoming light. The tawny male behind me called above the other birdsong all around. The scars left by the coppicing still showed though time would heal and cover them. I looked down over Lucy's last resting place to the tawny hen greeting her mate; the call and answer of their dueting seemed the spirit of eternity and the woods themselves.

One day years hence, this sett will recover its lost beauty; its badgers will once again have the protecting cover so necessary for their home. Lucy's death achieved one thing, it gave us an official warden. Nothing is free in this world and everything has a price. There had to be a sacrifice and that sacrifice was a badger. Sometimes it is difficult to see sense or meaning in things that happen. 'Life can only be understood backwards, but it must be lived forwards.'

As I write this it is August 1989 and I know but for her death we would still be waiting. The warden we have is interested, enthusiastic and concerned and already through his energy has breathed new life into Ashcroft Woods.

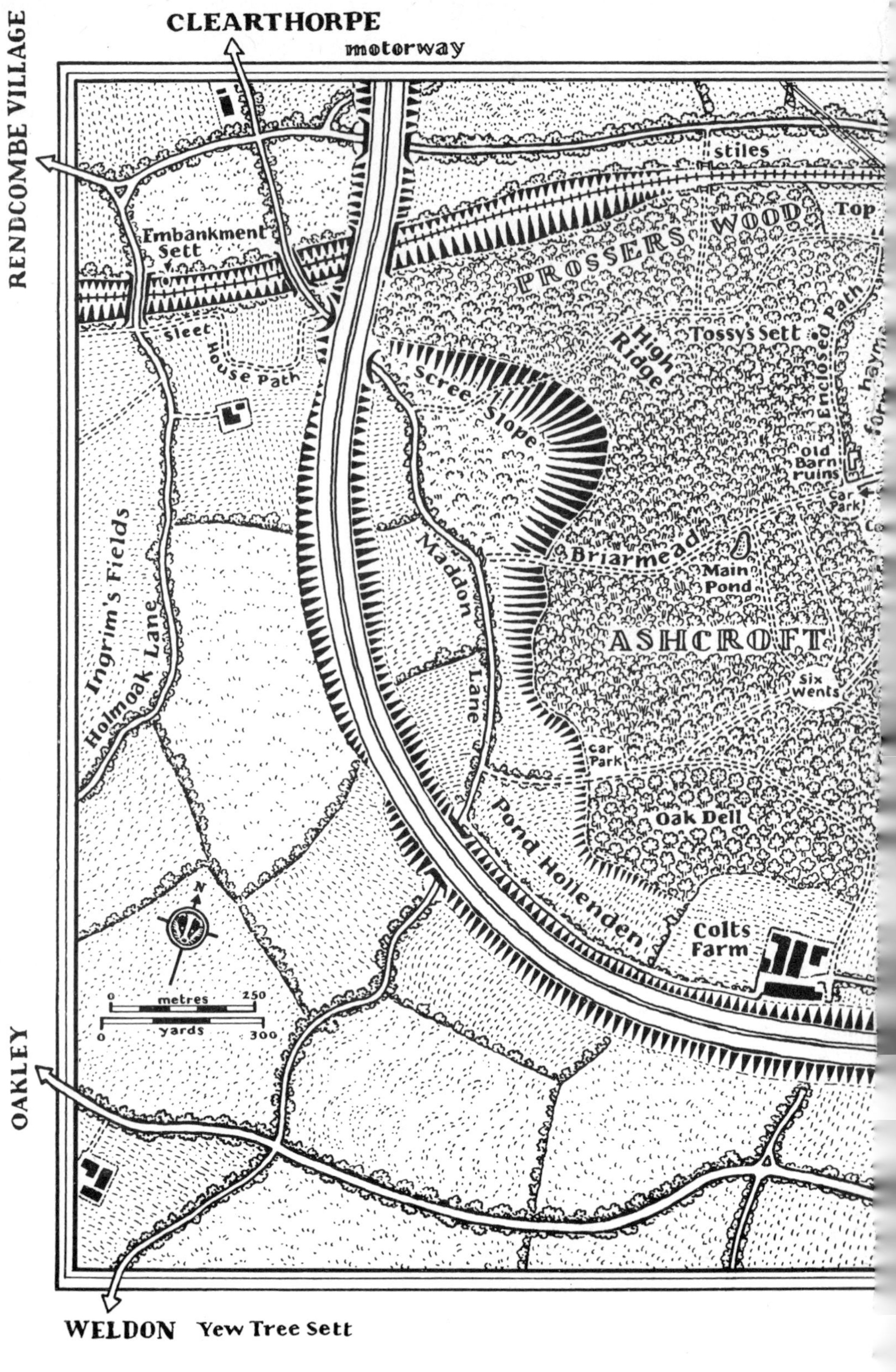

CLEARTHORPE

motorway

RENDCOMBE VILLAGE

PROSSERS WOOD

stiles

Top

Embankment
Sett

sleet

House Path

Tossy's Sett

High
Ridge

Enclosed Path

Old
Barn
Ruins

Car
Park

Scree Slope

Briarmead

Main
Pond

ASHCROFT

Six
wents

Ingrim's Fields

Holmoak Lane

Maddon Lane

Car
Park

Oak Dell

Pond Hollenden

N

OAKLEY

metres   250

yards   300

Colts
Farm

WELDON   Yew Tree Sett